MAXIMIZE YOUR LIFE
HOW TO DO EVERYTHING BETTER

MAXIMIZE YOUR LIFE

HOW TO DO EVERYTHING BETTER

BY THE EDITORS OF MAXIM

MAXIM
BOOKS

DDM Press

DDM Press
1040 Avenue of the Americas · New York, NY 10018 · 212.302.2626 · http://www.maximonline.com

For more information on Maxim Books, call 888-328-4380

ISBN 0-9675723-7-1
Printed in the United States of America

MAXIMIZE YOUR LIFE: HOW TO DO EVERYTHING BETTER

Maxim Editor-in-Chief Keith Blanchard

Group Creative Director Andy Turnbull

Art Director Jane Mella

Assistant Art Director Kevin Beard

Contributing Editors Leslie Yazel, Gene Newman, Jordan Burchette, Eric Alt

Photo Editor A.S. Brodsky

Illustrator Lyman Dally

Cover Photographer Gene Bresler

Writers Paul Bibeau, John Seder, Charles Coxe, John Walsh, Patricia Ryan

Copy Editor Larry Lerner

Proofreader Elaine Heinzman

Fact Checker Jaime Lowe

DDM PRESS

Chairman Felix Dennis

President Stephen Colvin

Chief Financial Officer Paul Fish

Publisher Steven Kotok

Managing Editor Andy Marinkovich

Direct Marketing Manager Joanna Molfetta

Directors Robert G. Bartner, Peter Godfrey

CONTENTS

One eyeball martini, please.

Get bucked up.

CHAPTER 4 MONEY EDGE **56**

CHAPTER 5 STREET EDGE **74**

CHAPTER 6 HANDYMAN EDGE **90**

"My God, he's such a stiff..."

CHAPTER 10 LEISURE EDGE

Havana daydreamin'.

150

CHAPTER 11 SPORTS EDGE

170

"I'll be good, mommy."

CHAPTER 12 SEX EDGE

182

GIVE YOURSELF AN EDGE...

Who would you rather have tell you how to keep burglars from robbing you blind, a cop or a burglar?

Who should you get advice from on what to wear on a first date, a style guru or your potential honey?

And if you had your choice, which would you consult about how to minimize your taxes without getting audited and/or thrown in jail, an accountant or the IRS?

The gang here at *Maxim* went on this quest to get "the edge" in life because we realized that between the Boy Scout Guide, Sunday school, and that big party known as college, some truly useful and crucial stuff may have slipped through the cracks. So we cracked open some beers and sent our interns out to interview the best sources on a ton of subjects to bring you a book that doesn't have the words "dummies" or "idiots" in the title for a reason—because you already know a lot. Now it's just time for you to maximize your world.

Life in the 21st Century should be a breeze. Picking up hot babes should be easy (Page 104), you should win big whenever you play bar pool (Page 160), and you should be able to buy a wide-screen TV for cheap (Page 63). You should also be able to play the confident hero if your girlfriend gets whacked in the nose with a football (Page 24), and be sensitive enough to stop Junior from crying so you can get into his hot mama's skirt (Page 120).

But there are obstacles to the good life—days where you may find yourself trapped in the wilderness without a tent or any source of fire, and days where you need to destroy the competition at work so you're the one moving on up. That's why we wrote this book. To give you the maximum edge when it comes to money, dating, sports, survival skills, style, career, and, most important of all...sex!

We hope that after reading this book you will enjoy life on the inside track, ahead of the pack and supersized, with more fun, babes, and money than you deserve.

Steven Kotok
Publisher, Maxim Books

AVERAGE JOE

All men are not created equal (Ron Jeremy is proof of that). Although we're certainly not the people who should give you a working definition of normal, here are your average Joe's body measurements:

HEIGHT 5' 9"

CHEST 37"-39"

PENIS CIRCUMFERENCE (SOFT) 3.75"

PENIS CIRCUMFERENCE (HARD) 4.85"

WAIST 31"-34"

PENIS LENGTH (SOFT) 3.89"

PENIS LENGTH (HARD) 6.21"

HIPS 36"

TESTICLE DIAMETER 1.2"

THIGH 21"

WEIGHT 180 LBS

MAX OUT!

We've found the maximum levels you can hit, if you're good enough—the stats you'd need to earn a perfect score on the U.S. Army physical fitness test. (Yikes! Better increase those workouts!)

Push ups	Age	Amount
	25	80
	35	73
	45	66

Sit-Ups	Age	Amount
	25	87
	35	78
	45	69

Two Mile Run	Age	Finish In
	25	12:36
	35	14:00
	45	15:06

FITNESS EDGE

Building Your Temple

You're not the most slovenly guy in the world, but you could use some extra room in those 501s. You need a plan, but first you need to figure out where you stand. Size yourself up, then bulk up, trim down, and/or minimize gasping with exercises designed to cut through the fitness noise.

WHEN SUCKING IT IN DOESN'T WORK ANYMORE.

Starting Point: Find Your Fitness Level

You're never gonna get where you're going if you don't know where you're at.

HEIGHT/WEIGHT CHART

Congratulations. If you've been saying for years that those height and weight charts at the doctor's office are bullshit...your opinion is supported. Statistics show that people who live the longest in each height category are actually heavier than the "ideal," and fat-asses everywhere are praising the Metropolitan Life Insurance Company for revising their famed height/weight charts. Check yourself out under the new standards, which still look ridiculous to those of us who are happy with our 5'9"/210-pound frames.

Height	Small Frame	Medium Frame	Large Frame
5'2"	128–134	131–141	138–150
5'3"	130–136	133–143	140–153
5'4"	132–138	135–145	142–156
5'5"	134–140	137–148	144–160
5'6"	136–142	139–151	146–164
5'7"	138–145	142–154	149–168
5'8"	140–148	145–157	152–172
5'9"	142–151	148–160	155–176
5'10"	144–154	151–163	158–180
5'11"	146–157	154–166	161–184
6'0"	149–160	157–170	164–188
6'1"	152–164	160–174	168–192
6'2"	155–168	164–178	172–198
6'3"	158–172	167–182	176–202
6'4"	162–176	171–187	181–207

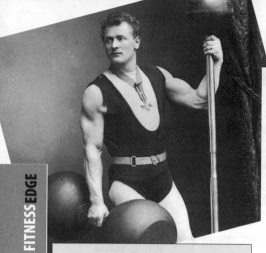

Pump Fast

A little something for every muscle group.

What do you need to start? Exercise guru and editor of *Muscle Media,* Bill Phillips, says it's a set of regular old dumbbells. They allow you to move as you want to move, which is better than trying to fit yourself into the guided movement of a fancy machine. This means your wrists and other joints can be in their most natural, comfortable position while you do your exercises. Dumbbells enhance coordination and balance, and allow you to work out faster so you can burn more calories and get a greater cardiovascular workout. Best of all, they're cheap, and they work well for beginners and experts alike.

In other words with a set of dumbbells, you have absolutely no excuse not to look buff like a vampire slayer. Get a set of adjustables that go from 2.5 lbs up to 50 lbs each (depending on your strength). Also, you will need a flat or adjustable home bench. These are the workouts you can do to build muscle the fastest, cheapest way possible:

CHEST LIKE SUPERMAN (BENCH PRESS):
Lie on your back on the bench, dumbbell in each hand. Bring the weights to just above your shoulders, keeping your palms toward your feet and elbows out. Press the weights up straight until your elbows lock, with the dumbbells over your collarbone. Slowly lower them to the starting position, feeling your chest muscles stretch outward as your elbows go below the bench. This may feel clumsy, but it works the muscles all over your chest much better than a barbell press, and it's easier on your shoulders. To do it right don't lift your head up while pressing, and don't let the dumbbells drift up toward your head while they're in the air. If blood starts shooting out of your neck, go to the next lowest weight.

SHOULDERS LIKE ATLAS (SIDE RAISE):
Stand with your feet shoulder-width apart and your arms at your sides. You should be holding a dumbbell in each hand, with your palms turned in toward you. Keep your arms straight, and lift the weights out and up to the sides until they are right about level with your chin. Hold for a count of "one." From this position, lower them slowly back to your sides. Make sure you *lift* the dumbbells on the way up—don't swing them, lean your body forward, or bring the dumbbells down in front of you. The trick is to isolate this move so it just blasts your shoulder muscles. The other trick is not to drop the fuckers onto your feet.

ARMS LIKE THE MIDDLE EAST (ARM EXTENSION):
Many exercises can help you build up your biceps, but triceps are a major part of arm bulk. To get yours in good shape lie on the bench, with a dumbbell in each hand, arms extended over your head (not pointing up in front of you but reaching above your head parallel to the floor). Your palms should be facing each other, inward. Bend your elbows, and slowly lower the bells toward your shoulders. Your upper arms should remain still, and you must keep your elbows tucked in and pointed up, not back, to get maximum benefit from this exercise. To make it even better, rotate your palms inward as you lower the bells all the way almost to your shoulders. As you lift, rotate your palms out again.

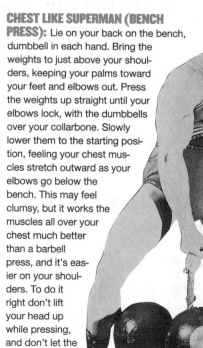

"The swelling is a nuisance, but the spare is handy."

BUST THAT GUT:
Tips to Train Your Abs.

Crunches and leg raises are workhorse ab excercises—they get the job done. But according to *The Fitness Bible* by Peter Anthony, there are a couple of rules to follow to make your paunch-eliminating exercises the most effective they can be:

■ **Warm-Ups.** Do your cardio training first to get you pumped up and limber. It enhances blood flow and makes you feel good about all the pain you're about to experience.

■ **Feet first.** The lower ab muscles (which are blasted best by leg raises) are the hardest to work. Focus on those first, before you start with crunches, which target your easy-to-work upper abdominals. Both of these are important for all-over tone, so don't cheat, weasel!

■ **Go slow.** All stomach exercises should be slow and deliberate so you can fully contract the muscles. If you bounce around, you'll use other muscles—such as your back—and end up in pain, riding the couch alone.

■ **Breathe right.** Inhale on the relaxing phase, and exhale on the exertion. This will help your muscles fully contract.

■ **Burn, baby.** Go for the burn on each set. Your stomach muscles are among the hardiest in your body. If you're not feeling that sucker-punched sensation, you're either way too lazy or using other muscle groups to cheat for your tummy. Cut it out.

Exercises in Futility

Cut out these time-wasters and still look like six million dollars.

■ Crunches
You'll spend 20 minutes building muscles you'll never see unless you get rid of the fat on top of them. Burning calories on a bike or treadmill is a more practical part of an "ab building" exercise program.

■ Concentration curls
Those bicep curls you do in The Thinker pose are great but only work about one-50th of the muscles within your body. A simple pull-up incorporates those same muscles while working one-10th of your body's muscle mass.

■ Leg extensions
A lot of guys like this exercise because it lets them watch their thigh muscles. What they don't see is that the inside surface of their kneecaps could be wearing away (Can you say "knee replacement"?), while the patella tendon, a muscle that supports the knee, wears also.

■ Weight belts
These manly items help you do overhead presses and squats, but most guys unnecessarily wear them throughout their entire routine—a move that may actually make their bodies weaker.

"With the right shoes, it could work."

DOWN ON THE PHARM

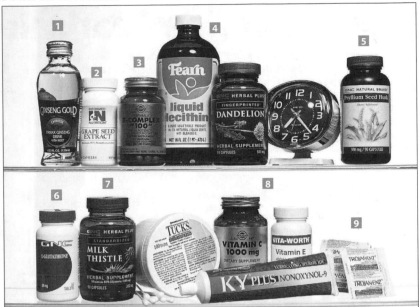

FLIRT WITH DEATH, STAY ALIVE

Stock up your medicine cabinet with the following goodies to help offset your Orson Welles-like habits.

1. **Ginseng:** An adaptogen herb that will lower your stress level while raising your energy.
2. **Grape Seed Extract:** May protect you from the ravages of tobacco.
3. **B Vitamins:** Alcohol flushes B vitamins from your body. Keep plenty of supplements on hand.
4. **Lecithin and Dandelion Supplements:** These will help scrub your liver clean after a hard night of drinking and debauchery.
5. **Psyllium Seed:** A natural high-fiber laxative that'll help to flush out all the junk food you've been scarfing.
6. **Glutathione Supplements:** These help your body break down alcohol efficiently—and minimize the toll on your kidneys.
7. **Milk Thistle:** Helps to avoid liver congestion.
8. **Vitamins C and E:** Smoking depletes the body's reserves of these crucial vitamins, leaving your immune system weakened.
9. **Condoms:** If you can't keep it in your pants, at least keep latex condoms in your medicine chest so you can always stay safe. Remember, use a water-based lubricant such as K-Y jelly—oil-based lubes break down latex.

Make Any Exercise Work Better

DO IT BACKWARD. Not for beginners, this trick forces your muscles to work in new and painful ways, and keeps you developing. Since muscles are grouped in pairs of opposites, this method gives you full value for your effort. Say you've been doing presses. Instead of doing a normal press, start from the top and lower the bar instead of raising it, only this time as slowly as you can, holding it in place at as many points as possible as you bring it down. You will not be able to do it many times, but it blasts your muscles and makes you hurt. And hurt is good.

Keep Your New Year's Resolution

Can self-hypnosis help you quit smoking, gain confidence, lose 15 pounds, and beat the crap out of your boss? Sure, why not? Jim Fortin, a hypnotherapist at the Hypnosis Institute in New York City, shows you the way with a 10-minute program designed to help you achieve a goal through auto-hypnosis—in this case, to shed 15 ugly pounds. You are getting sleepy...

STEP 1: LOSE THE SWINGING POCKET WATCH.

Forget that image of being under the spell of a hypnotist bent on making you cluck like a chicken. Modern hypnotherapy is about the power of positive thinking and imagery. "People think that with hypnosis you're losing control, but you're gaining control, since it helps you become more aware of what's going on in your head," says Fortin.

STEP 2: STATE YOUR GOAL POSITIVELY.

To make this work don't wish that you could ditch the repugnant slab of flab housing your abdomen. Instead think that you have reached your ideal weight. Stare into a mirror and visualize yourself with a more aerodynamic physique.

STEP 3: TALK TO YOURSELF.

For two or three minutes, give yourself specific instructions out loud, such as "I hate cigarettes!" or "I don't enjoy Ding Dongs!" This will "program" your subconscious to help you reach your goal.

STEP 4: RELAX, RELAX, RELAX.

Stare at a fixed point—if you have a poster of Alyssa Milano, her navel ring will do just fine—and take a deep breath. Close your eyes, count to three, and slowly exhale. Feel your body relaxing. Do this for a minute, then stop or you might tip over.

STEP 5: REINTRODUCE YOUR GOAL.

Imagine having reached your goal and state how you feel about it in the present tense (e.g., "I'm lean and I like it, damn it!").

STEP 6: RELAX AGAIN.

Close your eyes and count slowly from zero to 100 and back. Your conscious mind will become bored, but your unconscious mind will feel calm, happy, and suggestible.

STEP 7: LOOK INTO THE FUTURE.

For the next two to three minutes, focus on how being fit has changed your life. Picture chicks groping your taut bod and your bosses handing you fat raises just for looking so damn marvelous. "Your unconscious mind understands visual imagery and will know what to do from there," Fortin says.

STEP 8: CLOSE THE DEAL.

State your goal again, revel in your imagined body, and voilà: an affirming perspective on the new you. Sure, you'll still need to exercise and pass on the second pizza, but now let's hope those things will start to seem almost bearable. Repeat until blue jeans fit.

GET THE MENTAL EDGE

"10-4, good buddha!"

Whether you're training for a marathon or just trying to get a little more toned, your head is one muscle that can help you move mountains. Here's how to use it.

■ **Blow off steam.** When you're in the middle of an intense workout and you feel as if you want to quit, instead take a deep breath and blow it out hard and loud. This is a mind-clearing technique called the explosive exhale, used by competitors in all kinds of sports.

■ **Think form.** Imagine that the weight you're lifting is sliding on a track, with perfect smooth form. If you're running, do like Olympian Frank Shorter and imagine your legs are bicycle wheels, rolling gracefully around and around. This exercise will help keep your form perfect and effortless.

■ **Sweat the small stuff.** Arthur Ashe used to put a little note that said, MOVE YOUR FEET under the umpire's seat where only he could see it. Focus on the nitpicky details and you'll not only prevent screwups; you'll forget to be nervous.

■ **Visualize.** In one study people were asked to try different strategies of pumping a grip meter as hard as they could. Another group did nothing but count backward from 20. One group got mad at the meter. But the group that outperformed the rest simply visualized pumping the meter all the way down.

■ **Om it.** Frank Zane, a professional bodybuilder known for his pioneering work in concentration in bodybuilding, recommends a simple meditation. Sit comfortably in a quiet place, clear your thoughts, and mentally repeat a standard mantra, such as Om or a word of your own that has a pleasant sound. Do this for 15 to 20 minutes to start, twice a day, ideally before a workout. As you progress you should be better able to focus on one thing for a long period of time and ignore distractions. After a while, you'll be able to work out for longer periods with perfect focus, even losing track of time in the process.

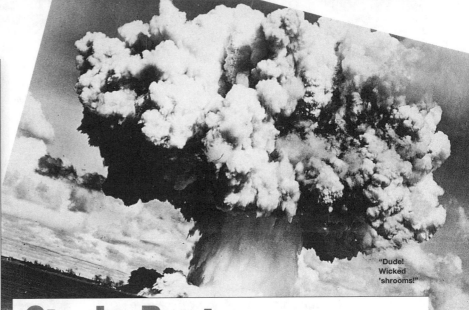

"Dude! Wicked 'shrooms!"

FLEX FOR SEX

Turn your routine into a love warm-up!

According to a study of 8,000 women by Linda De Villers, a Santa Monica, California, sex therapist, 40 percent of women who workout regularly report increased arousal, and 31 percent have sex more often. Here are exercises to get you ready for all this potential booty:

■ Create the mood.

Testosterone levels—yours and hers—skyrocket within an hour after aerobic exercise, according to Howard Devore, Ph.D., a clinical psychologist and certified sex therapist in San Francisco. Run together, but don't push it too hard, and you two will have no problem continuing the workout (and increased pushing) back at your place.

■ Get flexible for the kinky stuff.

Stand between two chairs, gripping the top of each firmly for support. Lunge back with one leg, then stand up and repeat with the other leg. Start with one set of eight, and build up until you're doing three sets of 12. After a few weeks of this, your thighs will be strong and flexible enough to bounce a quarter off of. Or anything else, for that matter.

■ Get hard and stay hard.

Practice working the muscle you use after you've had 10 beers and are waiting in a 20-person line for the bathroom. Seriously! Flex that muscle between your legs, known as the pubococcygeal muscle, and work up to three sets of 12 whenever you can—at work, on the bus ride home, sitting in the tub. This will give you greater staying power and better erections. It also makes your orgasms more intense.

Now prepare the massage oil and the Barry White tapes, and get down to business, ya big rock star.

Strain-Buster

Whether you spend a lot of time working out or sitting on your ass typing, you put a lot of strain and tension into your body.

Whether you spend a lot of time working out or sitting on your ass and typing, you put a lot of strain and tension into your body. Later in life this will turn you into a stooped, tired old man. Regardless of your future, here's some ways to get in tip-top shape:

To get rid of a sore spot on your back, put a tennis ball into a sock. Hang it down beneath your shirt, to where it hurts, and roll it against the wall. Wow, doesn't that feel better than a massage from a Thai whore? Well, maybe not. But your back feels better, doesn't it?

Pressure points. You know what people do to screw themselves up but good? Keep a wallet in a back pocket while sitting. The unbalanced pressure on your ass reverberates through your whole spine. Do that a little bit every day and it's trouble down the road. So ax that overstuffed condom carrier, and use a money clip in the front pocket instead.

If you have to stand for long periods, put one foot on a box or rock or short stool from time to time. Take it down and put up your other foot. This relieves a great deal of tension in your back. Plus, it makes you look folksier if you want to make a stump speech.

Here's a good exercise you can do at your desk to get tension out of your shoulders. First, with your right hand gently tug your left arm down and across, behind your back. Lean your head sideways toward the right shoulder. Hold this for 10 seconds. Then repeat on the other side.

If you work a keyboard all day, this is a nice way to relax your mitts and prevent carpal-tunnel from setting in. Place your hands palm to palm in front of you, as if you're going to say a prayer—only don't...it's too late to save your soul. Now move your hands downward, keeping your palms together, until you feel a nice stretch in your wrists. Keep your elbows up and even, and hold for five to eight seconds. If you want you can rotate them down and hold for a few more seconds. Or you can flex your palms from side to side. Vary this motion until you're so loose and cool, you can pick a lock with one hand and unsnap your girlfriend's bra with the other.

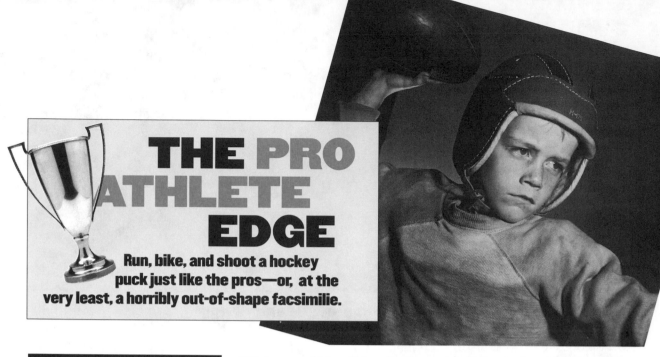

THE PRO ATHLETE EDGE

Run, bike, and shoot a hockey puck just like the pros—or, at the very least, a horribly out-of-shape facsimilie.

RUN LIKE MICHAEL JOHNSON

1. **"Use your upper body to power the lower,"** says Olympic gold medalist Michael Johnson. "Your arms and shoulders power you through and keep your body upright and in good form as your legs start breaking down at the finish line."

2. **Go slow, but rep fast.** Johnson doesn't run all out when he does wind sprints, but he waits only two minutes between sprints, instead of the traditional three.

3. **Stretch out and wait.** Johnson does thorough stretches, holding each for a couple of seconds, relaxing, and repeating 10 times a leg.

4. **Train hard!** According to one runner, a good training exercise for power sprinting is jumping rope. He recommends starting out with a series of jumping jacks to get the blood pumping. Then, when jumping rope, try to make each jump high—between 10 inches and a foot at least—for three or four minutes. This will really burn your thighs, which are the muscles you use to surge ahead in short concentrated bursts.

BIKE LIKE GREG LEMOND

1. **Fuel up.** Most athletes rely on high-energy gels and bars during a race, and an offtrack diet heavy in carbs. But according to U.S. Women's cross-country champion Ruthie Matthes, you should balance it with fruits and vegetables, and make sure you get your protein. Even though carbs help you get energy, eating regular amounts of lean protein during training helps you repair muscle tissue and build mass, which is important for high-speed cycling.

2. **Water, water everywhere.** Water improves your aerobic output, and a lack of it during intense biking can drop you on your ass faster than an armadillo crossing Interstate-10. During competitions, cyclists start with a few cups and then keep drinking often.

3. **Sprint work.** This was the standby for Major Taylor, one of the first bike champions in the 1890s and early 1900s. It builds quads for the heavy work and gets you in condition to burn fast. Taylor knew that back before anyone had ever heard the phrase, "personal trainer."

4. **Team up.** On a flat road wind resistance accounts for 70 percent to 90 percent of the resistance you feel when pedaling. And it's not just the air pushing back against you— when you have poor aerodynamic form, the air in back of you creates a low-pressure zone, which sucks you backward. If another cyclist slips into that area, he or she will be able to reach top speed. But it works for you too—by filling the void, the cyclist behinds you minimizes the suction. So you both win.

SHOOT A PUCK LIKE ERIC LINDROS

1. **Line it up.** What makes the wrist shot so lethal is its deadly combination of accuracy and quickness. "Accuracy is definitely more important than power, and a wrister is your most accurate shot," Lindros says. "Winding up and taking a slap shot usually gives the goalie too much time to get in the right position—goalies are so good today, you need a shot you can get off

quick." Since a defenseman won't often give you a clear look at the net, once you see an open spot not protected by the goaltender, take quick, careful aim and don't take your eyes off the target.

2. Load. Once you know where you want the shot to go, keep your weight over your back skate and pull the puck back behind your center of gravity. The point here is to get as much power as you can while simultaneously keeping the puck away from the defenseman. "Sometimes you can't use your body at all and you'll have to shoot off your wrong foot," Eric points out, which will undoubtedly sap strength from your shot. To ensure that you get as much power and accuracy out of the shot as possible, make sure the puck is cupped in the middle of the curve of your stick blade.

3. Let 'er rip. Sweep the stick forward, shifting your weight from your back leg to your front leg together with the motion of the stick. "It's not so much upper body strength as legs" that puts the power behind the wrist shot, Eric says. As the

over the shot, the puck will go low; keep the blade open and you'll roof it. "Most NHL goals are scored low," Eric points out, "but when you're playing in the beer league, with lots of good-looking women in the crowd, that top-shelf goal is pretty tough to resist."

SHOOT FREE THROWS LIKE REGGIE MILLER

1. Set up properly. The first thing you need to do, after staring the other team down, is relax. Then get your body square to (facing) the basket, get a secure footing, and distribute your weight equally on both feet. "It all starts with the feet," Miller says. "If your legs aren't balanced, everything else in your shot will be off." Your feet should be positioned shoulder width apart or farther; if they're too close, you'll end up off balance after finishing the shot. "The most important thing is to find the stance that works best for you and stick with it," says Miller.

feet—but don't jump. Push the ball toward the basket until your arm extends completely. Some free-throw champs swear by keeping their elbows in—it restricts their shooting to a vertical plane, so at least they can't miss left or right. But Miller doesn't buy it. "People always say, 'Keep your elbows in,'" he says. "But there are guys who stick their elbows out and sink 90 percent. Why should they change? Again, just do what's comfortable."

4. Follow through. As you release the ball, snap your wrist down to create backspin. This softens the shot (i.e., keeps it from careening too far back over the basket if it hits the rim) and produces that sweet sound of victory—swishhh. The secret to consistent success? Repeat 50,000 times. "The key is practice, practice, practice," says Miller, who cut his teeth shooting 200 free throws every day after school, rain or shine. Looks like our unkempt lawn's just gonna have to wait.

"The secret to consistent success? Repeat fifty thousand times. The key is practice, practice, practice."

puck passes your front skate, snap your wrists over as though you were swinging a baseball bat. To strengthen your wrists ("You guys aren't gonna make a masturbation joke, are you?"), try Eric's technique: "My brother and I would practice with weighted pucks in our garage. Of course when we moved out, there was a little woodwork to be done."

4. Follow through. As your weight carries forward over your front foot, turn your body into the shot, letting your back leg extend behind you for balance. Follow through with your wrist, pointing the stick at your target. This is where you decide the shot's direction: If you curl the toe of the blade

2. Concentrate. Don't read too much into the name of the shot. "Too many guys take for granted that it's a free throw," Miller says. "There's no defense, the clock's stopped, and it's a wide-open 15-footer—what's the big deal, right? Wrong attitude. You have to concentrate on every shot." Miller says he focuses by dribbling six times and taking a deep breath. "Then I lock on the basket." Pay no attention to the obnoxious fans behind the net waving Styrofoam wiggly wands.

3. Shoot. Hold the ball on the fingertips, not the palm, of your shooting hand. Aim just over the rim, bend slightly at the knees, and push off the court with your

SMACK HOMERS LIKE ALEX RODRIGUEZ

1. Get comfortable. With balls whizzing toward you at 95 miles an hour, you've got no time to be tense. Purge every thought from your mind, relax your body, and breeze up to the plate. "It's really like I'm swimming or dreaming," Rodriguez says. Bend your knees and get balanced, but don't squeeze the life out of the bat. Rodriguez holds his with the last three fingers of each hand, his thumbs and forefingers barely touching the bat. "Really soft," he says, "as if a 10-year-old girl could come up behind me a second before the pitch is thrown and slip the bat away from my hands." You heard it here first, folks.

2. See the pitch. Watch closely to see how the ball comes out of the pitcher's hand. If you see two fingertips a slight distance apart on top of the ball, a fastball's coming down the pike. If they're touching, expect a curve. If you miss the release, try to pick up on the ball's rotation: A fastball will show backspin, while a curve will turn toward you. (Oh, and you have about two-10ths of a second to do this.) "Your eyes are muscles, and some days they're able to lift 100 pounds," says Rodriguez. "Other days they won't see it quite as early." If you wait any longer than that fraction of a second, you may as well keep 'em closed.

3. Pull the trigger. Bring the bat back, flex, and strike ("like a snake," says Rodriguez), using your hips as well as your hands. "Like a golfer, your hips go back, the torque comes in, and whoosh!" Rodriguez says. Uppercuts may get oohs and aahs from the crowd, but Alex tries to swing down at fastballs to maintain a line-drive stroke. Stand square to the pitcher, aim straight up the middle, and for God's sake keep those hands soft. "If you squeeze just before contact," Rodriguez says, "the bat head will bounce an inch or two." And your calculated sweet spot will go sour.

4. Stay loose. So you've made contact. Congratulations, hotshot. Even though technically your job's done, don't pat yourself on the back just yet. Good follow-through mechanics can mean the difference between a pathetic dribbler for out number three, and a Sosa-esque monster shot. Rotate your body smoothly, making sure your hips go through their full range of motion and your arms extend fully. Go ahead and let it all out. Rodriguez exhales on every swing, because holding his breath keeps him bottled up and tense. "I feel an illusion in my mind," he says, "like I'm blowing the ball out of the ballpark." If only it were that easy.

CRASH LIKE EDDIE THE EAGLE
Nah, we're kidding.

YOU ARE WHAT YOU INHALE

Friendly Fast Food

A trip to the Golden Arches doesn't have to be a life decision. Here are meals you can order with 50 percent less guilt than the leading slop.

TACO BELL: CHICKEN BURRITO
This offers a full serving of protein and carbs, and is fairly low in fat, as long as you ask them to hold the cheese and sour cream. Load up on salsa, get extra veggies if you can, and you've got a meal. A grilled-chicken soft taco is just as good.

LONG JOHN SILVER'S: BAKED FISH AND A POTATO WITH SALSA
The one thing on the menu that isn't deep fried. Get the salsa with the potato and you have tasty carbage without the sour cream lard-ass effect.

MCDONALD'S: GRILLED CHICKEN DELUXE
Tell them to hold the special sauce, and order extra lettuce and tomatoes if you can talk them into it—or just swipe some from someone's salad. The grilled chicken is high in protein and carbs, with minimal fat. You can also have someone ordering a salad steal you an extra lite Italian dressing packet for flavor.

ARBY'S: TURKEY DELUXE
Without the mayo, this gives you a full serving of carbs and protein.

BURGER KING: BK BROILER
Tell them to hold the mayo on this chicken sandwich and replace with mustard. And get yourself a hat while you're at it.

Get a Workout Anywhere
Now you've got no excuse for not getting in shape. Sorry.

Staircase Stretches (legs)
Let your heel hang off the step. Drop your heel until you feel a stretch in your calf and hamstring. Hold for 30 seconds, then release. Repeat with other heel. After the stretch run up and down the stairs. Bonus: The dog will go insane chasing you.

Broomstick Twists (abs)
"They allow you to work your abs by twisting left to right," says Don Hamlet, fitness manager at New York Sports Club. Then work your obliques by bending from side to side. Bonus: Mom will think you're helping out with the cleaning.

Bed Crunches (more abs)
By hooking your feet under the frame, you avoid cheating. Keep your abdominal muscles tensed throughout two minutes of crunches (use the bedside alarm clock to time yourself). Bonus: Discover all those old porno mags stashed under the bed.

Water Weights (biceps)
Take two jugs of water or milk, and presto, an instant river of resistance. Do curls or any other exercises you'd normally do with free weights. Just make sure those caps are on tight. Bonus: Liquid refreshment's at your fingertips.

Steering Wheel Push-ups (chest and triceps)
Grasping the sides of the wheel, press your body toward it, resisting with your arms. Then pull your torso away, again using your arms to resist. Bonus: Other drivers will see your grimacing and assume you're about to kill them.

What Else to Eat

Food, glorious food. Though your frequent over-indulgence makes you resent it at times, food can be your greatest ally during physical and emotional stress. According to his book *Doctor, What Should I Eat?*, Isadore Rosenfeld, M.D., tells what foods he found work best to get you through the tough times, and why.

MAIN EVENT	HOW TO CHOW	HERE'S WHY
You're flying to Singapore to research whether they really have the world's hottest brothels. You want to bypass that pesky jet lag and get right to the action, so prepare your Eastern-time-zoned body ahead of time.	3 days before the flight: Feast on fish, chicken, eggs, yogurt, pasta, and potatoes. 2 days before: Fast with salad, clear soup, plain toast, and fruit. 1 day before: Feast again. The day of the flight: water only until arrival.	This feast-fast-feast method seems to reduce the severity and length of jet lag. It is believed to affect the enzymes that regulate the amount of sugar stored or released by the liver.
The boys are back in town, and you need to prepare yourself. Day one nearly killed you, and it ain't over yet. You want to make friends with your liver again before you send it back out to the wolves.	Eat a power-packed breakfast (even if it is noon) of flavored yogurt (non-fat and sugar free), poached eggs, and whole wheat toast.	After one or more bouts of constant heavy drinking, your liver may become inflamed and you could suffer from protein malnutrition. Protein-rich foods aid in the restoration of your once-healthy organs.
You've been chosen to make the big presentation. A nerve-wracking speech can, well, wrack your nerves, and you want to avoid shitting your pants in front of a large group.	Start the day with a meal consisting of fresh fruit, eggs, whole grain toast, and cottage cheese.	Low blood sugar will make you feel anxious and shaky. A high-complex-carbohydrate breakfast will prevent low blood sugar later in the day, leaving you less panicky.
Your persistence and/or pathetic looks have finally paid off. You got that hot secretary from the next building to go out with you, but your love engine is in dire need of a tune-up.	Snack for a few days on a combination of chicken, peas, cheddar cheese, bananas, and cashews (dry roasted).	Think zinc. Some urologists recommend foods high in zinc to men with impaired libido. Even a mild deficiency in this mineral can lower your testosterone level.
It's time again for the battle of the sexes at your work picnic, and this time you can't be shown up by Nelson down in accounting.	Load up on brown rice, baked potatoes (skin on), corn, peas, and bagels.	Lots of carbohydrates allow you to produce energy quickly. Carbs work double-duty to prevent or reduce fatigue.
Time for another fun-filled, seven hour car ride to her Aunt Betty's. Better pack a few extra shirts. Whoever said, "Getting there is half the fun," never suffered from car sickness.	Drink gingerroot tea. Just steep slices of the fresh root in a cup of boiling water. You may want to make a big batch and put it in a thermos so it's handy in the car.	Researchers are trying to decide if gingerroot acts on the inner ear, nervous system, or stomach. Most people don't care what the reasoning is; they're too busy thanking God it works.

"I drink to forget, but...what?"

HEAVY DRINKING
Not that you drink heavily, of course.

When it comes to eating like a swine and drinking like a Viking, you're the man. At least you can be with tips from Paul Fegen. Touted as The Party King of L.A., and attorney for Hollywood Madam Heidi Fleiss (our ultimate party girl), Fegen tells us how he's made it through decades of being one of the boys.

■ Drinking on an empty stomach is every amateur's downfall.
So make sure you eat plenty, but don't do what women do: eat a big meal at home, then continue to nibble throughout the evening. You don't want to be so stuffed that you can't breathe, or worse yet, drink.

"Extra large, please."

■ Be careful about the foods you choose to line your stomach with.
Eat lots of gut-loving avocado and fruit. Most importantly, don't forget the bread, which really helps to soak up the suds. Foods to stay away from are the obvious choices that ordinarily leave you smelling like a neglected infant. Beans, tacos, and burritos are out... even if it is Cinco de Mayo.

Tuscan MILK VITAMIN D

Tuscan

MILK

An udder necessity.

■ Get milk.
Milk coats the stomach well and adds healthy fluids you're going to wish you had more of the morning after.

■ Sleep well the night before.
You need to log some serious R.E.M. sleep if you want to be the last man on the mountain. Rob yourself of precious sleep the week before and you're likely to be the asswipe who wakes up with pissed pants and your hand in a bowl of warm water.

■ Have sex!
Fegen advises having sex before the party so all that's left to concentrate on is the important stuff: the boys and the booze. Being physically and emotionally satisfied will add to your preparedness and will quell any anxious feelings you may have.

■ Stay out of the medicine cabinet.
You don't want any adverse interaction between the booze and the drugs (think Marilyn Monroe, Jimi Hendrix, and Janis Joplin, for example.). But you'll want to have plenty of pain-soothing pills to alleviate those nagging suicidal tendencies the morning after.

■ Drink mixed drinks over shots to make your stay last longer.
Downing the shots early is a good way to end up praying to the porcelain god before the midnight hour. Go with mixed drinks, and force yourself to sip them slowly. Always choose mixers that are carbonated—as opposed to acidic, heartburn-inducing fruit juices.

ASK ANYTHING
Is there any truth to the old saying "Beer before liquor, never been sicker. Liquor before beer, never fear"?

The Maxim staff has made numerous attempts to settle this matter, but we've repeatedly been denied the federal funding needed to complete our study. However, some real scientists think they know why the adage holds water: "If you drink beer, it takes awhile for the alcohol to be absorbed," says Walter Hunt, Ph.D., a senior science advisor at the National Institute on Alcohol Abuse and Alcoholism. "But if you take a shot of bourbon, you can feel the alcohol very quickly." Scenario one: You chug a brew, chase it with bourbon, and get hit with a double whammy as the drinks sabotage your system simultaneously. Scenario two: You drink liquor, then start on the beer, which hits you just as the liquor is wearing off. For full effect try out both scenarios with Pabst Blue Ribbon and Everclear and see which leaves you retching in the bathroom—and which leaves you dancing naked on the table.

Man Chowder

Still wondering why your little missus doesn't put her mouth to the south too often?

"You can't fool me, I've tasted chicken before, and..."

Stop trying to figure out what's eating her, and concentrate on what *you're* eating. Fortunately, nutritionists have studied women's opinions on how food alters the taste of your Johnson's juice.

FOODS TO STAY AWAY FROM:

■ Alkaline-based foods like meats and seafood tend to produce a (surprise!) fishy taste. You may lose all grounds to complain about *her* essence if you violate this one.

■ Dairy products (because of their potentially high bacterial levels) are noted as contributing to the most repulsive of tastes. This may mean you actually have to eat a real meal on the Big Night. Cold cereal or the wheel of cheese you snagged from the office party is out.

■ Likewise, asparagus is reported to generate God-awful tasting elements. This is fairly easy to believe for two reasons: It's got a fucked-up flavor to begin with, and it turns your pee that frightening neon color. Foul-tasting cum is just another reason to steer clear of this ironically phallic veggie.

■ Chemically processed liquors bring about a rush of acidlike tang. If you like the heavy stuff, it's best to stick with brands that use the old-fashioned distilling methods. If not, it's like laying her tongue across a 9-volt battery, and you can expect her to pull away fast.

■ Coffee and cigarettes are both said to be major sponsors in the "He tasted fucking nasty" contest. Of course if you smoke and drink coffee regularly, you may be more apt to get the blow job anyway. She'll probably go down on you just to escape your breath.

BEST BETS:

■ Stick to sweet acidic foods such as fruits. By giving bodily fluids a pleasant, sugary flavor she'll love, fruit may replace Doritos in your snack hierarchy. Go with fresh fruits instead of canned for optimal effect.

■ Naturally fermented beers will give your juice a subltly sweet, pleasing flavor. Drop the Meisterbrau and switch to a higher-quality brew, if only for tonight. Don't overdo it, though. Being sweet is one thing, but you don't want to look like an import-drinking poser.

HACK JOB
Beat the office cold.

Your workplace is a breeding ground for disgusting parasites (but enough about your boss). Ever notice how some people are always ailing for one reason or another, while others never seem to get bit by the bug? To be one of the latter, stay away from the former, and use this no-wuss, no-fuss guide to germ warfare. Prevention is the key to saving your sick days.

CLOSE YOUR MOUTH. Germs are everywhere, including the air. In fact they can fly as far 30 feet. So if you're forced to sit near someone who's coughing, wheezing, or sneezing, keep your mouth shut and breathe through your nose, where tiny hairs act as filters to keep out the germs.

HYDRATE. Your nose will filter germs more efficiently if you keep it lubed. The easiest way to do that is to drink over eight cups of water a day. In addition, have one 16-ounce bottle of Gatorade (you know, the thirst quencher) a day to replenish your salt and potassium stores.

WASH YOUR HANDS. You infect yourself by touching hard surfaces such as the coffee maker, the Xerox machine, elevator buttons, and doorknobs, where filthy, germ-encrusted coworkers have inadvertently left behind viral critters that can live for hours. A 1997 study conducted by Purdue University says the key is to wash your hands often with antibacterial soap and warm water.

HIT THE GYM. Moderate exercise two or three times a week will help ward off a cold: A mellow workout increases the circulation of your immune cells, but throw in the towel after an hour: According to Appalachian State University exercise science professor David Nieman, that's when stress hormones that actually suppress your immune system kick in.

GET A WINDOW SEAT. You want to avoid stagnant, germ-laden air at all costs, so always try to be near an open window during office meetings. If you must share an office with a bona-fide sicko, try wearing one of those heavy WWI-era gas masks, or at least keep the window open and the air moving. (A tiny desk fan can work wonders.)

ASSEMBLE A BEVY OF BUDS. More friends equals fewer colds, according to a Carnegie Mellon University study, because your pals help you deal with immune-system-suppressing stress. And knocking back a couple of stiff drinks a day may help keep the colds at bay (some docs theorize that alcohol alters a cold virus' ability to reproduce). But too much alcohol weakens your immune system, making you more vulnerable to the nasties.

GO AHEAD, KISS HER. Good news: Smooching is still relatively safe, since 90 percent of cold viruses lurk in your snot, not your spit. But again, opt for making out in the supply room with the window cracked rather than atop the hideously germ-soaked photocopier.

SHIT HAPPPENS

ER Advice

Ever dreamed of using your bravery and/or bullshit to save the day? We asked Bernie DePalma, physical therapist and Cornell University's head athletic trainer, how to play doctor.

The situation: *Your buddy was inadvertently fed the ass-end of a pool stick. His busted tooth needs saving.*
Your technique: If the tooth is partially broken, have him bite down on a towel, shirt, or wad of tissue to stabilize and maintain pressure on the roots. For a completely knocked-out tooth, have him put it back in place and apply pressure. If he's still kicking someone's ass over it, save the tooth in a bath of water or cold milk.

The situation: *Of course juggling chain saws looks easier than it really is. Now it's your job to stop the gushing blood.*
Your technique: Apply direct and firm pressure to the wound. If possible elevate the bloody stump above heart level until help arrives.

The situation: *A little tap with the ball, and your girlfriend's going Marcia Brady on you. Hearing "Oh, my nose!" over and* over is making it hard to hear the next play. You need to determine if it's broken.
Your technique: Ask her exactly where the pain is. A fracture can be expected if there is severe pain around bone sites. It takes a lot of experience to determine a fracture by simply feeling around (sorry, Mom), so stabilization and an x-ray are your best bets.

The situation: *Your pal "Sonny" has busted his leg and his femur is sticking out farther than his overly waxed skis.*
Your technique: Help him maintain consciousness, then stabilize the fracture site. Create a makeshift splint using clothing, newspapers, or whatever else is handy.

The situation: *You could have sworn the little dot on the spray-paint can was facing out. Not only do you have one Bashful Beige eye, but it feels like it's on fucking fire.*
Your technique: Immediately flush the eye in the downward-most position (so you don't flush the chemicals into your other eye, Dummy). You can't over-flush, so keep introducing the water until help arrives. Cover the eye with a wet cloth and apply pressure.

The situation: *There's a reason it's called a skill saw: It's supposed to be used by someone who has skill handling it, not the stockbroker next door who fancies himself "handy." You hear "Where's my fucking*

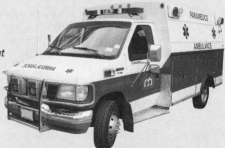

finger? Oh, Jesus Christ, my finger..."*
Your technique: Pick up the digit (go on, chicken, it won't bite), wrap it in cloth, and put it on ice, if available. Help him keep pressure on the wound with a clean towel, call a doctor, and set a date for the garage sale.

SURVIVE A KICK TO THE NADS

Her boots weren't just for walking, apparently. Your angry ex attempts to heighten your arousal in a whole new, and excruciatingly painful, way. Since chasing her down is not an option at this point (unless you're looking to end up in the custody of Johnny Law), take care of your boys instead.

■ Check for both testes first. If one or both have taken a trip up north, better see a healthcare professional, like, *now*.
■ If everything's in place, check for bleeding. You may want to see a doctor if you're bleeding from anything more than an obvious scrape.

■ Apply ice as soon as possible. You should check in on the little ones frequently, just to make sure no major changes take place. Then use your newly acquired free time to rest, read, clean your gun...whatever.

Kick Insomnia's Ass

Top tricks and advice to help you get into Club Dreamland, where the women are prettier and the booze is free:

COUNT BREATHS.

This is a great way of disrupting all the nagging thoughts that come into your head when you want to nod off. And it's better than sheep, because the breaths you take are real, not weird, fluffy, and cartoonish. Count an inhale as one, the exhale as two, the second inhale as three, and so on. When you get to five or 10, you can go back to one. Breathe slowly and deeply.

TRY A SWEEP.

Move your attention slowly and deliberately up your body as you flex and then relax each part. Start at your toes, then continue with your feet, legs, etc. Breathe deep and slow. As you move up your body, feel it getting heavier and sinking deeper into the ground. When you reach your neck, gently work all the different muscles there. Ditto your face and head. Now give yourself a temple massage. Using both thumbs press on each eyebrow. Starting at the the nose, apply light and steady pressure, and move back toward the ear. Stop every quarter inch and hold it for about 15 seconds. Then use the rest of your fingers to continue the process, running back from the ear to the nose.

NOTICE WHAT YOUR EYES ARE DOING.

According to some experts, there are links between nervous states of mind and nervous eye movements. Try to focus on keeping your eyes still, relaxed, and closed. This method can dampen your hyperactivity, and let you get some...well, shut-eye.

OTHER TIPS:

Face your clock to the wall to reduce stress, and watch the amount of alcohol and caffeine you consume in the hours before bedtime. Exercise in the evening is good, but vigorous exercise within a couple hours of bedtime can keep you awake. Also make sure you use your bed for sleeping, not lounging around—that way, when you go to bed, your body has a crystal-clear signal that it should be shutting down.

LETTING ONE RIP...

When somebody farts and you smell it, aren't you really breathing in tiny molecules of shit?

Don't worry, there aren't molecules of shit in there—just molecules of intestinal gas that smell like a barnyard in August. Farts are precursors of poop: They're the body's way of saying, "Shit's about to happen." They don't contain digested food or food by-products, but whether they stink (and how fiercely they stink) does depend on the food you ate beforehand. If you eat a balanced meal, the bacteria in your gut will produce odorless gases that slip into the world inconspicuously. But if you gorge on certain proteins, the bacteria will churn out hydrogen sulfide and other noxious sulfur gases, which explains why your girlfriend won't sleep with you after all-you-can-eat wing night. These odoriferous offenders come in trace amounts but pack such a powerful punch that you can sniff them from six movie rows away.

"Daddy's eating beans again!"

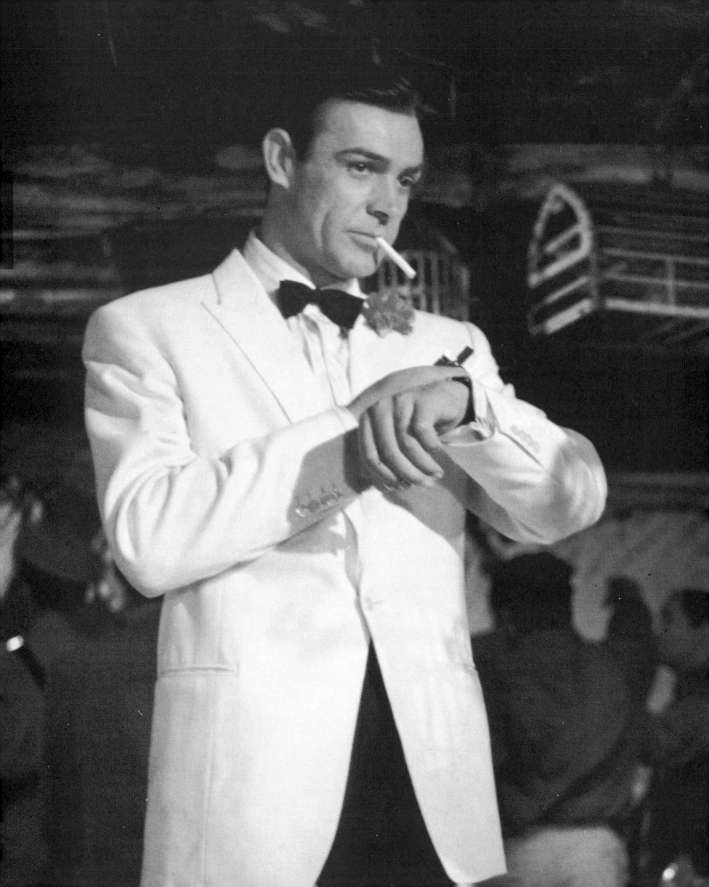

STYLE EDGE

Because it's much more important to look good than to feel good

Whether you need a whole-image overhaul or just a few tweaks, we'll help you dress better, groom groomier, and use your charm to win friends and influence people. Remember:

Landing jobs, getting noticed at clubs, and making women tear their own clothes off and ovulate on command is tough work, but someone's got to do it. We'll help you do it with style.

"Scotty...I just beamed out, and I'm chilly."

Make the Threads Count

Every girl's crazy 'bout a sharp-dressed man.

The Scoop on Buying a Sport Coat
Even if your wardrobe consists mainly of worn jeans and sweat-stained Motörhead T-shirts, you need a quality sport coat for those instances when you're around people who don't accessorize their latest tattoo with leather chaps. The trick is to find a jacket that fits into your meager budget, without looking like a defendant on *The People's Court.*

■ If you're only getting one jacket, pick a navy blue number. It goes with everything else and looks less grim than black. And according to studies on the psychological effect of colors, navy blue is a shade that conveys power and authority. Just ask a cop.

■ If you're not sure whether it fits, always try on the next biggest size. Guys try to

squeeze into a jacket that's too small because they don't want to admit they've gained weight. Fact is, nothing makes you look chubbier than wearing something tighter than a sausage casing. Give the waist button a tug; if it barely moves, you're kidding yourself.

■ Show some shirt. Half an inch of shirt collar should show above the jacket. The end of the sleeve should fall an inch above the base of the thumb. This will display half an inch of cuff. Also a jacket collar should lay smoothly around the neck. No gaps between it and your shirt, or the jacket doesn't fit right.

■ The waist button tells all. On the classic two-button jacket, this will sit an inch below your natural waistline. Too high and you'll look like you've got a stubby torso. Too low and you'll look like you're walking on your knees.

■ Check length. Put the thing on. Measure the distance from under the jacket's back collar to the floor. Now divide by two to get the right length.

■ Shoulders are key. The seam of the jacket's shoulder ought to lie just past the end of your own. Too wide and you'll look like a pinhead. Too narrow makes your head look bigger than Rush Limbaugh's. Also avoid overly square or padded shoulders, unless you're fronting for a 1980s cover band.

■ Lapels should be slightly rolled and extend halfway between the collar and shoulder line. When you squeeze a lapel, it will return to its original shape without any wrinkles.

■ Side vents on jackets should be lined up evenly and be anywhere from three to nine inches in length. Center vents should be seven to nine inches long.

■ Wear solid-color trousers with a sports coat, or else you'll look like you've got a side job making balloon animals.

Sexist Shirts?

Why do men's shirts, but not women's, button right to left?

It's all about gaining access to the chest. In the 17th century, when men started wearing button-up jackets, they buttoned them right to left in keeping with the pattern used for armor, which was designed to make it difficult for a right-handed opponent to thrust a sword into the seam. Theories vary as to why the sides were reversed on women's shirts, according to Deirdre Donohue, the librarian of the Costume Institute at New York's Metropolitan Museum of Art. Perhaps the switch made it easier for maids to dress their mistresses, or perhaps it helped mothers breast-feed with the left breast, located over a woman's heart and more comforting to babies. Horny male tailors may have had something to do with it: If a woman's shirt buttons left to right, a right-handed man can get at her mams more easily.

Tie You Up, Tie You Down

Here's why these fuckin' nooses exist.

If there's one item of clothing nearly every man despises, it has to be the wretched necktie. Undeniably useless, our oh-so-important business accessory causes us unending frustration, expense, and discomfort. At least the lady's counterpart, the scarf, does serve a purpose: It can be used to cover her head in the case of a rainstorm. All a necktie doubles as is a head band for a drunken prom-goer. In our quest to find the bastard to blame for the modern noose, we found ourselves up against an army.

Through the 1600s Croatian soldiers were presented to nobility in Paris with linen and silk scarves wrapped around their necks. Whether the *cravat* (named after the Croats for their inspiration) had any real military function or was simply the first lasting fashion statement, no one is sure. It has been reported they could be wrapped solidly to buffer a sword's blade, or be soaked in water to keep the regiment cool. No matter: The always fashionable French liked what they saw and began incorporating the style into their everyday lives. It didn't take the English long to jump on the band-wagon, thus associating them-selves with both the mas-culinity of soldiers and the refinement of royalty (albeit *French* royalty). Lesson: Never trust the French.

Now, for the practical stuff: how to tie the damn thing.

You should always wrap it around your finger and bring the skinny end up to the fat end at an angle—as you've seen people do before—because no tie looks exactly the same tied as hanging down off the rack. You should take a quick gander before you get it home and it's too late.

For a nice finishing touch, get the dimple centered just below the knot. If you like the way a tie clip holds a tie in place, but you think jewelry on guys is best left to Mr. T, try this: Pass the narrow end of the tie through the label, then use your tie clip to secure it, under the label and behind your tie. The clip won't be visible, but your tie will stay in place.

The tie should come down to the very top of your buckle—any lower and it will look like you're four years old and messing in dad's closet. Higher and you'll look like a New Orleans D.A.

Style Check

How to tell if your suit is older than your pick-up lines.

The happy times, before *Pennies From Heaven* and *Caddyshack 2.*

WACKY COLORS ARE OUT.

You are not a *Dick Tracy* villain. Beware of plaids and bold stripes, and immediately burn all "novelty colors"—lavender, pink, seafoam green—unless you and Tubbs are about to bust a huge coke drop on Miami Beach, Florida. Next time stick to the Civil War spectrum: blues and grays. "The classics never go out of style," says Ralph Lauren executive John Haarbauer. "That means solid colors: navy blue, gray, black."

SHOULDERS CARRY WEIGHT.

Those heavily padded suits you bought in the late '80s and early '90s were great when you played defensive line for the Green Bay Packers, but today they've gone the way of Ray Rhodes. Be careful, though: If the shoulders are too thin, you're treading on Pee-Wee Herman territory. An imaginary line running perpendicular from the shoulder seam to the ground should just graze the outside of your arm.

Hey, we said *imaginary* line—if you draw on the suit, you're paying for it, buddy.

LAPEL SIZE MAKES THE MAN.

The standard width for lapels has long been agreed upon as four inches (it's in the Warsaw Pact. We checked). If yours are three inches or less, it looks self-consciously cutting-edge: great if you're a club kid; risky if you actually have a job. Lapels that exceed five inches say, "Well, you can tell by the way I use my walk / I'm a woman's man: No time to talk." And with that look the women won't have time to talk to you, either.

SHIRTS AND TIES CAN HELP.

Even if you've got the right suit, you can still be done in by accessorizing incorrectly. Dark suits (blacks and grays) can never go wrong with a white shirt—see how easy that was?—while navy suits look best with shirts in lighter shades of blue. Stick to this simple solid palette and practically any non-fish tie will work; go crazy and treat yourself to a silver one. But be careful to avoid looking too "Regis."

Ditch Your Iron
Ironing without all the, you know, ironing.

"I shall flatten your underwear with pleasure."

Since pulling off a polished look with minimum effort remains the *true* measure of the man, we contacted Fran Sadler, technical information specialist with the International Fabricare Institute, for tips on how to look well-pressed without ironing.

Tip #1: Get space-age threads.
Ever notice how on *Star Trek,* no one's clothes are ever wrinkled? Manufacturers including Hagar, Savane, Arrow and Van Heusen sell treated pants and shirts that resist wrinkling. If the idea of synthetics makes you itch, try a polyester-and-cotton blend, which shows fewer creases than all-cotton fabrics. And stay away from linen, unless it's under your dinner plate.

Tip #2: Be a softie.
When washing clothes use liquid fabric softener during the rinse cycle. Note: Softener sheets don't have the same wrinkle-erasing effect—stick with the liquids.

Tip #3: Rinse, snap, spin.
Resist the urge to chuck that big wet ball of clothes into the dryer. Instead, when removing clothes from the washer, separate out each garment from the others, give it a quick snap, and lay it gently in the dryer. A minute here can save an hour of ironing during the game.

Tip #4: Hang 'em while they're hot.
Convenient though it may be, try not to leave your clothes in the dryer after it stops. "While your clothes are still warm, give everything another snap and hang 'em up," advises Sadler.

Tip #5: Take advantage of your bed.
Start using the space between your mattress and box spring for more than stashing Victoria's Secret catalogs. Slip your pants in there overnight and when you wake up, presto, they're pressed.

Tip #6: Give 'em a tumble.
The ol' hang-your-threads-near-a-hot-shower trick works to a point, but here's a better one: After you shower throw any clothes with nagging wrinkles into the dryer with your damp towel. Wait a few minutes, then take them out: The dampness and the heat should roll away the creases.

Tip #7: Get steamed.
Invest in a portable steamer, the magic wand for wrinkled clothes. Wave it in front of a garment and, quicker than you can recall that childhood fantasy about the *Bewitched* babe, your creases will disappear.

Size matters
Settle down. We mean clothes here, sport.

If you've got some dough to spend on clothes, make sure you pick stuff that works for your body type or you'll look like a teeny, tiny dog wearing a sweater: uncomfortable and full of spit. Here's a handy breakdown:

BODY TYPE	SUITS AND JACKETS	COLORING	FABRIC
AHNOLD	Get a special athletic-cut suit that has a "drop," or jacket that's a different size than the trousers. Or buy a matching jacket and trousers separately.	Dark colors and subtle or no patterns. Why? Because when people see a big, brightly colored swatch of fabric, they think it's a flag.	Medium-weight or light-weight works best to minimize your stature and make you look less scary.
TATOO	Fit is crucial or you'll look lost in your clothes. Side vents and center vents add to the vertical, but avoid pocket flaps and wide lapels. Pick a two- or three-button single-breasted, or a double-breasted job (you'll need to button the lower button). This makes you look a little taller—unless you're standing next to Ricardo Montalban.	Pinstripes are good for obvious reasons. And when you wear a sport coat, make sure there's a little contrast between the jacket and trousers. A sort of "Hey, look at me down here!" approach to fashion.	Light- or medium-weight—otherwise, you'll get lost in the texture of the fabric.
LURCH	Two-button single-breasted suits are a sure bet. If you wear a double-breasted number, button the middle button. "Tall"-size suits have a longer jacket length and a long rise in the trousers. With sport coats shoulders should be squared and slightly padded, and the fit at the waist should be loose or straight. Flapped pockets fill you out.	You can wear plaids well, but avoid stripes. A contrast between your coat and trousers is good, and think about bold patterns and colors if you're wearing a sweater or casual shirt.	Medium to heavy fabrics. And even bulky old tweed looks good on you.
BALLOON MAN	A three-button jacket will add height. Double-breasted can cut away thickness. Slanted flapless pockets make you slimmer. Avoid ventless jackets if you've got a big ass. But don't go too far: Think roomy, not baggy.	Simple patterns. Solids in dark colors. Vertical stripes. These all minimize your bulk. Not too much contrast between your jacket and pants or it will draw attention to your middle like a T-shirt that reads, BABY INSIDE.	Medium-weight or light-weight. Avoid tweed, unless you want to look like a bushel of wheat.
TWIGGY	Avoid three-breasted suits or jackets. Try shoulders with soft padding, wider lapels, and double vents. Patch- and flap-pockets also bulk you out a little.	Try bold patterns or contrasting jacket and slacks.	Tweeds are good. They add to your size and make you look professorial.

SHIRTS AND TIES	TROUSERS	SHOES	ACCESSORIES	GLASSES	TOPCOATS
Try a straight point collar instead of a spread. Vertical stripes are good, because of their slimming quality.	If your lower body is as developed as Jennifer Lopez's, try dark colors for camo.	Avoid a heavy, clunky look, unless you're going for Herman Munster chic.	Try suspenders, which minimize your chest bulk with their vertical lines.	People with large faces should avoid little specs. If your features are really square, try glasses with rounded edges to soften your look and make you appear cuddly for the ladies.	Single-breasted with set-in sleeves. You'll still look like a wall—but a well-dressed wall.
Wear thin, short ties.	They should have a medium break on the trouser bottoms. And cuffs are fine, as long as they're between 1" and 1.25"	Substantial, even clunky. And nothing with a curled point and bells.	Like somone with an athletic build, you can use the vertical line that comes with suspenders.	Avoid the big, overdone, Sally Jesse look. Think trim, lightweight, and metal.	Keep it at knee-length. Anything longer and you'll look like you're dressing in Dad's clothes.
A wide spread collar and/or a tie with a big honking wide knot like a Windsor will work well, because they widen your face and neck. Horizontal stripes are a plus, but you probably knew that.	Beware of high cuffs, unless you want to look stretched. Make sure the pants have a long rise, which accommodates big pins nicely.	Substantial, which draws the eye down and balances you out.	Belt, especially with a little contrast between it and the pants. This can add a nice horizontal line, which makes you seem less sequoia-like.	Pick slender frames. Try to get types with the temples placed near the middle of or low on the frames. A low bridge helps minimize a big schnozz.	Loose-fitting, double-breasted, which fits nicely with a tall frame.
Regular point collars are best. No bow ties, unless you're going for that Oliver Hardy look. Make sure the tie comes down to your belt buckle. And avoid short sleeves, even with casual shirts.	Wear your pants in line with your natural waist, lined up with your belly button—this will prevent gut spillage over your buckle.	Dark and thin-soled is fine.	Avoid anything brightly colored or contrasting with your other clothes.	Try something with high temples and a high nose bridge to give a round face more edge. Rimless glasses are good, too.	Single-breasted with a set-in sleeve.
A spread collar will broaden your face, and a wide knot will make you get horizontal, baby. If you have a long neck, try a tab or pin collar.	Get cuffs at about 1.25" to 1.5"	Something wide with a heavy sole.	Vests and V-neck sweaters add some weight to you.	Full rims around the lenses will shorten your face. Mid to low temples are good.	Raglan sleeves and double-breasted types are perfect.

MAXIMIZE YOUR LIFE **31**

Five Tips to Banish Pit Stains Forever

Some summer days it doesn't matter how well you looked when you put yourself together—one commute later and you're like Michael Douglas in *Falling Down*. Here's how to fight pit stains:

ONE: Keep your shirts starched. They won't cling and soak up your sweat. On the contrary, there will be more room for air to circulate around your body.

TWO: Stay away from nylon and polyester fabrics. Cotton is good. For a more formal office, invest in a tropical-weight wool suit.

THREE: Invest in some baby powder to prevent heat rash in your pits or groin. Unless you like scratching there.

FOUR: Wear a T-shirt underneath your dress shirt. It keeps your shirts from soaking you up. Avoid coffee until after you get to the air-conditioned office. It's a diuretic and revs your system up—so when you leave your home and hit that hot air, your sweat glands just kick into action. Wait for your caffeine buzz until you're safely indoors.

"Yes, Regis, that's my final answer!"

"Uh...club soda? Quick?"

Get Out a Stain

We can dress you up, but we can't take you anywhere.

Just before your big interview, a ketchup-drenched hot dog squirts out of its bun and slimes your $90 shirt. Don't panic—here's help.

Lipstick on Your Collar
Solution: Rub with dish detergent and cold water; if it doesn't work, try scrubbing it with rubbing alcohol.

Red Wine on Your Tie
Solution: Pour white wine or salt on stain.

Grass on Your Ass
Solution: No quick fix; apply a "stain stick," such as Dow's Spray 'N Wash stain stick, and wash as usual.

Gum on Your Shoe
Solution: Rub with ice to harden, then scrape off with dull knife.

Ballpoint Pen on Your Shirt Pocket
Solution: Saturate with alcohol-based hairspray or sour milk.

Hamburger Grease in Your Lap
Solution: Chew, damn it. Or: Rub talcum powder into grease to absorb it, then wash as usual.

Chocolate in Your Pocket
Solution: Soak in cold water for at least 30 minutes.

Dog Piss on Your Pant Leg
Solution: Blot with towel, then wash with a mix of one tablespoon white vinegar and one cup lukewarm water.

Semen on Your Intern's Blue Dress
Solution: Just tell her to tuck it away and forget about it.

Blood on Your Belly
Solution: Sop with one tablespoon of ammonia; stitch up slash in shirt.

Make It Last

■ Look for buttons that have a hand-finished loop on the inside. They're more durable and won't fall off at the dry cleaners.

■ When you take a suit or sport coat to the dry cleaners, pay extra to have it hand-finished rather than run through their pressing machine. That machine will tear your suit up in the long run.

For the Hygienically Challenged

You might be the best-dressed guy in the world, but without good grooming habits, you'd be unkempt and smelly (and probably French). Here's how to keep your birthday suit just as polished as the rest of your wardrobe. (Caution: Hide these items in your medicine cabinet or face endless ribbing from your pals, fancy-boy.)

Facial Scrub

Brand: Exfoliant from Aveda
This is a gel that clears dead skin cells away, leaving your face fresh and ready for treatment or moisturizer.

Facial Moisturizer

Brand: Face Protector from The Body Shop
After washing or shaving, this helps keep your skin moisturized and smooth. It also has sunscreen to give you a little UVB protection.

Skin Toner

Brand: Turnaround Lotion from Clinique
Firms up skin tone and reduces fine lines and past sun damage. Robert Redford never used his, and now look at him.

There. Just don't tell anyone we told you.

So? Sew!

'Cause you can't ask Mom anymore.

In golden ages past, women did stuff like this for us. Ask today's woman to sew and she's likely to stitch your scrotum to your stomach. Face it, you're on your own.

Thread the needle:
Cut a foot of like-colored thread, wet the end, and poke it through the needle, pulling half the thread through.

Double-knot both ends together:
Wrap them around your finger rolling the wrapped thread down your finger, and sliding the bunched thread tight.

Sew your button:
Place the button (get one that's the same color, fool) where you intend to sew it, putting a toothpick between the button and the material (this gives necessary slack). From underneath the material, push the needle up and through one of the button's holes. Pull until the knot stops the thread, then go down through the button's next hole.

Tie her off:
Once you've completed about six stitches, end with the needle on the fabric's underside and remove the toothpick. Pull the button so the stitches are taut, then run the loose line around the line beneath the button. Run a few more securing stitches through your other stitches on the underside of the fabric, and cut off any remaining thread.

Propecia vs. Rogaine Extra Strength

STATS

Pro: Merck, the manufacturer, said in studies 83 percent of those who took the drug maintained or increased hair count in two years.
Ro: Pharmacia & Upjohn, the maker of Rogaine, reported that 80 percent of users reported the product slowed or stopped hair loss.

DOSAGE

Pro: A pill you take once a day. Available by prescription only ($50 a month).
Ro: A liquid you apply to the scalp twice a day with a dropper or spray. Available over the counter ($30 a month).

SIDE EFFECTS

Pro: Can cause decreased sperm volume but doesn't affect sperm count. Small numbers of men report a drop in libido. If a pregnant woman is exposed to it, it may deform her fetus.
Ro: Can cause itching or dryness of the scalp.

BOTTOM LINE

One independent study reported that Propecia was more effective, but that taking both drugs at the same time gave men the maximum effect. Also, the earlier in your hair loss you start treatment, the better chance you'll have for success, since both drugs are more effective at stopping further hair loss than actually regrowing lost hair. If you're already resembling Kojak or George Costanza, you may just have to deal with it or book an appointment with the wig maker.

HAIR TODAY...

We hate to bring this up, but...

You have approximately 100,000 hairs on your head, each going through a mini life-cycle: being born, growing, dying, and being replaced. In a typical day, a person with a healthy tuft loses 50 to 100 hairs. A person suffering the onset of male pattern baldness loses up to 250.

There are many reasons for hair loss, including scalp bacteria, stress, hormonal imbalance (thyroid), and poor nutrition. But 95 percent of hair loss seems to be caused by damned, stupid genetics. Here it is—the ugly truth they won't tell you in commercials. Take a look at the men in your family: That's where you're headed.

Is there hope for the follicle-challenged male? Besides going to the extremes of follicle transplants or fitting yourself for a toupee (don't do it!), there are two drug treatments that may help curb your hair loss and possibly even grow back some of those suckers. On the previous page we give you the lowdown on Rogaine and Propecia to help you decide which—if either—is right for you.

Shaved and Confused

Shave closer...bleed less.

You've got a big date—the last thing you want to do is come out of the bathroom looking like Leatherface went to work on your face. See how these tips feel:

■ **Wait at least 30 minutes after you wake up before cutting.** While you're groggily reaching for the remote, your body fluids puff your skin up. If you shave before the skin settles back, you won't get a close shave.

■ **Make it a night shave.** In the summer shave in the evenings—the heat and sunscreen will irritate your skin if it's shorn early in the day.

■ **Don't just use plenty of cream, use plenty of water.** This is what fluffs up the hairs and makes them cut 70 percent easier. It also gets excess oil and dirt out of the way.

■ **Shave easiest areas first.** The harder spots will have a longer time to soak.

■ **If you drop your blade, replace it.** The blade is just as easily damaged by being banged around as it is by being used. Also rinse it dry; don't wipe with a cloth or towel.

■ **If you nick yourself, put a little Vaseline or antibiotic ointment on it instead of TP.** After you finish, wipe it off. It will clot the blood without getting you all scabby.

■ **If you've got the time, try this method to get a close, comfortable shave:** Lather and shave carefully with the grain. Then lather again and shave at a slight angle across the grain, but not against it. Repeat, feeling your

face to find spots, then lathering, then cutting cross wise. Smooth.

■ **Is it hot face, cool blade, or...?** Experts differ on how hot the water should be on your face, and on the blade. But we back Johnny Caspar, the gangster in *Miller's Crossing,* who tells an underling he should splash hot water on his face and cold water on the blade (hot water opens the pores, and cold water contracts the blade). Of course right after he gave the advice, he got whacked. But check him out—the man was smooth-skinned throughout.

"We're looking for this woman, Glenn Close..."

GET INTO A NIGHTCLUB
You look the part. Now act it.

Somewhere among college athletes who never made it to the pros, sadistic New York City cops, and feral apes lie bouncers. Cross a failed model who can't orgasm with Sally Field and you get a hostess. When the two team up at the door of a nightclub, they passively aggressively ignore you as you stand in the rain watching models and Euro-trash whiz by. You're pathetic. But you don't have to be. Here are our proven tactics to help get you past the velvet-rope squad:

AVOID RAT PACKING.
The Catch-22 of clubs is that they need men to drop big dollars, but they don't want to let any of them in. They hate men. If you're going with a bunch of guys, break up into pairs. Try to spot some ladies heading the same way and ask if you can go in with them.

STOP BEGGING.
Don't claim to know the bartender or to be on the guest list. Bouncers know that you don't know anybody, that you are nobody, and that if you really were on the list...you'd be on the list. These guys are told to keep a crowd outside the place to make it seem happening, and they'll let beggars languish all night.

LET MONEY TALK.
Yeah, you know about this gag, but you've always been too cheap or too much of a wuss to try. It works, and you'll look cool if you're with a date. Go up and ask the bouncer how long the wait is, to which he'll reply, "Don't know." Just calmly ask him how much it'll cost in order to not wait all night. Now, most bouncers want $20 per head passed to them with a sly handshake. Tell him you'll be right back. If there are two of you, walk away and fold up $30. Return to the door, say hi, and slip him the money. He'll act like your old friend, put the cash right into his pocket, and wave you in—never knowing that you stiffed him $10.

CRACK THE GUEST LIST.
Send one of your friends to hang by the door and listen for two or three names given by people on the guest list. With the names in hand, chill for an hour at a nearby bar and then head back to the club. After a while, the list starts to become pretty marked up, and you should be able to get in with an old name. The only risk here is getting busted and having the bouncer snap your neck like a chicken's.

LET YOUR FINGERS DO THE TALKING.
Call the place around 5 P.M. and say that your phoning from one of the more popular music or lifestyle magazines (but not *Maxim*—that's our scam). Tell them that a couple of writers are in from out of town and ask if they'd mind putting them on the guest list. To sound more authentic, ask if they would like a formal request on letterhead. Of course if they do, you'll spend the evening bowling. This ploy works only as well as your ability to bullshit. Good luck.

Stinking All the Way to the Slammer

Can you really be arrested for issues of cleanliness? According to dumb-laws.com—which doesn't guarantee these laws are still in effect—you can.

- **In Athens, Greece**, a driver's license can be lifted by law if the driver is deemed either 'poorly dressed' or 'unbathed.'
- **In Long Beach, CA**, you cannot bathe two babies in the same tub at the same time.
- **In Prunedale, CA**, two bath tubs may not be installed in the same house.
- **In Indiana**, baths may not be taken between the months of October and March.
- **In Gary, IN**, persons are prohibited from attending a movie house or other theater, and from riding a public streetcar, within four hours of eating garlic.
- **In Topeka, KS**, the installation of bathtubs is prohibited.
- **In Massachusetts**, it is illegal to go to bed without first having a full bath.
- **In Nebraska**, a parent can be arrested if their child cannot hold back a burp during a church service.
- **In Waterloo, NE**, barbers are forbidden from eating onions between 7 A.M. and 7 P.M.
- **In Marion, OR**, ministers are forbidden from eating garlic or onions before delivering a sermon.
- **In Port Arthur TX**, obnoxious odors may not be emitted while in an elevator.
- **In Vermont**, lawmakers made it mandatory for everybody to take at least one bath each week—on Saturday night.
- **In Milwaukee**, it is illegal to be in public during the day if you are physically offensive-looking.
- **Cheyenne, WO**, citizens may not take a shower on a Wednesday.

How To Be a Man of the World, in Quick, Easy Steps

Tip incorrectly in your native land and you're a hapless moron. Tip incorrectly abroad and you risk disrupting the course of international relations. Here's a cheat sheet for tipping abroad from the travel gurus at Fodor's.

CITY: BERLIN
Service charges are usually included, but in restaurants, you'll want to leave an additional 5 percent or round up to the nearest deutsche mark. But don't leave the tip on the beer-garden table or it could disappear faster than pieces of the Wall. Shell out a few marks for the hotel staff, too.

CITY: LONDON
Tip the cab driver and the waiter who brings your steak and kidney pie 10 to 15 percent, but only when a service charge hasn't been included. Don't tip the bloke behind the bar—just buy him a drink every third round if you're feeling generous.

CITY: DETROIT
Here's a tip: Don't go.

CITY: MADRID
Tip up to 10 percent in restaurants and taxis, but don't be too flamboyant about it. Spanish workers are proud. If you're just eating tapas at the bar, round the bill up to the nearest 100 pesetas. Hotel employees usually get anywhere from 50 to 100 pesetas. Also washroom attendants should get 10 to 25 pesetas for doing their thankless job.

CITY: PARIS
Tips are lower here than in the U.S. because service charges are already included on bar and restaurant bills (it's the law). Leave 5 percent on top of the service charge at expensive restaurants; at moderately priced places, leave 50 centimes to a franc for drinks and 10 to 15 francs for a meal. Tip 10 percent for taxis. Piss on the seat before you get out.

CITY: MEXICO CITY
Keep in mind that many Mexican service workers get a daily wage less than your hourly pay and expect Americans to be big tippers. Consequently you may get called a cheap gringo even if you're tipping the norm of 10 to 15 percent. Slip a couple of bucks to the hotel employees, but don't tip the taxi driver unless he helps with your bags (five to 10 pesos) or introduces you to his saucy sister (use your own discretion).

CITY: JOHANNESBURG
South Africans are tip-happy, and unless a service charge has been added, tips are expected, even for services you usually take for granted such as maid service. Leave 10 percent for waiters and taxi drivers. Hotel porters merit one and a half to two rands per bag.

CITY: MOSCOW
Tip waiters, taxi drivers, coatroom attendants, and porters 10 to 15 percent in U.S. dollars or in another currency more stable than the ruble. If you pay by credit card, leave the tip in cash or the waiter who served you that vodka and borscht won't receive it.

CITY: TOKYO
Tipping is rare; expensive restaurants usually include a 10 to 15 percent service charge. You don't need to tip taxi drivers or bartenders. Tip airport and railway porters 200 to 300 yen per bag. Slip a gratuity of 2,000 to 3,000 yen—in an envelope—to any hotel staffer who makes restaurant reservations or puts up with lame jokes about Ginsu knives and Godzilla.

CITY: BUDAPEST
You only need to tip waiters, taxi drivers, and coatroom attendants. Give them 10 percent. If a gypsy band plays at your table, drop 100 forints in the plate provided.

CITY: ROME
Be prepared: Everyone from railway porters to theater ushers will expect a tip from you; but, as always, tip for good service. Service charges are included in restaurant bills, but an additional tip is expected. Tip 5 to 10 percent for taxis, and at coffee bars where you stand at the counter, tip 100 lire; if you sit down at a table, leave 500 lire.

CITY: HONG KONG
Leave about 10 percent in restaurants and taxis, in addition to the 10 percent service charge. (Since the change over, you may be able to leave a photo of Mao next to the remains of your pork-fried rice and be done with it.)

CITY: TEL AVIV
Tip 10 percent when service isn't included. If you've negotiated a price for a taxi, assume that the tip has been built in. Hotel bellboys get a lump sum of five to 10 shekels, regardless of how many bags you have.

CITY: SINGAPORE
You almost never tip here, and it's actively discouraged by the government. (Hey, they've caned people for less.) The only guy you tip is the hotel bellhop, and then only one Singapore dollar per bag. Locals get particularly peeved if you tip a taxi driver (they don't want it to become custom).

CITY: CAIRO
Tip every worker who does you a service. Dole out 10 percent maximum for personnel in restaurants and hotels (hotels add 19 percent for service and taxes to your final bill). One Egyptian pound will suffice for other services. It's also customary to shower the hotel staff with piasters before you depart.

CITY: SYDNEY
Service charges are not generally included, so you'll want to tip 10 to 12 percent for some shrimp from the barbie and the waitress' mesmerizing accent. Taxi drivers are happy with small change.

Be the Best Man

Watchin' your buddy take the plunge is not easy.

In the Dark Ages, you'd have been asked to defend the honor of your best friend's betrothed with a sword. Even today being the best man entails a number of sober responsibilities: carrying the ring, procuring stacks of one-dollar bills for the bachelor party, scamming cute bridesmaids—the works. Here's how to put together a clutch performance as the right-hand man.

THE BACHELOR PARTY.
Besides making sure the bash is well attended, organizing the entertainment, and handling the cash, you're responsible for showing him a wall-to-wall great time without overdoing it. Try to keep the big picture in mind: If the groom returns from your gig with a broken arm or a burning sensation when he pees, Love Muffin is going to look to you for answers.

THE WEDDING REHEARSAL.
Your buddy has too much on his mind to baby sit, so it's your job to make sure the groomsmen show up on time, sober, and dressed appropriately. If the rehearsal reminds anyone of a Keystone Kops routine, you have failed miserably.

THE CHURCH.
When you're backstage alone with the groom, help him prepare for that final curtain call. Straighten his tie; dry his tears; assure him that you have a getaway car just in case. Above all, listen patiently as he gushes about the fabulous woman he's ditching you for.

"All right, which one of you bastards ate my frosting?"

THE RING.
During the ceremony, do not fumble the hand-off. Brides are extremely superstitious: Drop the ring and give her an excuse to deem the wedding a disaster and your buddy will pay the price.

THE RECEPTION.
The groom will likely be too busy to enjoy his own reception, so it's your job to be the life of the party. Work the room; make sure guests are getting comfortably pickled; drag old Aunt Sadie gently out onto the dance floor.

THE TOAST.
Just be yourself...unless you're a long-winded blowhard that nobody likes. Keep it short, compliment the bride at least twice, and remember: no bestiality anecdotes.

THE AFTERMATH.
As the band gears up for one last rousing hokey-pokey, wrap up any unfinished business. Make sure the help has been tipped. Help find missing coats and cameras and inquire about the destiny of half-empty liquor bottles. Find yourself a cute bridesmaid and shepherd her back to her hotel.

Weasel Your Way Out

You're locked into plans that you can't break ... or can you? Let us show you more stylish ways of squirming out of responsibility.

BREAK PLANS WITH THE BOSS
Blame: The Girlfriend
Because: If the mythical funeral is in her family, you don't have to fake being upset.
Just say: "It's a tremendous loss. Her great aunt Gertie was, well, her spiritual mentor. I have to be there for her through this difficult time."
Never say: "Her old man bought the farm, so I have to stay home and play snot rag."

BREAK PLANS WITH THE GIRLFRIEND
Blame: The Workout Buddy
Because: She can't complain if you're exercising. After all, she wants you to have abs of steel.
Just say: "I'm glad you care enough about my health to reschedule. Besides, it's hard keeping up with your beautiful body!"
Never say: "Wench, bring me my steroids."

BREAK PLANS WITH THE WORKOUT BUDDY
Blame: Your Best Friend
Because: It's an accepted guy rule. Best Friend always trumps the casual kinship of The Workout Buddy.
Just say: "My buddy's been going through a rough time. You know how it is."
Never say: "Actually I gotta go meet my real friend tonight."

BREAK PLANS WITH YOUR BEST FRIEND
Blame: Your Family
Because: He has one, too. He knows the drill, the guilt, the hell of not being an orphan.
Just say: "Sorry. If my Mom were a better cook, I'd invite you over for chow."
Never say: "I have a really special relationship with my sister."

BREAK PLANS WITH YOUR FAMILY
Blame: The Boss
Because: They're out of your work loop, so they'll believe you. Plus, they want nothing more than for you to remain gainfully employed.
Just say: "I've taken on more responsibility at the office, and procrastinating will just make it worse—you taught me that!"
Never say: "Duty calls. Catch you on the flip side."

TUX FAX
Take off the training wheels, and strap into the real deal.

■ **Single-breasted jackets with peaked lapels and no vent are best. They work well with a vest.** If you want a cummerbund, get a single-breasted jacket with a shawl collar. But this is only for evenings. Oh yeah, and unless you want to look like Tony Orlando, go with black.

■ **Don't get trousers with a stripe down the sides.** Drum majors can ignore this advice. The pants should break right on top of the shoes, and they don't have cuffs.

■ **Get a black tie.** Get one of those jobs that's already tied but has a clasp that hooks just behind the neck. Try to muss it a little so it looks like the real thing.

■ **Shoes should be black pumps or patent-leather oxfords.**

Make sure your socks are black and made of thin silk, cotton or wool.

■ **Here's the only individual touch you can add:** a white linen handkerchief in the breast pocket. Fold it so the points show. Don't blow your nose on it, either.

■ **Jewelry.** Cuff links and studs should be black, gold, or silver, depending on the color of your glasses and watch. Nothing else—the only exception is that eyeball cuff links are permitted only during a meeting with your droogs.

■ **Look Good in Your Clothes**
Our last-minute advivce to keep you looking properly fitted and wrinkle-free

■ **A vest should cover the waist-band of your pants.**

■ **Wear worsted wool, woolens, and polyester-wool blends yearround; cotton, seersucker, rayon, linen, and silk are for summer only.**

■ **Hang suits on wooden or plastic contour hangers to help them keep their shape.** Leave the jacket unbuttoned and the pockets empty when you hang it and the thing will wear a long time.

■ **Leave plenty of space between hangers to keep the wrinkles away.**

■ **Allow your suit to air out for at least 24 hours after and before wearing.** It keeps it from getting funky (not in a James Brown kind of way) and relaxes wrinkles.

CAREER EDGE

'Cause minimum wage just ain't gonna cut it.

Sure, there's fame, sex, and good old-fashioned fun. But nothing beats power! We'll tell you how to get it, keep it, and wield it like the mighty sword that it is. From picking the right career and pumping out resumes, to acing the interview and getting on the fast track to a promotion, we'll help you stomp the competition and get to the top faster than you can say, "Bill Gates is a pasty toolbox."

PICK A JOB THAT RULES

You don't have to become a bean counter just because it's relatively stress-free and pays well. That's how your dad spends his days. You need a job that'll shoot you to the top of the corporate ladder without making your balls drop. *The Jobs-Rated Almanac* by Les Krantz rates 250 different careers for a whole shitload (that would be an American shitload, not one of those dinky metric shit-loads) of categories you might not have considered. We've crunched the whole thing down to help you do a little career tweaking. Give it a look. Thank us later.

YOUR CHOICE: Newspaper Reporter
BETTER CHOICE: Radio/TV Newswriter
WHY: Cold hard cash! Newswriter jobs have a salary range of $33,000 for mid-level people to $69,000 for top players; compare that with a $25K–$52K range for paper hacks. The big plus is that newswriters have a much lower overall stress level than those poor ink-smudged bastards, who face more pulse-pounding, stomach-tearing hell than major league umpires and corrections officers combined. (Or perhaps that's just what *we* have to deal with all the fuckin' time.)

YOUR CHOICE: Web Developer
BETTER CHOICE: Web-Site Manager
WHY: Sure, you wanna develop your own Web systems rather than work for some ugly, nasty corporation. But the Web-site manager career is the number one-rated job in the entire almanac. Expected job growth for managers is a whopping 500 percent, compared with 91 percent for developers.

And even though starting salaries for managers are lower than those of developers, managers earn a mid-level salary of $75,000 a year, while developer's take home $49K. And the master managers pull down $155,000 a year, compared with $77,000 for those measly developers.

YOUR CHOICE: Cop
BETTER CHOICE: Postal Inspector
WHY: Sure, it sounds wussy as hell. Fact is, postal inspectors are gun-toting lawmen who investigate everything from mail fraud and drug smuggling to high-profile cases like the Unabomber and Butch Cassidy and the Sundance Kid. Cops face long hours, abuse from in-your-face crazies, and life-threatening situations daily. It is considered the seventh most stressful job you can have, according to the almanac, just above NFL football player and air traffic controller (but below jobs like taxi driver, firefighter, and U.S. president). Also,

postal inspectors have a salary range that's $15,000 to $17,000 more per year than what cops make, with pay peaking at $83K.

YOUR CHOICE: Physical Therapist
BETTER CHOICE: Occupational Therapist
WHY: Occupational therapists, who design programs to help physically, developmentally, and emotionally challenged people, make about $8,000 a year more at mid-level than physical therapists. And even though physical therapists have great job security, they have a more stressful and physically demanding job than occupational therapists.

YOUR CHOICE: Catholic Priest
BETTER CHOICE: Protestant Minister
WHY: Catholic priests have a higher stress rating than Protestant ministers, according to the almanac, and earn $15,000 to $20,000 less per year. And considering priests can't have sex, and that no American has ever been named Pope in the Catholic Church's 2,000-year history, you may want to reconsider a career as a Catholic clergyman. (Then again, if you want to devote your life to any kind of religion, you probably shouldn't be reading this book.)

Careers for Crackpots

A link between insanity and people who choose creative jobs has long been assumed...

"Well, the man said Hollywood or bust..."

How many welders have you heard of who cut off their ears and send 'em to their girlfriends? Now, however, we've got solid proof that many artists and poets are, for the most part, some real twisted freaks! Arnold Ludwig, M.D., a professor at the University of Kentucky, studied the lives of more than 1,000 "original thinkers" of the 20th century and compared the rates at which they suffered from mental disorders. He found that poets, in particular, should be kept away from kids, sharp objects, and the keys to the Ferrari.

Ludwig's 1998 study, "Method and Madness in the Arts and Sciences," reports that nearly nine out of 10 poets surveyed have had diagnosable mental disorders, as compared with "only" 72 percent of nonfiction writers. A natural scientist (biologist, physicist, etc.), for the record, has only a 28 percent chance of flipping out.

So, do creative jobs make people crazy, or do crazy people tend toward creative jobs? Simply put: Yes! But it's easy to see how sitting around all day, trying to come up with sonnets about birds, could turn normal thinkers into shit-eating maniacs.

There's also another possibility: Social scientists, like Ludwig, have a 51 percent rate of mental illness—in other words, this study could be totally wacked.

"Bad news, Ma'am. It's deaf."

Careers That Make You Go Cuckoo!
Percentage of workers with mental disorders by occupation.

Occupation		Percentage
Architecture/Design		52%
Music Composition		60%
Nonfiction Writing		68%
Visual Arts		72%
Fiction Writing		73%
Poetry		74%

Lifetime rates of any mental disorders (Creativity Research Journal, 1998, Vol. 11, No. 2, pp. 93–101)

BLOWING PAST THE COMPETITION

Here's the inside scoop on scoring that job and leaving those other chumps in the dust.

Nailing the Cover Letter

He was deaf to the paper's anguished shrieks.

■ **Send it to the right person.**
Call the personnel department, and find the name and title of the person who can hire you. Letters to "Personnel" or "Human Resources" only come from losers.

■ **Don't waste their time**.
One page, with everything they want to know about you—anything more just makes their eyes glaze over. Always put the date on your letter, and include your telephone number in case it gets separated from your resumé.

■ **Give 'em what they're looking for.**
Underline key words and phrases in their job ad, and use them when describing what you have to offer.

■ **Wow 'em with your savvy.**
Use a meta-search engine like savvysearch.com to find information about the company on the Web, including the health of its stock and any important news items. Follow that up with a general search for articles and tidbits on the field in which the company does its business. At worst you'll have some nice details for an impres-sive cover letter; at best you might get lucky and discover why they're hiring, which will give you an edge that'll pay off every step of the way.

■ **Make nice.**
You don't have to suck up. (Save that for after you get the job.) Paying one good, specific compliment is far more effective than telling them over and over how "dynamic and exciting" their company is. If they've just expanded into a new market, congratulate them on their fore-sight. If their profits are up and their stock recently split, make sure they know you're impressed.

■ **Don't demand things—focus on them.**
Convince them that you're a smart, ambitious person who thinks their compa-ny is going places, and that you want to join forces because you can help them go even further.

OK, you're in. Men's room is on the left.

Liar's Poker: Acing the Resumé

You've got their attention; now kill 'em.

It's a sad fact that many people feel as if they have to pad their resumés with overly hyped and erroneous information in order to get a job. We'd never tell you to do this. In fact we'd like to advise you in great detail, exactly how to avoid this road to easy wealth and moral turpitude. Your soul depends on it!

DON'T LIE ABOUT YOUR PAST JOB PERFORMANCE AND PAY HISTORY!
According to a *Los Angeles Times* study, this is the sort of thing that most people fudge because it's almost impossible to check. Lawsuit-wary companies are afraid to give a bad recommendation about former workers or reveal what they earned. Whew! Aren't you glad you know?

rcle
California 95850
26

OBJECTIVE:

EDUCATION:

DON'T FUDGE THE STARTING AND ENDING DATES OF PAST JOBS!
This is often used to disguise that you took two months off to be a barfly and to make you look instead like the hard worker you know you can be. Though this cover-up rarely causes a blip on a personnel director's radar, what will your kids think?

System Science course work: S...
Statistics I & II; Applied Numerical Comput...
Mathematics course work: Real Analysis I & II; Fourier and Laplace
Transfers; Linear Algebra; Mathematical Modeling.

Company (Summer 1988)

EXPERIENCE:

DON'T FAKE EDUCATIONAL DEGREES FOR AN ENTRY-LEVEL PROFESSIONAL POSITION THROUGH A TEMP AGENCY!
One guy—we'll call him Tom—got away with this heinous falsehood and landed a high-paying job as a paralegal in a large New York City law firm. "It was horrible," Tom said. "No one checked that sort of thing at the agency, and the firm didn't either. Also, I said I'd graduated from a state college a friend of mine had attended, so he gave me a few tidbits about life on campus just in case the subject came up in conversation at the job. I got away with it clean, and made much more money than I should have. Don't make my mistake."

KILLS:

ACTIVITIES:

REFERENCES: Availab...

Whew! Glad we got that out of the way. Now here's the right way to do it:

CUT TO THE CHASE. Experts estimate that roughly one interview is granted for every 200 resumés received by an employer. To make matters worse, your mark will only take 10 to 20 seconds to read what you give him. Lesson learned: The pertinent shit better be at the top.

OFFER VALUE. Nicholas Corcodilos, professional headhunter and Web columnist, advises adding a category, Value Offered, near the top of your resumé that tells them what you'll bring to the table. It should be concise and specific: "I will expand your program into new market X." "I will minimize costs for Y." This will show initiative before you've even walked in the door.

NIX USELESS JOB EXPERIENCE.
No need to talk up the Denny's gig you had during high school. Instead use a category called Skills and Accomplishments near the top of the resumé that lists exactly what you can do. A two-column bulleted list is a good way to present this information. Then, below this section, list only your last two to three jobs and what you did there, which is all your prospective employer really cares about anyway.

CUT THE BULL. Forget about listing your GPA, honor society shit, activities, and hobbies unless you're fresh out of college and are looking for entry-level work. If you're 35 and have been in the job market for 13 years, potential employers aren't going to care that you chaired the debating club in college, and like to play the guitar and work in the garden in your spare time.

PROVIDE REFERENCES SEPARATELY.
Don't list your references on your resumé. References should always be provided as a separate document and only provided on request. Always have a copy on hand when going to an interview (in case they ask) if you want to appear like a serious and prepared candidate.

MAKE IT PURDY.
Your resumé should look clean and professional, and have plenty of white space. Pick a traditional typeface such as Times or Bookman, and always print your resume on a laser printer and on high-quality resumé paper. (If you don't have a laser printer, go to Kinko's.) If your resumé is too crowded, poorly typed, or printed on your 20-year-old dot matrix printer, it's like wearing a sign around your neck to your interview that says, "I'm a clueless, unprofessional moron."

BRINGING UP THE CAREER

Blitz the Interview
Talk good and get money.

"Go long, and let's talk benefits!"

PRACTICE YOUR MOVES.
About 60 percent of our communication comes from body language, says communications consultant Carolyn Koff. Your handshake should be firm, but not a crusher, according to the career experts at Thomas Staffing, a consulting firm that publishes interview do's and don'ts. Have a friend evaluate it. Also, while sitting in a straight-backed chair, go over your answers to questions you think they'll ask. Actually say your answers out loud and practice keeping still for long periods of time without fidgeting.

KEEP IT IN THE BOX.
When gesturing with your hands, make sure they stay within a box formed by your shoulders and waistline. If your hands stay in there, you look like a statesman arguing policy—in fact this is a trick that former President Clinton's handlers actually trained him to do. If your hands go out, you look threatening and scary, like a homeless person pretending he's a bird.

DON'T CROSS UP.
Your arms and legs should stay uncrossed, according to Koff. Otherwise you look defensive and nervous. But don't get too cocky. "I've seen people lean back and put their hands behind their head," says one HR professional. "It looks like they're taking a little vacation."

MIRROR.
You should adopt an attitude and body posture similar to that of your interviewer. This sends a clear, but subconscious, signal that you're friendly and unthreatening. Practice it a little with people you talk to, so you don't go overboard and look like a mime.

DON'T ARRIVE TOO EARLY.
Make sure you're on time, but if you get there 30 minutes before the thing starts, go somewhere else—a restaurant, the park, anywhere. Otherwise you'll put subtle pressure on the interviewer and his staff, according to Jeffrey Allen, author of *How to Turn an Interview into a Job.*

DON'T GET DROPPED OFF OR PICKED UP.
It's almost as bad as bringing your mom into the interview with you. It reeks of dependency and tells people you don't even have transportation to what you hope is your new job. If you must get dropped off or picked up, do it out of sight, like you did with good old ma did in junior high, so you can walk in like your own man.

NEVER BAD-MOUTH ANYONE.
Not your old boss. Not your old coworkers. Not your ex-wife who disconnected the brakes on your car. Every story has two sides, and by giving them one side of a bad tale, you make them wonder what the other one is.

WRITE A THANK YOU LETTER.
Because hardly anyone writes them anymore, a polite and enthusiastic thank you letter will help set you apart (in a good way) from the rest of the pack. Make it brief, but be sure to reiterate or follow up on any key points discussed during your interview. Always send it within a day of your interview, not two weeks after the fact.

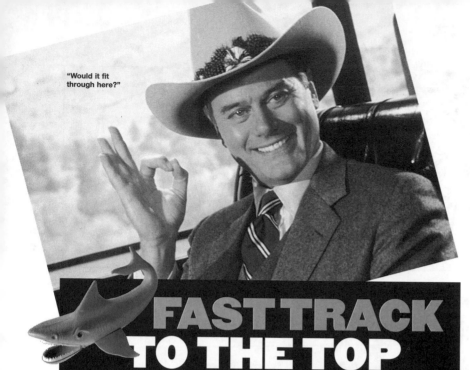

"Would it fit through here?"

FAST TRACK TO THE TOP

Now that you've got the gig, here's how to take advantage. Remember: It's not all about money. You wanna climb the corporate ladder by skipping rungs. Here's everything you need to swim faster than the sharks.

Get Cash Now! Ask Us How!

Because peanuts are for elephants and Snoopy.

Negotiate a raise the savvy *Maxim* way and they'll pay you more and like it. Here's everything you need to know:

■ Do your homework, part 1.

Call in your contacts and research other salaries in your field. Add the other jobs you do in addition to your job description, and come up with a reasonable figure. The Bureau of Labor Statistics Web site (http://stats.bls.gov/blshome.htm) has data on this. Consider applying for another job just to see what the market will bear, and plan on going out for an informational interview with someone from the competition.

■ Do your homework, part 2.

OK, you've looked down the block—let's look in the backyard. Think about how the company's doing. Are they expanding or contracting? Are they a fat, established conglomerate or a hungry start-up? If the company's lean and mean, you have to think in terms of what jobs you're saving them from doing. That way they see paying you more as saving money. Be ready for more responsibilities though. If the company's doing well, you have to sell yourself as quality merchandise they don't want to go to the competition.

■ Pick the right time.

The fiscal year has just cranked up, and there's usually more money in the budget than at any other time. Also, if you stake your claim now, all your future raise discussions will happen like clockwork in this bounty season.

■ Pick a Thursday.

No, not because there's some Norse thing involved. Studies have shown most bosses are in their best mood on this day. Hump day is gone, the weekend is coming up. Nice and easy.

■ Be an educator, not a fighter.

Assume your boss hasn't completely sized up your contribution. Build a case, using facts and figures to show what you've brought to the company in the past and what you're likely to bring in the future.

■ Ask for the highest offer you could get in another company.

As you negotiate, bring all the other benefits you'd like to the table. A particularly useful one is education—free college courses in your field or trips to seminars. A boss can't refuse a reasonable request to make you a better worker. At the same time this is exactly what gives you a better shot at getting higher pay in the future...or moving up with a competitor later on.

■ Walk out of there with something.

If the answer's no, find out why. Is it simply a bad time, and should you reschedule the conversation? Look at this as an appointment to help you get a raise: Get your boss to lay out the expectations you need to meet, agree on a timeframe, and then go for it.

Impress the Boss Without Actually Doing Any Work

Long hours and backbreaking toil are for suckers and brown-nosers. Lean back, put your feet up, and get ready to sample the many splendors of the corporate washroom without compromising your right to relax. Here's how:

■ **When you get up in the middle of the night to take a whiz, phone your boss's voice mail and leave a message.** The next morning, when he hears the time-coded message, he'll think you're a round-the-clock super-employee. Don't do it too often, though, or he'll think you're a no-life loser.

■ **Have yourself copied in on all memos your boss gets... even ones that have nothing to do with you.** When he eventually asks you about it, tell him you're trying to stay on top of as many aspects of the department as you can.

■ **Talk up your coworkers to your boss.** Pointing out the fine work others are doing shows you can keep your ego in check and work for the greater good...in other words, you're management material, baby. One thing: Praise only the small stuff. You don't want anyone promoted ahead of you.

■ **Five-finger a couple of sheets of a competing firm's letterhead.** Type up a glowing letter to yourself from a fictitious top-brass dude. Include "Been hearing great things about you" and "Let's do a retardedly expensive lunch." Leave the letter half covered on your desk until your boss spies it.

Does that "close door" button on the elevator do anything?

ANSWER: Well, it gives you something to do while you wait for the elevator door to close on its own. The button does work occasionally, but only when the elevator's not communicating with other elevators in a system to handle traffic, or when the landlord has special-ordered a button that works.

The rest of the time—and that's most of the time in the elevators you're likely to ride—the button is just a piece of plastic that happens to indent. "The computer system doesn't even recognize it," says Leonard G. LeVee, Jr., executive director of the National Association of Vertical Transportation Professionals. Saying "Come on, come on, baby" like a big jackass reportedly doesn't help, either.

Eat for Energy

We know this may sound fruity… because it is. But this stuff'll keep you going no matter what.

FOR LONG, HARD HEAVY-DUTY PROJECTS.

If you have the time, make yourself an omelet with egg whites, tomatoes, mushrooms, onions, spinach, and cheese. Get yourself some chopped honeydew or cantaloupe on the side. The eggs give you slow-digesting protein, which'll give you a steady stream of energy, instead of a quick burst and then a slump. The melons, veggies, and 'shrooms—not *those* 'shrooms, Jerry—give you a nice array of vitamins and minerals for brain work. And the cheese provides calcium.

BRACE YOURSELF FOR THE EARLY MORNING MEETING.

If you're in a rush, try this: Take a cup of yogurt, a multigrain frozen waffle with a banana, and grapefruit juice. The banana and juice, which are simple carbs, give your body a quick burst of energy, while the waffle has more complex carbs, which burn slower. The banana also has pectin, which expands in your stomach and keeps the grumblings away while you're sitting there in the office. And while the grapefruit has enough vitamin C for a full day, the yogurt has necessary protein. This meal is a good, quick source of energy.

FOR THE LATE NIGHTER.

Don't lean on the caffeine—it stays in your system for hours and hurts your chance of catching a few z's when you're finally done. Instead try a blended fruit smoothy with high-C juices like orange. It'll keep you awake but won't do a number on your system.

Fast times at the Betty Ford Clinic.

Here's one old bag you can live with.

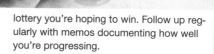

Scoring That Raise

You know you deserve it—and God knows you need it— so here's how to convince the boss to cough it up.

The reasons you need a raise could scarcely be more compelling: Your baseball-memorabilia habit; that fun, spur-of-the-moment tequila tour of the Yucatan; the payments on your 24-speed mountain bike (which weighs less than a puff pastry but is costing more than your first car). Collection agencies are sending death threats with crude diagrams of your route to and from the office. At times like this, you can hardly keep from bursting into your boss's office and dangling him out the window by his ankles as you bark, "Is now a good time to talk money?"

Asking for a raise is a crucial negotiation—and an easy one to botch. Do it wrong and you can find yourself on the street with a schedule more flexible than Gumby in a heat wave. Do it right and you'll secure your job, score a fat wad, and have the boss thinking the whole thing was his idea. Here are some expert tips on squeezing blood from a stone.

TIP #1 Start angling six months early.
Getting a raise isn't a skirmish—it's a campaign. "You've got to start sowing the seeds for your raise six months before your company does its salary reviews," maintains Kate Ludeman, author of Earn What You're Worth (Berkeley, 1996). For one thing, salary adjustments in most firms are locked in place, at least a month before you get the news...and by then it's too late to do anything but whine. For another, it may take that long to prove to your boss that you stand out from the herd.

TIP #2 Direct your efforts.
To make a positive impression, you've got to put your energy into things that will be noticed. And to do that, you must understand your company's overall mission and bottom line, not just your area of expertise. Christopher Hegarty, a management consultant and author of How to Manage Your Boss (Ballantine Books, 1985), asks company managers to define the tasks of their organizations, then asks line personnel to do the same, to see just how out of sync the two camps are. "The discrepancy is usually shocking," claims Hegarty. "It's like they're working in two different companies." Know your outfit and you'll know what your boss will value. If the firm is in growth mode, recruiting new clients is probably a priority. If cost overruns have been a problem, you'll want to find ways to slash spending in your department. You get the idea.

TIP #3 Have a game plan.
Get the boss to define as objectively as possible the criteria on which you will be judged. Say, "I'm committed to doing the best job I can. Let's identify the specific tasks that will allow us to evaluate my performance." For a salesman, perhaps it's bringing in a dollar amount; for an administrator, maybe it's meeting critical deadlines or coming in under budget. If your boss can't (or won't) give you written expectations, write a list yourself and ask him to revise and approve it. The point is to create a set of agreed-upon markers to hit on the road to your raise. It also lets the boss know that a raise is something you expect and deserve, not a lottery you're hoping to win. Follow up regularly with memos documenting how well you're progressing.

TIP #4 Get over yourself.
"It's amazing how many people think they deserve a raise simply because they've been at the job for two years, or because the company is making money, or because the guy next to them got a raise." Says Cliff Hakim, an executive development coach in Cambridge, Massachusetts. In the raise game, all this is irrelevant. From the company's point of view, a guy who's just doing his job is amply rewarded by keeping his job. Mo' money goes to the rock stars—those that perform above expectations. If you want to climb the pop charts, you've got to find ways to stand out.

TIP #5 Don't be afraid to get your nose brown.
For more bargaining power, become a student of your boss. Find ways to make him look good, especially in the eyes of his boss. Increase the trust between you by making him feel like your mentor, even if—hell, especially if—you're twice as smart as he is. Ask his advice on the best ways to tackle assignments, to bamboozle him into thinking you value his opinion. Find reasons to bring him good news, and try to structure your interaction with him so that you never hear the words But that's not how I wanted it done! The more comfortable he is around you, and the easier you make his job, the more value (i.e., monetary value) he'll place on keeping you on board.

TIP #6 Set the right mood. When you've laid the groundwork and are ready to close in for the kill, don't ask for a meeting to discuss a raise, advises Hakim. "That's too narrow—it paints you into a corner. Instead, say you want to talk to him about your accomplishments, goals, and compensation package." And when you go in for the meeting, advises Negotiating for Dummies (Hungry Minds, Inc., 1996) author Michael Donaldson, do something different with the physical environment. If you usually stand rigidly, assume a more relaxed posture; if you normally keep your distance, move in a little. "You're trying to subtly shift the atmosphere in this conversation, to put things on a more equal footing," Donaldson explains.

TIP #7 Know what you're worth. While sowing the seeds for a salary bump, keep tabs on what your services earn on the open market. Talk to friends at other companies, and scan the Sunday classified ads to see what salaries jobs similar to yours command. Even if you're comfortable where you are, apply for other jobs as a way of staying briefed on what your skills are worth. You may discover you're in a stronger bargaining position than you thought. Alternatively, you may discover you're damned lucky to get paid what you're getting paid. Either way, forewarned is forearmed.

TIP #8 Never say, "I need more money." Use this line, no matter how true, and your boss will guffaw and swat you back to your cubicle. At lunch he'll tell the story to his colleagues, and at the punch line ("He actually said, 'I need more money!'") they'll all be laughing so hard that their 20-year-old Scotch will spurt through their noses. "In the real world, everybody needs more money, including your boss," says Donaldson. "Michael Ovitz made $185 million last year, and I guarantee you he thinks he was underpaid."

TIP #9 Know your bottom line. Go in armed with a specific increase in mind (usually this falls between four and 15 percent), ranging from the minimum you'll accept to what you feel you ought to get in a fair universe. When your boss says there's no money for raises right now, be flexible: He may be telling the truth. If you're not ready to jump ship, negotiate. Ask about nonmonetary compensation: An extra week's vacation, an expense account or a transportation allowance, or tuition for a professional course that will increase your value to the company (and, for good measure, to other employers).

TIP #10 Flaunt Your Stuff. Say you'd like to be recognized for what you've done. Tell your boss what you've achieved in the past six months and have the hard data to back it up, whether it's an increase in sales, money you've saved the company with your incomparable ingenuity, or improved success in meeting deadlines. Be prepared for a counterargument listing the areas in which you were less than successful. Don't lose your cool or get suckered into that discussion. Instead, resist the temptation to defend yourself (remember, no one expects you to be perfect). Point out how you cut your losses and talk about what you've learned from your mistakes and what you're doing to make sure they don't happen again. Steer the conversation back to your achievements, and, whatever you do, don't be shy.

If the Boss Laughs...

Even with a stellar game plan, you can still get turned down. Your next move depends on how well you've prepared for this moment.

■ **The best-case scenario.** If you're already fielding better offers from other companies, it's time for a thrilling game of hardball. Gently but firmly break the news to your boss and tell him what it'll take to keep you on the team, then sit back and enjoy. Nothing makes the suits sit up and beg like the knowledge that somebody else values you more. If they meet your price, thank them and tell them you look forward to an even more productive relationship.

Congratulations: You've just beaten the bastards at their own game. If they don't decide to meet the offer, give your two weeks' notice and say you've enjoyed working there and wish them the best. This is, of course, code for telling them where to stick it. But it also leaves the bridges standing—always a smart move.

■ **The less-than-best-case scenario.** If other companies aren't exactly beating down your door, you can bluff...but it's a dangerous game. A lot of guys who think they're irreplaceable find out the hard way that the company machine runs on standard parts. Your best bet is to indicate in a non-threatening way that you're disappointed by the decision (the more composed you are when you do this, the more they'll wonder if you've got another offer percolating) and end the meeting. Step away and assess. It may be that you are indeed moving upward, just not as fast as you hoped. You may have some particular skills to learn or situations to master at your current level before management thinks you're ready for more responsibility. On the other hand, maybe it's time for a change of venue. If so, it's a hell of a lot easier to find a job when you've already got one than when you're sitting at home in your underwear, mass-mailing your desperately embellished résumé.

■ **In all cases.** There's nothing like asking for a raise to encourage a man to take a long, hard look at himself and ask what he really wants out of a job. As Robert Frost once noted, by working faithfully eight hours a day, you can hope to be made a boss and work 12 hours a day. Ask yourself: "Is this what I want to do? Am I headed toward something, or am I just eternally angling for as much dough as I can catch?" Quality of life and size of wallet overlap, certainly, but they're not the same thing. And you can take that to the bank.

GET MR. BIG TO TAKE YOUR CALL

Snotty assistants beware! We're on to you.

Getting through to an important person, or a person who thinks he's important, requires strategy and lightning-fast reflexes. This is how to get the honcho on the line every time:

■ Plan your attack.
Before you even deal with this guy's assistant, write down an opening line that'll quickly and clearly spell out how only you can solve an old problem or provide an unexpected benefit. Spit it out before he/she can say, "Let me transfer you to..."

■ Neutralize the guard.
Another trick to get past the inevitable call-screener is to give off the vibe of someone who talks with guys like the mark all day. "Bob," who's screened calls for high-ranking execs at one firm, tells how he spots a rube: "The people I screen out usually tip me off by sounding overly perky and nice." The best way to get through is just to say, "Is he in? It's John," in a low, hurried voice.

■ Zero in on the target.
If the screener tries to blow you off by telling you to call back, pin him/her down to a specific date and time, says Madeline Bodin, author of *Using the Telephone More Effectively* (Barron's, 1997). If the assistant's not helpful, call back at around seven in the morning. The president of one multi-million-dollar real estate firm swears most executives he knows show up early and pick up their own lines when no one else is there.

■ Strike quickly and make it count.
If you do make it through, your target's going to pick up the phone thinking, "This is a telemarketer, a wacko, or a guy who wants my money." You will have about 10 seconds to convince this hotshot that yours is the best call he'll take all day. And send a follow-up letter immediately, before the overpaid jackass forgets who you are and you have to start all over again. Good luck!

"Oh rats. You can see my nads in these pants."

Think Your Way to the Top

Just by changing the way people see you, you can clear a path to the corner office. Here are a few things you gotta remember.

LOOK FOR WAYS TO PRESENT WHAT YOU DO IN NUMBERS. Dollars saved, percent output increased, people helped, whatever. It all makes what you do seem more substantial.

KEEP RECORDS. Start two folders to record the qualifications that make you praiseworthy. The first one should have documentation on all your skills and experience. The second should have a list of all your accomplishments, projects completed, memos of praise, and good performance reviews.

FIND PEOPLE WHO DO THE JOB YOU WANT. Some might be in your company; some might not. Talk to them to find out what training they've had and what they do every day. Offering to take someone to lunch just so you can kiss their ass and loot their minds is a pretty big compliment—don't be surprised if some of your sources end up helping you get ahead down the line.

ORDER ONET. Go to the U.S. Department of Labor Employee Training Association (www.doleta.gov), and order ONet, a $26 database of skills needed to succeed in more than 1,100 careers.

CLIP AND INFORM. Clipping and displaying an article on the firm with which your employer is negotiating a deal shows you keep up to date, and will make people see you as more than just the step n' fetchit lackey you are. Send copies to the big-honchos throughout the company as an easy way to get noticed without being a total brown noser. Also, put your ideas down in writing. It forces you to organize your thoughts and gives everyone a record of why you're useful.

Your Better Image

"Sign here, Buck Rogers."

Here's some office equipment you probably don't have but should. This stuff makes for a more organized, snazzier you, and it's all pretty cheap. Buy or recommend these and you'll look in the know.

FACEPLATE HARD DRIVE COOLING FAN ($30)
(www.dirtcheapdrives.com) With hard drives running faster and hotter than ever before, this baby is a little piece of cheap insurance. Slot-mounted and small, it's an easy way to keep all that office hardware alive. Recommend this to the boss, and he'll see the upside.

LEVENGER SINGLE-SHEET CUTTER ($15)
(www.levenger.com) Zip it over the item you want to clip and it peels right out. Doesn't even touch the pages below. Cannibalize a newspaper in seconds and look insanely well-informed.

MOUSEKLIP ($3)
(www.mouseklip.com/index.html) This keeps your mouse cord from tangling and developing breaks as a pair of faulty headphones would. Makes your desk look neater too.

GYROPOINT PRO II ($99)
(www.ixmicro.com) The crème de la crème of wireless mouses (mice? meeses?). You'll be able to flick a cursor across the screen from 75 feet away. And the gyroscopic balance gives you control that's just plain ridiculous.

CLEARLINE CONCEPTS MODEL CL2009 ($50)
(www.damark.com) Forget those old laser pointers—they're only good for scaring pets or making a nuisance of yourself at a concert or sporting event. This baby has two lenses, and a switch that turns it into a laser underliner. This'll liven up your next presentation but good.

CROSS DIGITAL WRITER SUPERSTYLUS ($25–$60)
(www.cross-pcg.com) The pen maker Cross has come up with an elegant stylus collection for your PalmPilot to replace that plastic toothpick Palm gives you. It's softer and less likely to damage your screen.

TALK THE TALK

Step Up to the Mic

You could imagine everyone in their underwear, or just that cute blonde in the fourth row. Some tips for blabbing in front of crowds:

■ **Face your audience and make eye contact.**
Pick one or two people and "speak" to them.
■ **Don't memorize.**
Audiences can smell when they're getting something canned.
■ **Use notes sparingly.**
Spending too much time reading makes you seem unprepared.
■ **Dress for success.**
If you look like a clown, people will expect you to pull balloon animals out of your shorts.

"The new Bette Midler show... cancelled? But *how!*"

"Must... stay... calm!"

BYPASS BURNOUT

To win, you've got to think the long haul.

You can run from your job only for so long. Finding little ways to deal with stress will help you stay focused, sharp, and hardworking. Burn these tips into your frazzled skull and you'll be just as hungry a year from now.

DON'T STAY LATE UNLESS IT HELPS.
Sure, it's good to show the boss that you care. But when you spend more than 12 hours chained to your desk, you do more than hurt your chances of getting laid—ever. Because you know you're going to be at work until the wee hours, you subconsciously slow down, and goof off more. The result? During the time your boss does see you, you're at your worst.

WORK AT HOME FULL OR PART TIME.
With the advent of fax and e-mail, many employees are able to get their jobs done at home without fighting straphangers on the subway or battling rush hour traffic. The result? Calmer, more productive workers. Many companies these days are willing to work out part-time "work at home" schedules with their employees. Just don't start watching *Jerry Springer* and your favorite soaps when you should be preparing that latest budget.

TAKE LUNCH OUT.
According to Rosemary Maniscalco, executive vice president of Uniforce Temporary Services, you should get out of the building in the

"Sorry I'm late, I was working on my manifesto, out in the woods."

middle of the day, especially if you work in an office with AC, computers, and fluorescent lighting. That would be everyone except the monks. And if you're a monk, clean those grapes off your feet once in a while.

PUT A BIG CANDY JAR ON YOUR DESK.
If you're a known source of quick sugar, says career expert Karin Ireland, you'll get some camaraderie and stress relief. She's overlooking the fact that this is the single greatest way of getting interoffice gossip delivered to you, express.

ORGANIZE FIRST.
According to a general counsel of one real estate firm, it's the key to keeping your cool. "You are never too busy not to take time to find out what you're doing," he says. And according to psychologist and expert on "flow" Mihaly Chiksamihaly, doing easily accomplished, repititious tasks gets your brain geared up to handle the harder stuff.

VISUALIZE.
Conjure an image of the source of your frustration, and then imagine it disappearing gradually. For example picture your boss going down for the third

time in a giant vat of day-old coffee as you and your coworkers chuck staplers, Hi-Liters, and DON'T SWEAT IT! paperweights at his head. Feel the stress melt away like snow on a sunny day.

DO A "BODY SCAN."
Anti-stress experts advocate decreasing anxiety by doing a "body scan"—i.e., concentrating on and "breathing through" each part of your body in succession. Our simpler, more effective version: Do a thorough body scan of the new temp while breathing heavily.

"Look, Daddy! Mama's bustin' a cap in some punk's ass!"

USE ACUPRESSURE.
Make the ancient Chinese science of the "touch of health" work for you. To remove disturbances in your body's energy field and acquire a calmer, more positive disposition, firmly apply pressure to the dangly appendage between your legs for approximately 10 minutes. Note that some discharge may occur (possibly yours from the company).

Make Any Day A Sick Day

Why spend another perfectly sunny golfing day under fluorescent lights? Maybe it's time to call the boss and say bad morning and bed riddance. With the help of the *Springhouse Professional Guide to Diseases,* we found a few new afflictions that should send you off to greener pastures.

"That puny hip flask just didn't hold enough."

■ **Otitis Externa** Also known as swimmer's ear, (but much more impressive in Latin); you can blame this one on contaminated water you were swimming in. Chewing is tough, fever is up, and tilting your head may splash your desk calendar with ear drainage. While making the sick call, a "What?" now and then due to partial hearing loss is appropriate.

■ **Pityriasis Rosea** Although this all-over skin rash (most likely caused by a virus) isn't contagious, your boss won't know this—in the sick-day scam, *contagious* is your best friend. Plus, the label on the Benadryl that relieves the itching on your chest and back says you should not operate heavy machinery...like your computer.

■ **Gastroenteritis** This one covers the gamut—from food poisoning to traveler's diarrhea—of ailments caused by tainted food or water. Feel free to be creative about your symptoms, adding flashbacks and hallucinations to the heaving and the straddling of the toilet bowl. And not only is this an illness that

comes on suddenly; no boss will ever ask for more details about your bathroom anguish.

■ **Pleurisy** Caused by an inflammation of the pleurae that line the thoracic cage and envelop the lungs, this sharp and stabbing chest pain may develop after a bout with pneumonia, bronchitis, or a viral infection. So if you've used up a few sick days on the flu, this unexpected irritation is perfect: All you'll need is some bed rest and ibuprofen. After all, unless you're a porn star, the supine position at work just isn't practical.

■ **Corneal Abrasion** This is a scratch on the surface epithelium of the cornea caused by anything from a fingernail to dust around third base. You can earn a few laughs with the tale of your perilous but comical drive to the emergency room with vision in only one eye. Fortunately, some eye drops and a 24-hour patch will do the job and have you back to work the next day—but it's the perfect way to scam that sorely needed three-day weekend.

"The doctor said I should get plenty of greens."

Hysterical History: Are we working harder?

Even as a kid you recognized that gramps' recurring "you kids have it easy today" speech was staler than a stand-up comedy routine on airplane food. But did you know it was just plain wrong, too? True, stats indicate that the average U.S. worker's weekly hours nowadays are only minimally higher than figures from 50 and 100 years ago, and admittedly there are fewer seven-year-old coal miners now. Even so, studies show that today's average schmo faces more stress and a lower standard of living than his predecessors (read on to find out why). Can someone please pass the Prozac?

HOME WORK.

One reason we're working harder now than ever before, says national labor and employment lawyer Joe Fleming, is the ubiquitous hi-tech "conveniences" that fill our lives. But these things make our lives easier, don't they? Think again, O gullible wage slave. "No place is not a workplace today," Fleming notes, pointing to the proliferation of communications devices (cell phones, pagers, voice mail, laptops, the Internet, etc.) that turn us into walking offices and make us increasingly accessible to employers, customers, and solicitors of every stripe—and to all their requests and demands.

DOUBLE TIME.

Thanks to E-mail, fax machines, and the like, adds Fleming with cynical glee, expectations have changed about how long it takes to produce and deliver projects and documents. In other words, we're expected to do more in the same number of hours. Coronary, anyone?

TIGHTENING THE SCREWS.

Big deal. So you'll beat the system by pretending to be busy. Good idea...except for the current managerial trend toward using Big Brotheresque anti-slacking gadgets (surveillance cameras, phone and E-mail monitoring systems, etc.) to catch workplace loafers red-handed. On the plus side, you'll have extra time to waste while unemployed.

CAREFREE EXISTENCE.

OK, fine, so maybe we're working harder, but it all seems worth it when you come home after work to a piping hot meal cooked by your old lady. Yeah, right. Between the increase of women in the labor force, the decline of the male-as-exclusive-breadwinner family, and the 10-plus additional hours worked per week by the average couple since 1970, couples are feeling the time crunch, and domestic life is suffering as a result. If you want to fill your belly tonight, odds are you're gonna be making a run for the border.

"Dear Penthouse Forum..."

Spot a Psycho

Is that furtive, fatigues-wearing loner in payroll just a run-of-the-mill loser, or a psycho ready to blow?

"P-U! Don't go in there for a few minutes!"

In 1994, more than a thousand Americans were murdered at work; 160,000 were assaulted. Here are some warning signs your office buddy'll give before goin' postal:

CLUE NO. 1: He's got chronic girl trouble. "It's mostly young, single men who commit extreme acts of violence," says Norman Sussman, M.D., a clinical associate professor of psychiatry at the New York University School of Medicine. "They cannot establish a sexual relationship with the opposite sex, and they snap."

CLUE NO. 2: He shows you his Airborne tat and new Glock. According to The *SAM Advanced Management Journal,* a trade mag for office managers, traits of a "work-place killer" include military experience and a fascination with weapons.

CLUE NO. 3: He triple-locks his desk and often accuses coworkers of nosing about in his business. "People who express themes of persecution or conspiracies should be cause for great concern," says Sussman.

CLUE NO. 4: He always sulks after getting chewed out by the boss. Experts believe that a factor contributing to work-place violence is the "authoritarian-style management" found in many companies, the SAM journal reports. So whoever the poor slob is who's getting reamed, be nice to him.

CLUE NO. 5: He hits happy hour hard and follows pro bodybuilding with a vengeance. "Violence is commonly related to substance abuse and intoxication, including the use of bodybuilding steroids, which leads to 'roid rage," warns our friend Sussman.

CLUE NO. 6: Yells "Die! Die! Die! Nobody leaves! Everybody dies!" and cuts the water cooler in half with a spray of automatic gunfire. This is a moderate to strong indication of possible trouble. Time to call your contacts and get working on that resumé pronto.

TO BS OR NOT TO BS:
All You Need to Know About Being Someone You Aren't

Fibbing on your resumé is as American as Budweiser and pork rinds, if the studies estimating that 30 percent of Americans have tried it are any indication. Unfortunately for us...or, for certain people we know, the art of "creative embellishment" has been endangered by the multitude of new companies offering inexpensive, Web-based background checks. A few things to keep in mind if you're still determined to try it:

■ Reference checkers can easily verify job titles, academic degrees, past salaries, and dates worked at other companies. "Our basic, same-day degree checking costs $12.50, and employers can find out right then if the person's telling the truth," says Jack Weber, Executive VP of Degreechk.com, an Internet service run by the Illinois firm Credentials LLC. Our advice? Stick to fudging the details of what you did in your past jobs by using careful wording to make your menial accomplishments sound impressive—a practice most employers expect and are willing to forgive. Shouldn't be too hard, after all—isn't it the same thing you do on a date?

■ You say got away with it and got the job? Great. Now you can kick back and relax...Psych! But it ain't that easy. Problem is, sometimes reference-check results don't come back till weeks after your starting date. Guess what happens then? As Shakespeare said, just 'cause you're making lettuce don't mean the hatchet won't drop when the skeletons come out. (Well, he should have.)

■ Another point: If you ever try to sue your company for discrimination, wrongful termination, or anything else, you can bet they'll do a thorough background check. And if the bastards can plausibly argue they wouldn't have hired you had they known about the lies on your resumé, you're shit out of luck. Some companies will even reserve any goods on you they uncover, to use later in the event you ever try a lawsuit. Hmmm...wonder how much sympathy Judge Judy has for resumé frauds...

In general, the amount of trouble you'll face if you're busted will depend on your career type. In most cases, you'll simply get handed your walking papers, and maybe a few looks of self-righteous disapproval will get shot your way as you exit. But if your profession is in the public sector (e.g., journalist, politician) or involves other people's safety (civil engineer, bus driver), getting exposed can be a career-ender, regardless of whether you've shown you can do the job. In extreme cases, you may even be landed with a criminal impersonation rap. One consolation: If you aspire to be a mafioso or street-gang member, your career's just been made.

MONEY EDGE

How to make as much of it as humanly possible.

You don't want financial experts preaching at your ass, telling you to work hard and make nice with your boss. You have parents for that. You want quick tips to help you slash your costs, make your investments grow like a boner, and pay as little of it to your creditors or Uncle Sam as possible. And you want it to be as easy as dialing room service for more hookers and another gold-plated game of Twister.

Secrets of the Very Rich

In *The Millionaire Next Door,* Thomas J. Stanley, Ph.D., and William D. Danko, Ph.D., surveyed more than a thousand millionaires coast to coast to try to figure out how they got so damn wealthy. We filtered out the filler and are offering up the most useful findings.

■ **Make money for yourself, not your boss.** Two-thirds of the millionaires are self-employed.

■ **Live among people who are tighter than you.** The majority of the group were always surrounded by non-millionaires. Most of the people interviewed had a spouse who was more thrifty than they were. Drop those club-hopping friends of yours fast, 'cause they're just dragging you down.

■ **Buy cheap.** Most millionaires have never spent more than $600 for a suit or $200 for a pair of shoes, and they buy cheap American cars. They don't lease.

■ **Build a go-to-hell fund.** Most millionaires think of wealth in terms of financial independence, not cool shit in their homes. What they focus on is saving enough money that they can quit work, if they want to, for 10 years or so. Think about this the next time you've got to go out and get Mr. Big's coffee.

■ **Don't focus on making more money; focus on hiding it.** Millionaires minimize realized income and maximize unrealized income. Ross Perot, for example, built a huge fortune investing in tax-free municipal bonds, tax shelters, and investments with unrealized gains. You might not have that opportunity to start,

"But am I really happy? Shit yeah!"

but you probably have a 401K plan. In contrast, your realized income—the stuff you get every two weeks—is what the government is constantly levying. Shrink that category, and put more where the government can't get it.

■ **Invest slow and steady**. Ninety-five percent of the millionaires invested in stocks, and most have 20 percent or

more of their wealth tied up in publicly traded companies. But here's the rub: 91 percent of these guys hold their wealth in the stock for at least a year. Many stay in the same companies for six or more years. They focus all their time and energy researching a few good stocks to build a portfolio...and then they stay the course. No broker's fees. No short-term crises. Just a steady, obscene gain.

"Sac o' what?"

THE FACE OF CASH

Why Pamela Anderson's gorgeous mug isn't on the penny.

According to the Bureau of Engraving and Printing, the Secretary of the Treasury usually selects the designs shown on U.S. cash, and today's circulating portraits were picked back in 1928. The images on our money are of historically significant (but dead) people because the law prohibits portraits of living persons from appearing on govern-

ment securities. The U.S. Mint recently introduced the new golden dollar, replacing stodgy suffragette Susan B. Anthony with Sacagawea, the Pocahontas-looking hottie who saved Lewis and Clark's ass on their famous expedition. Interestingly, the picture of Sacagawea on the coin is not actually her picture since no record of her likeness exists.

Buck You!

The phrase *pass the buck* comes from...

It started as a poker term, according to Tom Dalzell's *The Slang of Sin*. In the mid-1800s, cardsharps placed a buck knife in front of the player who was to deal the next hand. When you passed the buck to another player, you were shifting that responsibility to someone else. "Eventually, poker players replaced the knife with a silver dollar," says Richard Lederer, author of *Crazy English* and *The Word Circus*. "That's how the dollar came to be called the buck." And, of course, "The buck stops here" means that the speaker takes responsibility for something—dropping the A-bomb, for example.

Read 'em and wipe

Life in Spendorama... Even More Reasons to Hate the Rich

There are plenty of reasons to hate the rich: better tax breaks, bigger write-offs, bustier women...but here are a few outlandish tales of wastefulness that'll make you sick to your generic-soup-filled stomach.

"Well, howdy-do Ms. Lewinsky!"

Trophy Wife Barbie

Girly author Danielle Steel's got one lucky kid. Her daughter Zara (OK, maybe not so lucky) "graduated" from kindergarten in 1993, and Mommy Steel's gifts included an obnoxious 18 Barbie dolls—all clothed in the finest gowns and furs. Twenty thousand dollars later, Zara finds the heads pop off just as easily as the rayon-skirted ones.

HOLY SHINDIG!

New York financier Saul Steinberg's 50th birthday boasted 250 guests who were seated under tablecloths fringed in real gold. Oriental rugs were placed across grassy areas so guests wouldn't get their feet wet while gawking at the identical twins dressed as mermaids in the swimming pool. An actress posed naked throughout the festivities for a living re-creation of Rembrandt's Danae. Steinberg's centerpieces were not those tacky floating candles, but actual treasure chests overflowing with pearls. Not a bad little social, for a scant $1 million.

HE'S A LONELY DORK.

Businessman Delbert Dunmire invited every Kansas City, MO resident to his wedding reception. An estimated 7,000 to 10,000 people took him up on it, running up a $1 million tab. A mere year later, Dunmire paid for a four-day cruise to the Bahamas for 420 classmates and their spouses in celebration of their 35th-year high school reunion. Close to a half-million dollars was spent reliving what must have been a painful era for a guy with a name like Delbert.

DUST CASTLES.

Castle-crazed William Randolph Hearst couldn't find exactly what he was looking for in an ancient dwelling, so he made do. Hearst bought Santa Maria de Ovila, a monastery founded on the Tagus River and home to Cistercian monks since 1180. Hearst spent nearly $1 million in total (that's in Depression-era money, mind you), including the cost for 65 laborers to dismantle it one piece at a time and number each for future assembly. Hearst's monastery was shipped to New York, stone by stone, in 10,000 carefully packed boxes. He never did anything with it anyway; the pile of rubble sold for $25,000 after a decade of collecting dust in storage.

THE POWER OF SEAMEN.

The *Christina O,* Aristotle Onassis' famed

The Need for Speed...

Tom Cruise rang in his 37th birthday much like most of us wanted to ring in our seventh. He took his son Connor and 16 friends and relatives to the International Karting Raceway in Sydney, Australia. The site was rented for five hours, and at close to $25,000, Tommy got to relive his Days of Thunder.

"Look, in the gutter! It's that guy who pantsed me in high school."

Golden Gates

Bill Gates' fortune may have been cut by a third, but he's still one of the richest men in the world, with an estimated worth of $60 billion. His $110 million suburban home has an annual tax bill alone of over $1 million. Gates' five-acre spread has 24 bathrooms, a 30-car garage, 150-seat dining room, a 20-seat theater, and its own trampoline room. The library houses the $31 million Codex Leicester (Leonardo da Vinci's, that is). In his leisure time, Gates can fish in his man-made trout stream, complete with its own salmon run. Now, if he weren't such a weasly, screaming dork...

Ellison beat Roy Disney (of the Disney Corporation) by several hours. This gave Ellison time to dock, get into his personal Cessna, hunt down Disney over international waters, and dive-bomb him. "It was one of those wonderfully immature acts for which you cannot pass up the opportunity," gloated Ellison, who incidentally, and frighteningly, has his own private air force.

yacht, included Ari's personal, if not bizarre, touch. The state rooms housed baths of pure champagne, and the indoor swimming pool featured a mosaic bottom that mechanically rose to become the dance floor. Our personal favorite: the bar stools upholstered in the skin of whale scrotums, reportedly so the tycoon could tell his female companions they were standing next to the most powerful penis in the world. And you wondered why Mrs. JFK didn't mourn for long...

CAKE ROT.

San Francisco entrepreneur Bernard Yim paid $29,900 for what most of us have the good sense to throw out. Yim purchased a long-stale

There are some things money can't buy. Like poverty

Whatta Bitch!

Australian Rose Porteous publicly announced she is leaving her legacy, nearly $1.5 million, to her pet pooches. Reported to hate people, Rose said, "I don't trust humans. My dogs mean everything to me." This preposterous squandering of dough didn't sicken us as much as the breed she chose to endow: poodles!

DIE, DISNEY, DIE!

Larry Ellison, 55, the playboy head of software giant Oracle, is estimated to be worth $47 billion. He got there by being one competitive bastard. In a 1996 Miami–to–Montego Bay sailing race,

61-year-old piece of wedding cake Sotheby's promised was from the Duke and Duchess of Windsor's nuptials. Yim justified his purchase, proclaiming his bacteria-infested little box a "romantic gesture."

Maximize Your Investments

Keep these maxims in mind and you won't go wrong.

Get paper trained.

START YESTERDAY.

Each decade you wait to invest doubles the amount of money you'll need to sock away to get the same retirement benefits. If saving 5 percent of your dough in your twenties is going to set you up right, you'll have to sock away 10 percent in your thirties, 20 percent in your forties, and so on until you're dead.

GIVE IT ENOUGH GROWTH.

Subtract your age from 100. That number is the percentage of your money that you should put into more volatile "growth" investments. If you're a by-the-seat-of-your-pants type and want to make more scratch, subtract your age from 120.

GET FOOLISH.

Buy the Motley Fools' guides to investing. Enemies of high-commission brokers, they teach you In quick, simple language how to buy and watch your own stocks, and give you a listing of complete no-brainers to invest in. Get updates from them by checking out their Web site at www.motleyfool.com.

LOOK FOR MERGERS.

These mean big profits! According to investment banker Scott Delson, a solid company that has suffered a temporary snag, scandal, or setback is ripe for one. The problem drives the buying costs

Invest in pork bellies.

Read the Papers

Helping you understand what all that stock gibberish really means.

■ Div: Dividend
The current dividend is the yearly amount, per share, that the company is paying out to shareholders. Check to see if there's a note saying it was recently increased—this means the company is becoming more profitable—which is a definite hold sign, and maybe a buy.

■ Yld: Yield
The effective yield the stock is producing is calculated by dividing the dividend rate by the current stock price. This gives you the percent you can expect to earn on your money if the stock price stays the same from year to year. Do you like this number? If it's high, you better, mister!

■ PE: Price/ Earnings Ratio
This is the ratio of the price of the company's total stock divided by its annual earnings. A low number indicates good, unexploited value. A high number—over 14—is only good if it's matched by high earnings growth rates over the past couple of years. No growth and a high P/E means that sucker's coming down.

■ Vol 100s:
The number of shares, in hundreds, that traded during the previous days' trading. The only time to pay attention to this number is if the price is changing by leaps and bounds—a drastic change with a high volume means something major is going on in the company. Don't act yet, but you better do some research to find out what's going on.

down and makes other corporations want to take on someone else's problem and make a profit. Also, communications, health care, utilities, and financial services are good bets. Finally check out stocks in industries undergoing deregulation.

DO YOUR RESEARCH.

Value Line (www.valueline.com) contains both Web-based and printed reports on 1,700 large- and medium-size companies, and provides plenty of stock and management information. An annual subscription to their service costs $570. But you can get a 10-week trial subscription—all reports updated for the entire period—for only $55. After that you can order information a page at a time for $12.50.

DON'T GET TAKEN IN BY IPOS.

IPOs were hot with the proliferation of Internet-related companies in the late '90s. But two university professors, Jay Ritter and Timothy Loughran, did a study on IPO return rates vs. comparable stocks, crunching data from all the way back to 1970. The average annual return for IPOs was 5 percent whereas the annual return for established stocks is 12 percent.

"Maybe I can help?"

End the Credit Card Nightmare

Cut high-interest rates faster than Freddy Krueger slashes through a bunch of high-schoolers.

Ever get the sneaking suspicion that the asshole in the next cubicle's copping a sweeter credit card deal than you? The bad news is, you're right. The good news is, you could be that asshole. Head for www.getsmart.com, answer a couple of yes-or-no questions about your credit history (such as "Have you had a bankruptcy in the last seven years?"), and rank a few credit card criteria—a large credit line, a low introductory rate, credits for free stuff—in order of importance to you. GetSmart will not only spit out your six best credit card options but also will hook you up with point-and-click online application forms so you can get a card pronto. Next stop: a Ferrari dealership. It's almost too easy...

See Your Credit Report

Don't forget to bring Kleenex...

Wondering why those nice Visa Gold folks told you to go screw yourself? The answer's probably in your credit report. You know, that sordid history of late mortgage payments, delinquent student loans, and credit card spending sprees that follows you around like that bull you just milked. If you're curious or wanna check for errors before applying for a big loan, send a written request, plus up to $8 (plus tax in some states), to one of the big three national credit reporting agencies and they'll shoot it out to you within 72 hours. (You're entitled to a freebie if you've been denied credit in the past 60 days, and six states—Colorado, Georgia, Maryland, Massachusetts, New Jersey, and Vermont—grant you at least one free annual copy.)

Below are the three major credit report companies, with Web site information, so you can order your credit report online:

■ Equifax: www.equifax.com (800-685-1111)

■ Experian: www.experian.com/personal.html (800-682-7654)

■ Trans Union: www.tuc.com (800-888-4213)

In addition you can get a combined report from the files of all three of these companies by contacting CREDCO at (800-443-9342). Even though their report costs a pricey $30.95, it'll give you the whole enchilada.

If you take steps to clean up an erroneous report, but the big boys aren't playing your ball, complain to the Consumer Credit Counseling Service, an arm of the National Foundation for Consumer Credit. Call (800-388-2227).

Pick a card, any card.

Fantastic Plastic

It's the best thing to happen to careless spending since the condom vending machine, but what you don't know about your credit card could be killing your cash flow. Here are some things the credit card companies don't want you to know.

■ Some cards charge you interest from the day of purchase, before they even pay the store on your behalf.

■ Check the fine print if you have a credit card and a deposit account with the same bank. Some banks reserve the right to dip into those deposit funds if your card is delinquent.

■ If you sign up for a card with an extra-low rate, when the rate expires, your existing balance is slapped with the new higher rate.

■ Some of the sweet deals on high-limit cards aren't so sweet when you realize there's no grace period on purchases. You pay interest starting the day you buy something.

■ Watch those cash advances: Some cards charge finance charges and a transaction fee.

SALE GET SHIT FOR LESS

Cut corners, buy cheap, and make a bundle!

The Waiting Game

How can you score killer deals on almost anything? All you need is a butt—to sit on and wait.

The only dignified way for a man to hunt down a discount is to kick back, polish his collection of miniature stagecoaches, and consult his calendar. Many deals have nothing to do with how hard you look; it's when you look that's important. Here's the best time to...

BUY A BIG-SCREEN TV:
A FEW DAYS AFTER THE SUPER BOWL

Yeah, yeah, you want it before; but a little patience will save you 10 to 50 percent, which could amount to $1,500. Why the postgame steal? "Big-screen-TV returns are high in January because kids buy them for the Super Bowl, throw a party, then return them afterward," says Gayle Marco, professor of marketing at Robert Morris College in Pittsburgh. The sets then go on "open box" sale, which means discounts of up to 50 percent. Worried that some drunk idiot broke the TV? According to *Consumer Reports,* most stores will replace the used set with a new one.

PURCHASE A PLANE TICKET:
JULY, AUGUST, AND DECEMBER

These are the months business travel drops and airlines offer deals, says David Fuscus, spokesman for the Air Transport Association, a coalition of U.S. airlines. For a last-minute deal on a weekend getaway, shop on Wednesday, when airlines often extend discounts as deep as 70 percent. Why Wednesday? "On Monday an airline typically kicks off a sale. On Tuesday other airlines start undercutting the first one's deal. By Wednesday the ticket war is at its height, and prices are down as far as they'll go," says Tom Parsons, president of Bestfares.com.

DRIVE 'ER HOME: SEPTEMBER

Most new models roll onto the lots in September. That's also when last year's models are rolled out—along with $2,000 rebates or interest loans of 1 to 2 percent, says Dave Van Sickle, consumer information director for the Automobile Association of America. "Given that the typical car loan is 7 or 8 percent, you can save thousands if you finance in September," he says. Hit the lots around the 29th or 30th, when salespeople scramble to fill their quotas. "The boss may be dangling a Caribbean cruise to the top seller or threatening to fire anyone who doesn't make the cut," explains Robert Moskowitz, author of *How to Organize Your Work and Your Life.*

JOIN A GYM: JULY AND AUGUST

In summer anybody with half a brain heads outdoors to exercise. "Since gym traffic is slow in July and August, gyms are anxious to sign people up," says James Auerbach, vice president of the New York–based World Gyms, a national franchise that historically has offered 5 to 15 percent off its annual fee during those months. In addition look for new gyms or gyms that are expanding their facilities, suggests Corey Sandler, author of *Secrets of the Savvy Consumer.* "Gyms need to generate cash flow the moment they open or expand," he explains. Shoot for a two-years-for-the-price-of-one deal.

BUY A COMPUTER:
RIGHT AFTER CHRISTMAS

When Santa heads back North, start hunting for a computer. Stores will be frantic to sell off anything left over from the holiday rush, often discounting machines by as much as 25 percent. But if you're willing to do a bit of research, the best deals arrive when new technology hits the stores. "As soon as Intel announces a new chip, buy the old one," says Wendy Taylor, editor of PC Computing magazine.

HUNT FOR A HOUSE OR APARTMENT:
JANUARY, JULY, AND DECEMBER

Against a backdrop of dismal gray light,

even the nicest house is less in demand because it looks about as cozy as a 19th-century English orphanage. Also fewer buyers are willing to battle the elements to see it. According to Ray Brown, coauthor of Home Buying for Dummies, this puts home sellers and landlords at the mercy of buyers and renters, who can sometimes negotiate an additional 10 to 20 percent off the listed price. Another good time to buy or rent a home is late summer, when most families who wanted to move before school starts have done so. Come mid-July, "landlords and home sellers who missed out in the early-summer rush will be desperate to sell," Brown says. You can take advantage of that desperation, and seeing a landlord grovel is one of life's rarer pleasures.

TRAVEL TO EUROPE: OCTOBER THROUGH APRIL

From May to September, tens of thousands of Americans invade Europe, driving prices up as they get shit on by French waiters. If you travel from October through April (excluding holidays), however, tourist traps may be half the cost, according to Eleanor Berman, author of Traveling Solo. And depending on where you go, the weather may beat that at home. Paris' average high temperature in March is about 52°F, seven degrees warmer than New York's. While it may not be balmy enough to let it dangle on a nude beach on the Riviera, you'll still get two weeks—or three Dutch prostitutes—for the price of one.

SHOP FOR A SUIT: NOVEMBER THROUGH JANUARY

If you're a Cosa Nostra consigliere, every day is the right day to buy a money suit; if you're not post-Christmas bargains are unbeatable, says Kenny Luck, author of 52 Ways to Stretch a Buck. You can also look for end-of-season "sample sales," in which manufacturers unload showroom merchandise at nearly half the regular price. A good place to find out where the sales are is www.samplesale.com, a wussy online guide that lists more than 100 sample sales held in major U.S. cities during

November and December (and 20 to 30 in each of the other months). Of course you should go to this site only when no other men are around.

BUY ELECTRONICS: FEBRUARY AND DECEMBER

Each January in Las Vegas, the Consumer Electronics Show unveils the world's next generation of electronic products. The month before the show, large electronics chains start slashing prices—up to 30 percent—on models rumored to be discontinued. Smaller stores, however, generally don't discount items until after the show, when they're sure which models are goners. Don't let the fact that items are discontinued get to you. "There's nothing wrong with discontinued products," explains Stewart Wolpin, executive editor of E/Town, a home-electronics Web site. "The technology on many items hasn't changed in aeons. Most modifications are cosmetic."

RENOVATE YOUR SHACK: JUNE, JULY, AND DECEMBER

During summer and at yuletide, people focus on seasonal activities: getting drunk on the beach and getting drunk at office parties. Nobody wants to focus on the butt crack of a construction worker who's raiding their fridge. And that's why contractors often shave 5 to 10 percent off their fees at these times. Not only can you save two grand on a $20,000 roof job, you'll also get a better roof. "During slow periods, contractors lay off the bad employees," says James Carey, host of On the House, a syndicated radio home-improvement show. That also means the rejects won't be peeping at your wife while she's showering.

GO ON A FIRST DATE: LUNCHTIME

On a dinner date you'll cough up half your paycheck for a steak the size of a saltine; but many upscale restaurants offer lunch for far less, according to Secrets of the Savvy Consumer author Sandler. For instance, at New York's famed Le Cirque, where a dinner entree can run more than $35, there's a $25 price-fixe lunch that includes entreé, appetizer, and dessert. Plus, this innocuous midday rendezvous will put a woman at ease. Date number two may be dinner at her place.

STEALS AND DEALS

Quality goods at Kmart prices.

■ **Bedroom sets.**
Hit the furniture stores in North Carolina. Stores around High Point, Hickory, and other towns in the area sell furniture for 40 to 60 percent off the manager's suggested retail prices. Even with shipping costs, it's big savings. You can get shopper's information packets for High Point stores by calling (336) 884-5255, or for Hickory, (800) 849-5093. Check out North Carolina Furniture Online at www.ncnet.com/ncnetworks/furn-onl.html.

■ **Vacations.**
Vacation Homes Unlimited (www.vacationhomes.com), or the International Home Exchange Network (www.homeexchange.com) are services that allow you to swap homes with like-minded folks in different parts of the world, for a modest $30 to $70 fee.

■ **Cigarette boats, lawn mowers, and brass tubas.**
Track down government auctions—you know, where they have cars, radios, clothes, and frozen pig heads go on the block for amazingly cheap prices. Here's the lowdown:

■ **Treasury Department auctions.**
For more info, call (703) 273-7373, or check out www.ustreas.gov/auctions/customs

■ **Marshals.**
For 50¢ the U.S. Marshals service will sell you a booklet of companies that sell confiscated property. Call (719) 948-3334, or look them up at www.usdoj.gov/marshals.

SLASH YOUR INSURANCE RATES!

Here's everything you need to know to get your rates as low as they can go.

■ **Pump up deductibles** Do this for collision, comprehensive fire, and theft costs. Hey, if something that bad happens, so you'll have to pay a little extra. Meantime you'll lower your rates by up to 30 percent.

■ **Drop excess coverage for junkers.** If you paid $1,200 for your car, nix collision and comprehensive coverage. You're going to pay that cost in rates pretty soon anyway.

■ **Eliminate duplicate medical coverage.** Check out your medical plan at work, and eliminate double dealing. You can only break your head once, my man.

■ **Take the extras.** When price-checking companies, ask about discounts on rates for low mileage, automatic seat belt systems, and air bags.

■ **Avoid stupid insurance.** Credit card insurance and insurance they tack on personal loans to pump up your monthly payments—think before you sign on to this stuff.

■ **Buy your home and auto policies from the same dealer.** Some companies will take 5 to 15 percent off your premium if you buy both. Ask for a toaster too!

■ **Check the construction.** Brick houses, which resist wind damage, are less costly to insure in the East. Frame houses are more ideal for the earth quake-ridden West. By choosing accordingly, you can save 5 to 15 percent.

■ **Check security.** Stuff like deadbolts and smoke detectors can save you 5 percent. Sophisticated sprinklers, or alarms that ring at the police or fire departments can save you 15 to 20 percent.

■ **Stop smoking.** You have one more reason. It accounts for about 23,000 home fires a year, and insurance companies sometimes give you discounts for quitting the weed. Do what you do with your girlfriend. Lie about it and smoke in stairwells.

Home, Cheap, Home

Need more beer money? Use these handy tips to save money at home.

DWARF AIR. Buy the smallest AC unit that can do the job, says the U.S. Department of Energy. Check www.energystar.gov for a list of appliances that are energy efficient and you could save hundreds.

INSULATE. Six-inch-thick rolls of fiberglass insulation in your attic can save you hundreds annually for as long as you live in your place.

CHECK WITH THE NEIGHBORS. In many suburban communities, with houses built at the same time, your neighbors and you could need repairs to roofs, driveways, etc., all at once. You can negotiate with contractors together and save by offering them a big deal.

RECYCLE GRASS. No, not that kind! Mulch grass clippings and it will cut your fertilizer needs by about a third. Updating your power mower with a mulch kit costs just $60 or so and saves in the long run. Plus, it's earth friendly—unless you throw a dog in there too.

Travel on the Cheap

What you need to do:

MEMORIZE THIS NUMBER. (800) 576-1234. Use it to order Insider *Travel Secrets You're Not Supposed to Know* by Tom Parsons. At $20 it's a steal. And he has a $60 subscription to his newsletter, which lists the best deals in hotels, planes, and other travel stuff.

TEACH THE WORLD. If you're a palmist, yoga instructor, astrologer, photographer, wine taster, marine biologist, bridge player, or anything else that bored cruise travelers might find interesting, call the American Council on International Studies at (800) 888-2247. They will help you find a way to get out on the high seas for free, using only your brain as barter.

BUY BACK TO BACK. If you travel to and from a destination frequently, buy tickets in pairs. This way you can take advantage of extra-low ticket prices that require you to stay over in the destination city on Saturday nights. The discount is often so low that even if you buy two round-trip tickets and throw away half, you still come out ahead. Some airlines charge fees for doing this back-to-back deal, in which case you can buy two tickets from two different airlines.

SPLIT THE FARE. A nonstop ticket is often hundreds more than two tickets with connecting destinations. Buy in little hops and you could get home with extra Ben Franklins.

  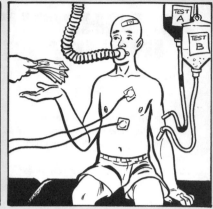

NEED A LOAN? YOU ARE ALONE

Fast Cash for Desperate Times

When time's short, funds are low, and you owe someone bigtime, here are some easy ways you can make moolah in minutes.

We don't want to know the disgusting details concerning your current plight. Let's just leave it at this: You need money and you need it fast. It's time to spring into action before some hairy-knuckled man named Bruno kicks down your door.

SELL YOUR POSSESSIONS.

Stuff just gets in the way. It slows you down. It needs to be dusted. It's time to sell anything that doesn't help you eat, sleep, get sex, or procure beer.

■ Start by loading up the car and heading to Play It Again Sports, a secondhand sporting goods chain (call 800-445-1047 for a store near you). They buy dumbbells for 15¢ per plate, lacrosse helmets for $16, ice skates for $6, starter sets of golf clubs for $50, your younger brother's hockey blades and goalie gear for $125. Resist the urge to splurge on a used snowboard.

Face it, you suck at golf anyway.

■ A pawnbroker will grudgingly shell out $30 each for once-loved pos-

sessions (your boom box), stuff you hate (the watch your stepmom gave you), and stuff your girlfriend hates (time to hand over the pistol). Your VCR will fetch $50-ish and your stereo a bit more. Sacrifice your Nintendo 64, Sony PlayStation, or Sega Dreamcast to the cause and you're looking at $60, plus up to $20 per game. Since your band, Snot Factory, has split up, sell the electric guitar for $75.

■ And what good is a computer if your fingers have been broken? Computer Renaissance (call 800-445-1047 to find a local store) pays about $50 for a 486 and up to $300 for a first-generation Pentium. As for your vast literature collection, expect $4 for John Grisham and Michael Crichton hardcovers at most used-book stores, and up to $10 for your parents' artsy-fartsy coffee-table books, which they'll never miss; paperbacks will get you 10 to 25 percent of the cover price.

The porn on your hard drive is worth more

SELL THE SHIRT OFF YOUR BACK.

You're probably holding onto your old rags because you've heard that "fashion recycles every 20 years." Get over it. In 20 years you'll be old and fat, and those clothes will look about as good on you as a lace corset.

Every day's casual Friday!

■ Open the yellow pages to "Clothing—Used." Now open your closet. Clear out half of your wardrobe and start referring to it as "vintage." When you bring it to the store, don't have it in a Hefty bag—you'll up your take by presenting it folded and clean. Redeem your 10-year-old leather jacket for $25 and your lone Armani suit for at least $100 (it didn't help get the bank loan, so what's it good for?).

■ You've probably heard that you can turn your old sneakers and jeans into serious money if you sell them overseas. Of course if you could afford a plane ticket to Tokyo, you wouldn't be hocking your crappy old clothes in the first place. Meet your new middleman: Atlas Clothing (www.atlasclothing.com) buys your '70s Nikes for $15 and '80s Air Jordans for $100 per pair and ships them to rich Eurodorks. And if the tag on your ass says "Levi's," you're sitting on a small fortune. A California company, Green for Jeans (800-538-4799), pays up to $15 for 501s in decent shape, which it sells for $100 to kids in Japan whose only goal in life is to look as cool as you. Finally your jewelry. No one is impressed with your class ring. No one! Sell it to Mr. Pawnshop for at least $30.

Save your ass: Sell your pants.

SELL YOUR SELF-RESPECT.

Now it's time to start trading on your wit, your charisma, your education, or, most profitably, your cojones.

■ Everyone loves to be entertained, and they are willing to pay dearly for it. For your lucrative debut, go drinking with a large group of friends. After three rounds mention that if paid enough ($250), you'd shave your head. Then suggest $50 as a fair price for each eyebrow. (At this point, if you're lucky, your girlfriend will offer you $400 not to do it.) This will incite a frenzy of dares, and you, brave soul, can accept them all. For $25, tell the chick across the room that your name is Michael Bolton and you'd like to be her "soul provider." Walk through the place naked for $100. For $150 circulate around the bar, whispering, "Penis and the buttocks. Penis and the buttocks," with a deranged look in your eye. Tomorrow you can blame it all on the booze.

If all else fails, hold a paper drive.

■ Once you've had enough of live entertainment, give journalism a go: You can sell lame sob stories to The National Enquirer (800-628-5697), which pays up to $500 for "stories of tragedy and triumph, courage and sacrifice, humor and outrage." Bombard Reader's Digest with amusing anecdotes, which sell for $400 apiece (www.readersdigest.com). Just keep it rated G—those old folks scare easy. And, as you're no doubt aware, Maxim shells out $150 for the Joke of the Month (jokes@maximonline.com).

■ Hollywood may be the most remunerative way to go. While your buddy stands by with a camcorder, "accidentally" throw yourself off the roof of a building while wearing a duck costume and quacking out the theme song to *Bonanza*. Send the tape to one of those World's Most Outrageous Video shows, which will gladly pay for the video of your unfortunate accident.

SELL YOUR BODY.

Your body is a temple, and now's the time to ransack it. You can make $300 to $500 a day as a male porno star. You'll need an agent who handles your brand of talent, like Jim South at World Modeling (818-986-4316). Of course he'll just tell you to screw yourself. ("We don't really like it when guys call here," says the receptionist.) A better way to land this job, according to the FAQs of porno knowledge (www.faqs.org /faqs/alt sex/ movies /part3/), is to find a cute wannabe porn queen who will perform only with you. Start with bus stations.

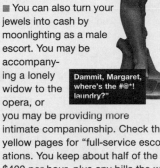

Dammit, Margaret, where's the #@*! laundry?"

■ You can also turn your jewels into cash by moonlighting as a male escort. You may be accompanying a lonely widow to the opera, or you may be providing more intimate companionship. Check the yellow pages for "full-service escort" operations. You keep about half of the $100 to $400 per hour, plus any bills the women fling at you with wild abandon. Bolstering your resumé with skills like "fluent in French" and "certified massage therapist" can only help your cause. And it certainly won't hurt if you look like Alec Baldwin.

Illegal. Immoral. Insane. And Highly Lucrative.

You may be hard up for cash, but you should never, ever do anything like this:

■ Buy alcohol for minors: $9 a sixer.

■ Rent out your apartment to horny teenagers: $20 per hour.

■ Hook your neighbors up to your cable: $90.

■ Snatch a Pekingese in the park and wait for the reward notices: $100.

■ Blackmail your ex with a naked Polaroid: $500.

■ Put talcum powder into small baggies and sell it as heroin: about $5,000... before a crazed but baby-fresh junkie cuts out your liver.

■ Carry out a hit for the Mob: $10,000.

■ Slam on your brakes suddenly and sue the schmuck who rear-ends you for whiplash: $500,000.

■ Start a cult: Unlimited money, unlimited sex, unlimited Kool-Aid.

■ Of course, you can look as mangy as Stephen Baldwin and still get a job as a nude model for a college art class. Call the school's art department to apply. It pays just $8 to $15 an hour, but a beer gut is not a problem: "You can be fat, tall, skinny, short, furry...Variety is good," says one art department staffer.

■ If you're muscular, though, you'll make more as a bouncer. The cooler the club, the less you'll get paid, but you'll average about $100 a night on the books, and losers who want to see the VIP room will grease your palm with another $200.

■ No matter what you look like or how you're built, drug companies are always looking for guinea pigs to test their new wares. They lure their prey with help-wanted ads in college and city newspapers that often begin with, "Looking for MEN 18–55..." Dermatological researchers at New York's Columbia-Presbyterian Hospital (212-305-6953), for example, pay you $15 to let them clip one of your toenails (to test for fungus), or $20 to $25 per visit to apply ointment to your athlete's foot. If they put four blisters on your arm and apply cream to them for a month, you can make $700. But if you live near the University of Texas at Austin, you just struck oil: A drug research company called Pharmaco will give you $300 per tooth to test painkillers while having your wisdom teeth pulled, or $1,550 to test acne drug L762973. If you agree to be quarantined in their cushy facilities—complete with big-screen TV—for several weeks, you can make $4,050 testing a new blood-clotting drug. (Call 800-773-2782 and ask for the automated "info hot line" to hear about similar upcoming studies so you can drive your ass to Texas.)

Money talks. Listen close

■ Plasma is always a hot commodity. Sell yours once every three days or so for about $35 a week...that is, if you don't mind the dreaded apheresis machine, which hurts like hell and can cause suspicious-looking track marks. Selling sperm is great work—if you can get it. Unfortunately, only about 5 percent of guys have the stuff it takes to get $35 to $50 a pop. If you're gam for a little adventure and want to flirt with death, you could always hop a plane and sell a kidney in the Philippines, where the market price is more than $25,000, and it's legal. Although illegal—and, at about $4,000, much less tempting—there's still a market for kidneys in Madras, India, as well. When you get to town, simply ask anyone to direct you to Kidney Street. Really.

"What can I get for this phlegm?"

Weird Jobs for the 21st Century
Make plans now to get rich in the future.

MAXIMUM-SECURITY TODDLER-PRISON WARDEN: With younger and younger children committing increasingly violent and heinous crimes, we can expect metal detectors in preschools by 2005, and a diaper-wetting prison population soon thereafter. As warden, you'll decide who needs major time-out in The Hole and which li'l felons just need a great big hug.

ADULT-DIAPER SERVICE MANAGER: When aging baby-boomers start making unscheduled backdoor deliveries, don't expect them to dump their ecological principles, too. No throw-away Depends for this generation's end game! They'll insist on reusable, organic cotton. By 2010, if you have an 18-wheeler, a washing machine, and immunity to the smell of shit, you'll be seated on a golden career throne.

SURVIVAL-GEAR FASHION DESIGNER: By 2017, contagious flesh-eating bacteria and terrorist nerve gas attacks will be daily threats. But just because we'll have to wear full biohazard suits to the office doesn't mean we'll want to look like styleless drones. The first guy to come out with a smart Italian-cut suit (double-breasted with an escape hatch in case of air filter failure), or microbe-resistant khaki for casual Fridays, will make a bundle of coin.

ATTENTION-SPAN TRAINER: Forget about Alzheimer's disease (if you already have, see a doctor now). The future's biggest problem will be young adults with brains so addled by Web surfing and music videos that they can't concentrate long enough to non-speed-dial 911. Trainers will work closely with clients on focusing skills such as selecting meals from non-hyperlinked restaurant menus and sitting through multisyllabic words.

SEX ROBOT/VIRTUAL GIRLFRIEND REPAIRMAN: Learn to say stuff such as, "You'll want to go with 10W-40 on that groin lube" and "These pneumatic nipples are still under warranty," and you'll command hourly rates that will make doctors green with envy. Then, of course, there are the test drives.

Why she wants to get into your pants.

"Gilligan, I think I'd like to meet your 'little buddy'."

Marry a Millionairess

Since you got nothing left to sell, the lottery's too unlikely, and crime can entail serious practical and logistical problems, why not marry into money? Here's some counsel on securing cash the cold-hearted way.

SHED YOUR INTEGRITY WITH YOUR NAME. To help you cast off your inhibitions and perfect your ruthlessness, Ginie Polo Sayles, who has spent 10 years teaching a course, "How to Marry the Rich," recommends dumping your name and acquiring a new one. "You'll feel your whole being shift into someone else," she says.

BE INFORMED. Your library can provide you with two important reference volumes. First, the annual issue of Forbes that lists the 400 richest men and women in America. The second is Helen Bergan's Where the Money Is: A Fund-Raiser's Guide to the Rich. Though meant for high-minded institutions, it will serve you nicely in your efforts to line your own pocket.

LOOK THE PART. Rather than just blend in with the crowd, Sayles advises, try wearing different outfits in different regions. "In the East the preppy look is dependable—say, a navy blazer and khakis. In the West and Southwest, you can go with the dark blue jeans, white starched shirt, and expensive belt. For California, maybe a black T-shirt and blazer, without socks." Marty Westerman, author of How to Flirt, is more succinct,

saying, "With a tan and an Italian suit, you can do anything." We go with Westerman here: Being slightly but tastefully overdressed is much less risky than possibly looking like the cabin boy, J. R. Ewing, or Miami Vice's version of a drug kingpin.

MOVE UPTOWN. "The first rule," says Sayles, "is to live where the rich live, even if you have to live in an attic." Other experts on marrying women for the wrong reasons concur. Even in the right neighborhood, however, you'll have to make an effort to mingle. Sayles suggests volunteering at a charitable organization, working in a museum, or taking painting classes. Westerman recommends attending vintage car rallies, polo matches, art auctions, and ("to find the rarin' widow") afternoon tea at the best hotels. He also advises crashing A-list parties: "Come in a tuxedo, with a bottle of champagne, and on crutches. No one will ever turn you away, and once you're there, you'll have no problems starting a conversation."

UNDERSTAND THE HUNTED. Sharyn Wolf, the author of Guerrilla Dating Tactics, suggests taking a year preparing to deal with the wealthy. "You'll definitely

need to know how to tango," she says, "so take some lessons before you start your dating." Westerman warns that the one thing moneyed women want is to be entertained. "Being rich," he says, "often means being bored."

REEL HER IN. Once you've started your relationship, you must get her so caught up with you that the only logical step is marriage, preferably without a prenuptial agreement. Sayles advises that you let her shape you in whatever way she desires. "Be a problem to her. She'll want to fix you, and you'll have her hooked." He adds, "It practically goes without saying that you have to give her great sex."

HONOR THY FATHER. This man can trip you up. "A woman's first marriage is always to a version of her father," says Westerman, adding that the more you understand him, the more thoroughly you'll be able to ensnare her. But fathers can also be a problem. Joe Bolker, a divorced L.A. real estate broker, married Christina Onassis in the '70s. She was 27 years his junior and heir to Aristotle Onassis' megafortune. Nine months later Bolker got another divorce. "When a billion dollars leans on you, you can feel it," he said.

"Here's a little ditty I call 'Blow Me, Mr. Taxman.'"

FRICKIN' TAXES!

Here's how to keep those IRS bastards from squeezing your teat till it turns purple.

Avoid an Audit

How can you give Uncle Sam as little as possible without triggering an audit? Here's some help:

RED FLAG #1: Big numbers
Large amounts of dividend income, medical deductions, and business-related entertainment or travel expenses, along with charitable donations of more than 10 percent of your adjusted gross income will mark you as auditable.

RED FLAG #2: Math mistakes
Though being a moron isn't illegal yet, it's an audit trigger. According to How to Beat the I.R.S. at Its Own Game, by Amir Aczel, arithmetic blunders suggest you're pulling funny stuff with the numbers. Use a calculator, check your figures, then check 'em again. Or hire an accountant, ya cheapskate.

RED FLAG #3: Inconsistencies
If your federal return doesn't jibe with your state return, you become a target. Similarly, if it fails to agree with past returns, it can trigger the goons. Attach a note explaining anything fishy.

RED FLAG #4: Too much income
According to stats in The Christian Science Monitor last year, the feds audited 2.85 percent of returns of people making $100,000 or higher—more than twice the rate at which they audited those making $50,000 to $100,000, and three times as often as those earning $25,000 to $50,000. Schmucks earning less than 25 G's were audited 1.17 percent of the time, but the rate almost doubled when they filed 1040A returns!

RED FLAG #5: Scheduling errors
According to Aczel's book, roughly 90% of all audits are triggered by bad ratios on schedules A, C, and F. His tips (figures may change yearly—so watch out):

■ Schedule A:
Divide your total itemized deductions (line 36) by adjusted gross income (line 33). Keep the number less than .35, and definitely stay below .44.

■ Schedule C:
Divide total expenses (line 28) by gross income (line 7). A number under .52 is OK. Anything more than .63 is like listing "underage Thai whores" as a business expense.

■ To audit-proof a Schedule F:
Make sure deductions stay below 59 percent of your income, and far from 67 percent.

Even White-Collar Crime Doesn't Pay

Sure, it's easy to cheat on your taxes, fudge your expenses, and dip into the petty cash. If caught, though, chances are you'll be promptly removed from society and found sporting a new girlfriend named Claude. Weigh your options according to the U.S. Sentencing Commission's punishment of white-collar crimes.

■ The average prison sentence being served for general tax offenses is just over one year. Pretty stiff compared with the potentially higher perks of embezzlement, which incidentally would run you a standard (and scant) six months in the pen.

■ Fraud convicts face $1\frac{1}{2}$ years, and bad news for the 30 percent of those eligible for non-prison sentences: They get sent to the Big House anyway.

■ Money laundering is twice as risky as fraud, having the potential to earn you more than three years' experience. With all sorts of things.

■ While racketeering and extortion still sound the most glamorous of all, those convicts average over eight years of incarceration. That's almost double the time a manslaughter sentence commands.

Audit-Proof Your Return

We interrogated the hell out of veteran tax preparer and deadly IRS-battler Shelley Jacobsen to give you the straight dope on who gets audited and why.

■ How do those IRS bullies decide whom to pick on?

Based on your return, the IRS calculates a magic number called your diff; a high diff spells doom. According to Jacobsen, your diff rises and falls depending on how your deductions compare with the national averages. So if most of your countrymen deduct three percent of their income for charities, but you generously donate four percent, your diff inches up toward the danger zone.

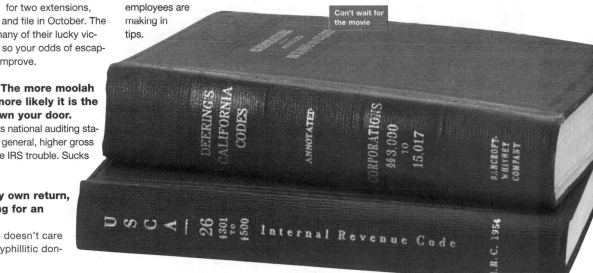

"Don't tell me... the dry cleaning isn't deductable."

■ When's the best time to file if I want to boost my odds of escaping an audit?

According to a former IRS auditor, your best bet is to skip the April rush, ask for two extensions, and file in October. The IRS goons select many of their lucky victims in September, so your odds of escaping the scythe will improve.

■ True or false: The more moolah you make, the more likely it is the IRS will bust down your door.

True. Jacobsen says national auditing statistics show that, in general, higher gross income means more IRS trouble. Sucks to be rich, eh?

■ If I prepare my own return, am I just begging for an audit?

Not at all: The IRS doesn't care if a three-legged syphillitic don-

key prepares your return. It's the numbers that count. But if you do get audited, warns Jacobsen, it's time to stop being the Lone Ranger. "The auditors are trained to ask you questions in a way that makes you incriminate yourself," she warns. Your best bet: Hire representation.

■ Does the IRS care if you round off your estimates of earnings and expenses?

Damn straight they do...revenooers are kinda meticulous-like. "Obviously If you pay for a college course and it costs $500, put down $500," says Jacobsen. "But if every number is round, it'll look like you made up figures willy-nilly."

■ If my job involves cash income (waiting tables, peddling crack outside grammar schools), am I at higher risk?

You betcha. "Certain industries, such as the restaurant business, have been targets for the IRS over the last five years," says Jacobson, who claims the G-men now investigate businesses to find out how much employees are making in tips.

■ True or false: The super-rich don't have to pay dick.

Used to be true, but now it's false. Ever since 1986 the Donald Trumps of the world have been subject to the Alternative Minimum Tax, which charges folks who gross more than $250,000 a tasty 39.6 percent off the top.

■ Once I get audited, the party's over, right? The IRS will be at my doorstep again and again till death do us part?

Relax. "It's not like there's a 'shit list' of people who've been audited before that the IRS refers to," says Jacobsen. However, it is common for people to 'get pulled' two years in a row, usually because they're filing the same type of high-risk return both years (e.g., you're a Fortune 500 CEO declaring only $12,500 in taxable income).

■ If I give my accountant a nice thank you gift at tax time, will he or she save me more money?

Well, says Jacobsen, it couldn't hurt.

Can't wait for the movie

DEERING'S CALIFORNIA CODES   ANNOTATED   CORPORATIONS $$3,000 TO 15,017   BANCROFT-WHITNEY COMPANY

U S C A | 26 $301 TO $500   Internal Revenue Code   I.R.C. 1954

Open Your Own Bar

When all else fails…
sling hooch for a living.

"So, wait…it's this second finger? That's the rude one?"

In the bar, the owner is king. And the bar is a good kingdom: Only you get to stock the jukebox, to dish out complimentary drinks as liberally as you please, to blithely ignore last call. So how do you get to be king?

STEP 1: COLLECT AN ENORMOUS STACK OF MONEY.

"I've made a small fortune running a bar. But I started with a large fortune," says Tim Hobart, owner of The Liberty Bar in San Antonio, Texas. Buying and renovating a space is just the beginning. You'll need to shell out for a liquor license ($2,000 to $100,000 or more, depending on your state), insurance (figure $15,000 or so a year for a bar generating $200,000 in gross sales), and other incidentals, like gas, water, and climate control. (John Mountain, owner of Dr. Joe's Intra-Coastal in Melbourne, Florida, spends about $900 a month keeping his patrons cool.) Even small items can add up: Glasses will break, knickknacks will disappear, towels and ashtrays will have to be replaced. Jeff Wright, 31, the owner of GT in Des Moines, spends about $75 a month on candles. Later your profits will take care of these ongoing concerns, but during your first, least profit-filled month, they can sting like swift kicks. If you don't have tons of extra greenery in your savings account, consider getting a partner.

STEP 2: KNEEL BEFORE THE GOVERNMENT.

Prepare to fill out a buzz-killing sea of government forms. If you skip this step, you will be punished: Wright started renovating the rented space where his bar now stands before he received a building permit. State officials halted construction, and that made picking up the other okays—from the health, zoning, parking, planning and fire departments—a painfully slow process. "The one thing that can get you shut down quick is to get crossways with the authorities," says Hobart, and all the other owners we talked to agreed. Find out what the applicable local laws are and stick to them scrupulously. And don't mess with the IRS: Apply for a federal tax ID number up front.

STEP 3: DESIGN YOUR DREAM.

Here's where the fun starts: Get creative and give your bar a soul. Wright was wild about auto and motorcycle racing, so he built a bar in which the beers are housed in one engine and another with light bulbs in its cylinders is suspended over the pool table. Hobart wanted to run a traditional saloon, so he bought one that had been in business since 1890. Think your concept through: Patrons may not flock, for example, to an "authentic" Irish pub in a strip mall next door to a Burger King. Also, pay attention to your bar's sound-track. "I tried running the music from behind the bar," Wright laments, "but too many drunks would want their request played immediately." He switched to a jukebox with a good mix including everything from John Coltrane to Fugazi. One bummer you'll face is that, sooner or later, an emissary from the American Society of Composers, Authors, and Publishers (ASCAP) will show up to charge you for each time one of its copyrighted songs is played (about $2,000 a year for a 50-person-capacity bar). This is an excellent time to complain that nobody ever uses the damn jukebox.

STEP 4: SAY ADIOS TO YOUR HOBBIES.

You have to marry any small business if you want it to succeed, so prepare to live in your drinking establishment almost around the clock, especially if you're too poor to hire a bartender. John Mountain figures he spent his first 18 months working 16-hour days. This has its upside. "A good bar takes on the personality of its owner," says Hobart. "If you're not there, the place won't have your character." What would Cheers be without Sam Malone?

STEP 5: MAKE IT LADY-FRIENDLY.

Without women, a bar gets either empty or out of hand. Hobart praises women for keeping guys in bars civilized. Wright agrees and says he keeps them coming back by keeping his bar clean—especially the bathrooms. As for the idea that a bar is like a giant Venus's-flytrap funneling babes into your life, it's true—but you might not have time to enjoy them. "You will meet women," says Joe Englert, who owns the Capitol Lounge in Washington, D.C. "But you'll still have to stay late and count the money."

STEP 6: HANDPICK YOUR TEAM:

If you do hire a bartender, Mountain suggests that you "look for the kind of person that other people like to be around." Wright adds, "We like inexperienced bartenders: They haven't learned ways to steal yet." There's a certain type of man that prefers to order drinks from a tank-topped female. (You know who you are.) This is the philosophy underlying Hooters, of course, and a dab of this may serve you well, as long as you don't turn off female drinkers. But think safety too: If you can't afford a meathead bouncer to keep out the riffraff, make sure at least one bartender is on the burly, fearless side. Or use Wright's method: "When someone needs to leave, I usually go back to the pool table, find the biggest guys there, and offer them a few free beers to help me out. They always do."

STEP 7: BASK IN YOUR GLORIOUS ROLE.

Wright estimates he gives away 20 drinks a night to regulars and people he'd like to see again. Such generosity is the noble duty of the bar owner: The king must be good to his people. "Everyone loves knowing the owner," says Englert. And when people feel connected, they come back...and they bring all their thirsty friends.

Open Your Own Swiss Bank Account

With a numbered Swiss bank account, you can store your wad for generations where it's safe from business partners, ex-wives, and the inevitable German storm troopers. Here's how to bank like John Gotti.

STEP 1: Contact the New York branch of a Swiss bank.
Call Credit Suisse, (646) 354-5000; Swiss Bank, (212) 574-3000; or Union Bank of Switzerland, (212) 821-3000, and grab the address and phone number of one of their Swiss offices.

STEP 2: Hop a flight to Geneva.
While your deposit can be wired in, you'll have to open your account in person. So look respectable: Says Swiss Bank spokesperson Jens Woehler, "Whether we will open an account or not may boil down to whether a situation or a person looks suspicious." If accepted you'll need to provide a signature sample and divulge personal info, including your real name, exclusive of Mob handles like "Sammy No-Neck."

STEP 3: Show Guenther the green.
Some Swiss banks require a minimum deposit of a quarter mil, but Swiss Bank will start you up with a savings account

for just $10. Your new account can be opened in any major hard currency: Yen, yes; the hilariously named Vietnamese "dong," no.

STEP 4: Keep your nose clean.
The U.S. and Switzerland recently signed an agreement limiting Switzerland's ability to keep banking secrets. Now you'll have to declare that your cash doesn't come from criminal sources; they can rat you out if they find you're lying, and the authorities can freeze your funds. Also: You must declare worldwide income on your IRS returns.

STEP 5: Kick back and pay.
Up to a hefty 35 percent of your account's interest could be withheld by the Swiss taxman, and assorted fees can tack on another $170 a year. Upside: The next time a global financial panic or a world war breaks out, you'll be sitting pretty.

BEYOND THE SWISS

Those cheese-making, watch-hocking bastards not doing it for you? Stash your cash here!

You gotta set up a chop account, which you can do in Hong Kong and banks around the Pacific Rim for as little as $20, according to Jerome Schneider, author of *The Complete Guide to Offshore Money Havens.* In fact large international banks like Citibank and Bank of America are adopting chop accounts.

A "chop" is your equivalent of a serial number, which protects the secrecy of your money. Far from being high-tech, it's a group of Chinese characters, carved into a piece of stone, which becomes your personal signature. It's thousands of years old, practically impossible to duplicate, and the next wave in private accounts... as well as a cool thing to show people at parties.

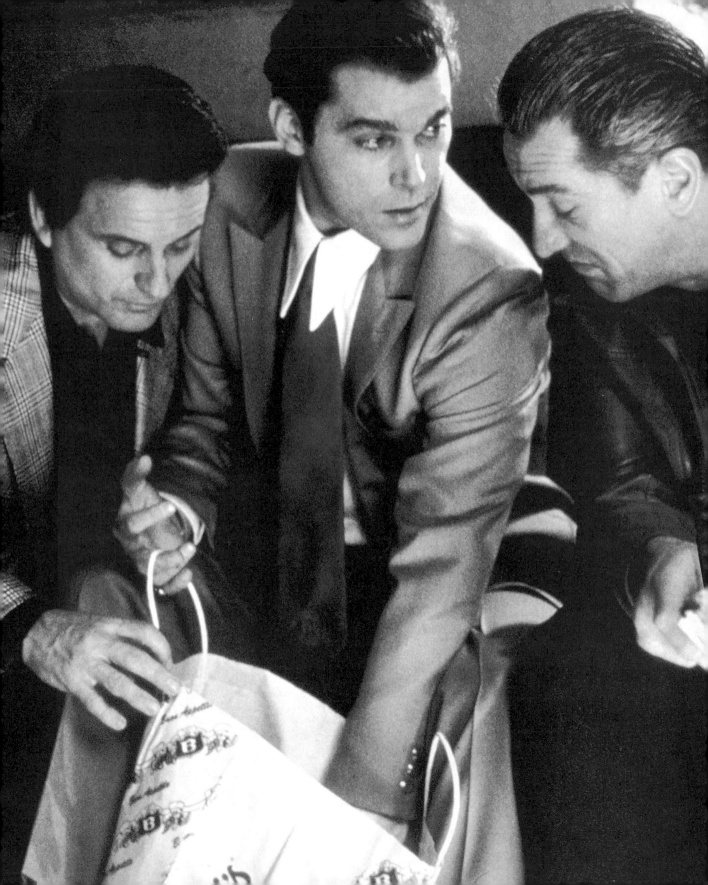

STREET EDGE

'Cause you belong to the city. You belong to the night...

Ever have one of those days when it seems like everyone's fucking with you? From the bartender who conveniently avoids your gaze to the guy driving 11 miles an hour in front of you in a no-pass zone, there's gotta be a better way to navigate through bad treatment in the urban jungle—or any jungle. Here's how to keep your nose clean and be a hero to your babe while other guys flounder and fail.

"Oh great. Now how'm I supposed to masturbate?!"

How to Take a Punch
Confucius say: "He who slam face on fist, get bloody nose."

Even saintly types, like us, occasionally get decked. But when your turn comes, you needn't go through the rest of your days sounding like Sylvester Stallone. That's 'cause your reaction to getting punched can be the difference between a two-day shiner and a lifetime of drooling.

ROLL WITH IT, BABY.
Longtime Los Angeles boxing coach and trainer Teddy Groat explains the concept of "rolling with the punches" by comparing it with being rear-ended by a car traveling 60 mph. If you're at a standstill, you're probably going to wind up as roadkill. But if you're traveling in the same direction at 55 mph, you'll hardly feel the impact. (Unless you're driving a Pinto, that is.) Likewise, when an unavoidable punch is thrown at you, rolling with it—moving your body in the same direction that it's heading—absorbs the momentum, thus neutralizing its force. Result: You retain consciousness, having

sustained minimal damage, and depending on what the situation calls for, retaliate with a devastating series of flying karate kicks and 1-2 combos, or flee and be grateful you've managed to retain your facial structure.

TAKE AN ALTERNATIVE VIEW.
Some people say it's better to move *into* a punch, a concept that is actually based on a sound premise. The basic idea is that when a straight jab or roundhouse punch has less distance to travel, it builds up less momentum and thus strikes its object with less force. Get it? So when the son-of-a-lunchlady aims one at your head, clench your neck and jaw, and step in as though you were trying to give him a kiss. While doing so attempt to partially deflect the blow with your arm, and if possible, turn to the side so that his fist glances off your forehead or, better yet, the back of your head. Exception: If you enjoy bird watching or stargazing, try to catch it on your nose.

"No big deal. I can't read anyway."

YOU CAN KEEP IT

Protecting Your Crap From Thieves

AVOID MUGGERS AND PICKPOCKETS.

Knowing that a pickpocket rarely works alone is your first step in preventing your wallet from being snatched. Pickpockets usually work in teams of two or three, each person having a different role in the operation. "The blocker" usually gets in your way or distracts you long enough for "the snatcher" to grab your wallet and then pass it off to "the shill" in case you catch on to what's happening. If a person blocks your way and pretends to move out of the way while still blocking you, there is a very high probability your wallet is being snatched. When this happens immediately turn around and try to catch them making the pass. Other ploys used by these vermin to distract you range from stopping you to ask a question to causing a commotion by spraying your shirt with ketchup or spilling a beverage on you.

STOP, THIEF!

Mugging and levying taxes aren't the only situations in which someone's after your property. Keep your possessions in your possession with the following tips:

■ If traveling use traveler's checks or credit cards as much as possible. Don't flash your cash around in public, and always keep one credit card and picture ID separate from wallet or purse. Don't stand around gapejawed while looking at the sights, and never wrestle with a tourist map in the middle of a crowd.

■ Avoid alleys, especially if somebody asks you to step into one. Yes, the chance of actually buying a Rolex for $10 is tempting, but wake up, ya friggin' cheapskate.

■ Look confident and be aware of the environment around you. Walk briskly, preferably with someone (especially after dark), and stick to the middle of the sidewalk. Face traffic and stay visible. Avoid isolated areas and avoid cutting through parks, vacant lots, and deserted areas.

■ Don't get involved with any betting on the street. Even if you happen to win something, good luck collecting your winnings. Most of these operators have their pals nearby, participating in the game as shills who'll happily separate you from your winnings with a few kicks to the groin.

■ If you're staying in a hotel and must leave money or other valuables in your room, try using a can safe to thwart hotel staff crooks. Made from actual product containers (Right Guard, 7-Up, Planter's Peanuts, etc.), these puppies have twist-off bottoms that reveal hidden compartments. Get one for $20 at www.securerite.com/products, and store it on the shelf next to the can o' nuts exploding-snakes gag until your next trip. Or use the room safe if there is one.

■ Foil pickpockets by having Grandma sew strips of heavy-duty Velcro (available at most camping stores) into your pocket openings and leave a finger-size pull-gap for easy noisy, opening. Added bonus: Play with your pockets until the ripping sound drives your fellow travelers insane.

■ The best anti-burglar device? Making 'em believe someone's home. Have a neighbor bring in newspapers and mail, put indoor lights on timers, leave a radio on (Rush Limbaugh will give 'em a double scare), and if possible, park a car in your driveway. If you're the type who leaves "I'm out of town till Wednesday" phone messages, you deserve to be burgled.

■ Ever notice how bike messengers' cycles are so dirty and greasy, you can't even read the brand? That's cuz flashy bikes entice baddies—so uglify yours with thick coats of car wax and/or latex house paint. As for locks, your best bet is a narrow U-type (e.g., Kryptonite Evolution 2000, $19), which is too skinny to wedge a car jack inside. In general the less room you leave inside a lock, the more frustrated the hoodlum—another reason to lock *both* wheels, you lazy sod.

■ Computer dealer trying to sell you on a slick leather laptop case with 18 side pouches? Tell him to stick it up his Zip drive. Save $200 on the expensive "steal me" bag and $1,500 on your laptop by using an old beat-up briefcase, backpack, or courier bag instead.

Big Guns

Unless you're from Montana, you probably don't know the difference between a machine gun, a submachine gun, and a machine pistol.

Asking about the difference between these three peacemakers is like trying to determine the difference between Roseanne and a 400-pound tuna; it's all a question of scale. All three guns use the word *machine* because they can fire either automatically (blasting a round of bullets with a single trigger squeeze) or semiautomatically (with the standard one bullet per squeeze).

The machine gun fires rifle ammunition, can weigh more than 100 lbs., and has a range of up to 1,000 yards.

The submachine gun fires handgun ammo, is held with both hands, and has a range of up to 200 yards.

The kinder, gentler machine pistol takes handgun ammo, is fired with one hand, and has a range of 200 yards.

Basically, soldiers carry the first two types of guns, police officers usually carry the third, and right-wing wackos stock up on all three.

Master the Car Chase

OK, you beat the gridlock, but there's some trouble ahead: The malicious trucker you flipped off is fixing to rearrange your skeletal structure, and six irate machine-gun-toting G-men are hot on your ass. If you hadn't read this section, you might actually be worried.

■ Test his testes
Give your vehicular pursuer a taste of fear. In quick succession:
1. Abruptly hit the brakes so he's forced to do the same to avoid a collision.
2. Hit the gas and leave him sucking up your dust. This little display of cockiness ought to make the bastard think twice about ridin' your tail.

■ Exit road, left
Get in the exit lane, feint left, then swerve onto the exit ramp at the last possible second, leaving no time for your adversary to follow. Get back on the interstate at your leisure, or pop into the rest-stop fried-chicken joint for an extra crispy three-piece chicken and biscuit with hot sauce on the side.

■ Just say S
As any greyhound will tell you, it's harder to follow a zigzagging rabbit than a mechanical one. If you're being chased through the city or a residential area, head for the twisty roads and make like a Jheri curl.

What some people won't do to avoid a parking meter.

■ The Bomb move
You've just taken a fast corner, thus momentarily removing yourself from your pursuer's visual range. If it's night kill your headlights and, using your emergency brake to slow down (if you pull up gradually, you won't fly through the windshield), glide into a parking space, driveway, or other cul-de-sac. Why the emergency brake? No telltale red brakelight, that's why. Do it gracefully and your pursuer will fly by without ever seeing you...and shortly start wondering how you evaporated into thin air.

HOME PROTECTION

Just in case you need something on hand to defend the homestead against zombies, aliens, or missionaries.

NAPALM
Soak a ball of wax in gasoline overnight. Put a wick in it, light, and throw. A flaming, sticky mess! Not real fun at parties, though.

DRY-ICE BOMBS
Put dry ice into a towel and crush into pebbles. Fill a two-liter soda bottle one inch with dry ice. Top off with hot water, cap the bottle, and run away. Loud and obnoxious mayhem!

HOMEMADE SLIME
Add one cup water to one tablespoon Borax. Stir until dissolved. Then make a 50-50 solution of water and white glue, using a quarter cup each. In a Ziploc bag, add equal parts Borax solution to equal parts glue solution. A half cup of each makes one cup of slime. Add food coloring. Seal bag and knead mixture. Repeat process until 50-gallon drum is full and ready to be dumped from your roof on the evil bad guys below. A good alternative to scalding oil.

Owning the Road!

Beating tickets, bypassing gridlock, and blowing past Smokey.

Traffic's moving at horse-and-buggy speed, and your wife's in contractions! Or maybe you're just an impatient bastard (or a New York City cabbie). Whichever it is, you don't have to blow a cylinder when you're stuck in gridlock. These tricks for weaving in and out of the mess will get you there faster—assuming you don't wind up in a holding cell.

■ Don't blink twice.
Think people will let you into their lane more willingly if you signal? Think again, Miss Manners. According to auto mechanic and illegal street racer Casey Hudson, frustrations run high when the traffic's heavy, and signaling only tends to make the guy behind you in the next lane speed up to prevent your entry. Forget about cueing him with your blinker; just cut the douche off.

"We're never meanin' no harm!"

■ Strut your struts.
People shy away from aggressive drivers. To pass in a tight space, get right on the bumper of the car in front of you, then nudge your way over. Says Hudson of this technique: "By the time they get their finger up, I couldn't see it if I tried."

■ Zen it.
A relaxed reckless driver is a quicker-reacting reckless driver. Whether you're cutting

someone off, swerving over two lanes, or braking from 80 to 0 in a short stretch, use smooth, fluid motions. You won't skid, you'll keep your car happy, and you'll decrease the odds of ending up in a body shop, operating room, or jail. Hudson suggests imagining there's a sleeping passenger, riding shotgun, whom you're trying not to wake. We suggest Catherine Zeta-Jones.

■ Speed past the pumps.
Waiting to turn at a red light or stop sign by a gas station? Don't. Just cut through the gas station onto the other street, and be on your merry way. Don't stop to take a leak.

■ Getting a little on the side.
If there's a shoulder or breakdown lane and you're feeling frisky, hit your hazards and go for it. Don't overdo it, though; too much speed can kick up rocks or dust and cause a skid. Don't get caught, either: Tickets for this li'l' maneuver tend to be in the three-digit range.

■ Ambulance chaser.
When a screaming ambulance or fire truck parts traffic, quickly jump in and fill the vacuum they leave behind. If the authorities nab you for this, be aware that a jovial "Nice one!" and slap on the back are unlikely.

■ Mind if I cut in?
At the end of a long line in the turning lane? Slip around 'em, then slide in at the front of the line wherever a space opens up. If you hear beeping, don't be concerned; it's probably because of your HONK IF YOU'RE HORNY bumper sticker.

■ The inevitable disclaimer.
"Honestly," says Hudson, "the best advice I can give you is, don't be in a hurry." Stats show aggressive drivers in gridlock situations get there no sooner on the average than calm, grandfatherly types. Sorry to brake it to ya.

Break-Fast Time
Punk-ass kid wants to race you off a light, eh? Show the little whippersnapper the meaning of the words ignition, blastoff.

IF YOU DRIVE A STICK.
Let the clutch out and rev the engine steadily at a mid-level rpm (2,000 or so). Meanwhile keep your eye on the opposite light; when it turns yellow, get ready for takeoff. Start letting up on the clutch so that, as the light turns green, you begin to lurch forward; at this moment lean on the accelerator. Be warned: Too many RPMs can cause tire-spin and skidding; too few and you'll stall. But get it right and you'll shoot off quicker than a 17-year-old in a whorehouse.

IF YOU DRIVE AN AUTOMATIC.
Wimp. OK, now that we got that out of the way: You can achieve a similar effect by revving the engine while keeping your left foot on the brake just enough to prevent forward movement. Don't be alarmed if you feel the car rearing up like an agitated mustang; that merely results from load-up on the torque converter. (Feel better?) Wait for the green, release the brake, and become a speck on the horizon.

"Last one to hit that nun is a rotten egg."

Speeding Wisely

We'd never advocate speeding, because if we did, we'd have to suggest the following methods to avoid getting caught.

"Hurry or we'll miss *Golden Girls!*"

HEED SIGNS OF LIGHT. Oncoming drivers flashing their headlights as they head toward you are saying: "Cop ahead." And if the red brakelights of cars in front of you start coming on for no apparent reason, the drivers are probably tapping them instinctively after having just spied a cop.

TRUST THE TRUCKERS. Big-rig drivers may have awful taste in music, but when it comes to speed traps, they know their shit. "Truckers always know where the traps are because it's their business to," says Todd Franklin of the National Motorists Association, the folks who lobby for your God-given right to use a radar detector. "If they're going 15 mph over the speed limit, you're safe. But if they start to slow down, watch out."

GO SLOW: LATTE ZONE. Hey, if you worked a cop's hours, you'd inhale coffee and doughnuts, too. 7-Eleven, Starbucks, Dunkin' Donuts, and other such establishments are notoriously filled with java-guzzling patrolmen, so don't pull any Evel Knievel moves in front of these joints.

U'S COMMON SENSE. If you see a NO U-TURN sign as you come around a freeway turn, beware: U-turns mean upcoming crossovers, where police cars often await their prey.

GOT RADAR LOVE. Don't forget what you learned on *CHiPs:* Quota-hungry cops associate the left lane with high-speed hijinks and the right lane with solid citizenship. If possible travel in the far right lane on multilane highways, since cops usually focus their radar on the passing lane. Bonus: If the cop's scanning from the median, trucks and other vehicles will partially shield you from the radar. *It was the other guy, Judge!*

GET OUT OF A SPEEDING TICKET

Once you see those flashing lights in your rearview mirror, your goose is cooked…right? Wrong! We asked state troopers and other cops how some offenders escape with warnings and others end up with a big fat fine.

DO: Slow down. Contrary to popular belief, cops aren't watching to see if your brake lights go on. Take the hint and slow down yourself and many cops will let you roll on by.

DO: Ditch the radar detector as discreetly as possible. It's an unspoken rule that possessing one mandates a ticket.

DO: Be extremely polite, and apologize for disturbing the cop's day.

DO: Deliver your cockamamie excuse (see page 81) *before* the officer returns to the squad car with your license and registration: All summonses have to be accounted for, and once written out, they can't be ripped up.

DON'T: Make it tough for him. Just pull over, turn on your interior lights, and put both hands on the wheel. Showing him you're not a threat is the first step toward putting him in a good mood.

Training Wheels

If you're already a risk-taking driver, and you wanna take it to the next level, you probably need professional help—the vehicular kind, that is. The Sports Car Club of America (http://www.scca.org/index.html) offers a national listing of autocross sessions and high-performance road-racing classes taught by pros for around $50. For some inside info on street-racing schools, try Thunderhill Park (http://www.thunderhill.com).

DON'T: Deny you were speeding. If they didn't have proof, they wouldn't have stopped you.

DON'T: Drop any doughnut remarks, no matter how hilarious.

No Brakes? No Problem

Dang those twins and their childish pranks—last week it was the plastic-explosives-in-the-toolshed gag, and this time they've cut your brake lines! And here you are, barreling down the interstate at 70 mph. One thing's for sure: If you get out of this one, *someone's* getting a stern talking-to!

TAKE A BRAKE. Your first recourse is to give the old emergency brakes a test. Turns out you don't *have* to yank it like a slot machine handle and exit dramatically through the windshield, though if you do have the urge, feel free. Otherwise head for the emergency lane, pull the brake up slowly, and glide to a gentle stop.

SHIFT YOUR THINKING. Depending on how much room you have to stop, gradually shift from higher to lower gears, and let the engine do the work of slowing your vehicle down. Drive an automatic? Same deal. Use those little "2" and "1" gears you never bother with. Riddle: What does using this technique have in common with holding in a wet fart? (Answer below*)

THOU SHOULD SHOULDER NOT. Hitting the soft shoulder to stop a runaway car is not a smart ploy. The reason? When your left tires are touching pavement and your right tires are trying to grab onto something softer such as gravel or dirt, the left ones will speed up to compensate for the loss of friction, and the back of your car will subsequently fishtail to the left.

BE SECOND SWERVE. If the cliff edge is coming up faster than lame dialogue in a Hollywood action flick, swerving back and forth before you get there will increase the distance you travel (and hence, the total friction). So start making some Z's. If you go over anyway, dive out in midair and use your pocket-pen parachute to float down safely—but look out for the piranhas before you reach the waterfall...

TRY THIS KEY MOVE. You can reduce your speed considerably by killing the ignition while in high gear, then quickly turning it back on. How does it work? We're told it has something to do with engine resistance. Why should you bother to turn it back on? Here's a hint: Ever notice how a steering wheel locks up when the ignition is off?

RAMP IT UP. If you're really, really lucky and you drive by one of those runaway truck ramps with the 50-degree incline, use it. Likewise if there's an exit ramp with a giant circus net at the end, head that way. (After you avert disaster, don't forget to stop at the nearest 7-Eleven to pick up a lottery ticket, you lucky bastard.)

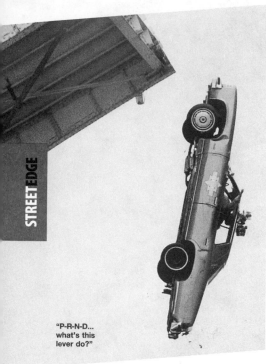

"P-R-N-D... what's this lever do?"

ASK ANYTHING

: When running on fumes, what's the best strategy to stretch the last of your gas?

ANSWER: "Don't race to the finish," says David E. Foster, director of the University of Wisconsin's Engine Research Center. High speed covers the miles faster, but it's too expensive in terms of fuel. (The national speed limit was imposed in 1974 specifically to save fuel, not because of safety concerns.) Slow and sensible has its limits, of course: At 5 mph, you're underutilizing the engine's power, and wasting even more gas. The ideal? Keep it between 35 and 50 mph, switch to neutral on long downhills, and don't stop and start unless you have to. And next time fill 'er up.

*You won't leave skid marks.

Mechanic Shenanigans

Sure, your mechanic calls you buddy, but is he really just a snake in dirty overalls? Here are some common scams to look out for.

■ **Good to the Last Drop.** A convenient squeeze bottle under the hood and, voilà, a "serious leak."

■ **Shavings and a Haircut.** A handful of random metal shavings "discovered" in your transmission pan looks like trouble.

■ **Hole in One.** When nobody is looking, a quick jab with a sharp object can turn any engine part into a hazard.

■ **The Makeover.** Just when you thought that old, worn-out part had seen its last drive, a fancy paint job makes it look (and cost) brand new again!

■ **Voice of Doom.** The last-ditch effort to get into your wallet further usually involves a frightening tale of losing all four tires and exploding into a fireball if you don't get that fan belt replaced immediately.

Identify the Enemy

To identify unmarked cars, look for late-model, stripped-down, domestic four-door cars with multiple antennas, a one-tone paint job, no fancy trim, and a spotlight sticking out of the driver's-side front post. One clue to spotting 'em before they spot you: Only two kinds of people still drive Chevy Caprices and Ford Crown Victorias... police and the elderly. If the guy in the driver's seat of one of these models doesn't look like a cast member from *Cocoon,* odds are he's a cop in an unmarked car.

GO UNDETECTED.

If you use a radar detector, mount it so you can quickly remove and conceal it if you get pulled over. Otherwise when the cop notices it, you'll see little dollar signs begin to flash in his eyes.

TRY THE OTHER SUPERHIGHWAY.

You can do some serious speed-trap snooping on the Internet. The Speed Trap Registry (http://www.speedtrap.com/choice.html) is the ultimate source for pinpointing where cops lurk, from L.A. to East Bumfuck, Wisconsin. The National Motorists Association (http://www.motorists.com) also provides useful tips and resource links.

Ah, crap! Its Boss Hogg!

Handle a Hit-and-Run

The situation: You blow through that all-too-familiar crosswalk and feel a sickening thud. After repeating, "Oh...fuck, oh...fuck, oh...fuck" religiously, you figure out the best thing to do (for the victim's sake, asshole). Our expert highway patrol guy, Mike Metcalf, a deputy sheriff for L.A. County, says to do the following:

■ Stop the car immediately!

You don't want to run him over again, and besides that, you'll want to save that "Leaving the Scene" ticket for something *really* bad.

■ Don't move the victim.

You never know what kind of injury you're dealing with, so don't risk making the victim's physical complications worse by pretending you're saving Private Ryan.

Just stay nearby and make sure no one hits him again.

■ Check for vital signs.

You need to tell the medics whether or not the person appears to be breathing or has a pulse. Pray, of course, for at least one of the two.

■ Call 911.

Use the nearest phone, and make it snappy. Remember, this is the moment you've been waiting for: Your outrageous monthly cell phone charges have been justified at last.

■ Finally, head for a car wash.

Metcalf advises you go to an automated one, which will do the best job cleaning the undercarriage. Apparently clumps of hair have a tendency to stick to the muffler.

STOP ME IF YOU'VE HEARD THIS ONE

COCKAMAMIE EXCUSES
Use one of these babies and that state trooper will be ripping up that ticket in record time.

1. ROAD WARRIORS.

"Oh, man, some guys in a blue minivan were tailgating me. Then they pulled up beside me and started throwing coins or cans or something. Maybe I accidentally cut them off or something. I tried slowing down and everything...they must have gotten off at the last exit...but anyway, it's a good thing you stopped me!" (Your exasperated, anxious tone works every time—unless you have alcohol on your breath.)

2. NATURE'S CALL.

"I'm sorry, please give me the ticket—quick! I really gotta get to a bathroom—I've got, I've got diarrhea! Sorry I was speeding." Unless the cop is sadistic, and you didn't just pass a rest area, he should let you go. (If you've got a girl in the car, you can try the period-pain excuse: "Her cramping is getting really bad; she took some Tylenol, but it's not working. I'm just trying to get her home.")

3. MEN IN UNIFORM.

"I'm sorry, didn't mean to be speeding. Hey [look at his nametag], Roberts? Weren't you a first lieutenant at Fort Bragg? No? Oh, you look just like one of my old commanding officers there. His name was Roberts. Anyway, sorry." (Oh boy, if you were in the army, you were practically a cop—it would be sacrilegious to give you a ticket.)

How Car Dealers Rook Your Ass

Get yourself some wheels— without having to learn to drive without an arm and a leg.

"Oh, you want seats? That'll cost a little extra..."

Don't Get Taken Every Time, by Remar Sutton, is a sleazy, ugly, eye-opening guide to the games car dealers play to fuck with your head. Here's what you need to know:

■ Add ons:
Rustproofing, undercoating, conditioning fabric—any of those "services" are designed to maximize profit. They cost the dealers a couple hundred. They try to sell them to you for thousands.

■ Extended warranties or service agreements:
Most cost the dealer under $200; you'll get them for $600 to $1,800.

■ Four-square system:
The sales guy draws a little cross on a sheet of paper, making four squares. He asks you what you'd like to pay, what you think your trade-in is worth, and how much you can afford a month. You say something you think is ridiculous, and the guy just writes it down, as if it were completely on the level. He gets you to sign the piece of paper and fork over a hefty deposit, while he goes into the main office to fight for you. When he comes back, though, he scratches out each figure and works you over, getting you to give more and more on each category, as if they were completely unrelated.

■ Notes:
Your salesman goes in with your offer and sends a note back asking for you to meet them halfway. You agree, and another note comes back, asking for just a little bit extra to clinch the deal. This goes on until they've got almost everything they could squeeze out of you, but you walk out, thinking you were a hard negotiator. Why? The series of notes gives you the feeling you were haggling, whereas the price was only ratcheting one way: up. The notes are written almost word for word in some sales training books.

■ Social Security scam:
The dealer asks for your social security number to "check records" or some such bullshit. But what they're actually doing is running a credit check on you without your knowledge. When they come back to the table, these guys know you're nervous about getting financing, and they use the leverage against you.

TO BUY OR NOT TO BUY?

You buy a car in order to invest money as an asset that will give you a return—a few years of driving plus value when you turn the sucker in for a better model. A lease gives you lower monthly payments, plus a new, shiny toy every year or so. Whether to buy or lease depends on these major points:

■ If you drive more than 12,000 miles a year, consider leasing, according to Jack Nerad, author of *The Complete Idiot's Guide to Buying or Leasing a Car.* That's the point at which those fees for extra miles are going to kill you.

■ If the vehicle you're considering might not be reliable over the long-haul—say you've heard rumors the radiator develops seal problems easily—leasing is definitely the way to go.

■ If the leasing company has extra costs—such as an acquisi-tion fee at the start of the lease, a disposition fee for people who don't opt to buy, or an early-termination charge if you turn it in early—consider it against the cost of buying. Also see if you can bargain these charges away—sometimes leasing companies see them as taxes for stupid people.

■ If you have 10 percent of the purchase price of a new vehicle, either in cash or in trade-in, consider buying. You're almost there financially.

■ Leasing can give you a greater tax bonus come April 15...if you use the car for business only.

■ One thing that might make a lease cheaper is if you can get a good price by financing through a bank or leasing company instead of some shady-ass dealer. Try it and see if the numbers pan out.

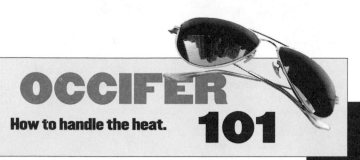

OCCIFER 101

How to handle the heat.

PIG OUT

Handle the Interrogation

Some basic rules of thumb that can, at the very least, decrease your chances of an intimate encounter with a nightstick.

"You guys are all named Marsha!? Weird."

HERE'S THE SKINNY.

Now that you've got Officer Smedley's exclusive attention, it would be best to tread lightly. Whether you've committed public urination, triple homicide, or nothing at all, how you conduct yourself during this interview may determine whether the end result is an apology, a warning, a night in jail, or a new sievelike appearance.

SHUT UP.

"The more you talk, the more likely you are to put your foot in your mouth," advises Rick Puller, a Baltimore safety consultant and ex-cop with 20-plus years of experience. He advocates treating a brush with the thin blue line like a professional business transaction you're trying to wind up with the least possible fuss. However sus-picious or intimidating your interlocutor's demeanor may be, your innocence (assuming it exists), will generally emerge. Show some ID, speak when spoken to, and wait it out. Same goes if you *do* have something to hide—the less you do to arouse attention, the better the odds it'll stay hidden. And if you're caught doing something red-handed, a lot of fast-talking is about as effective as it is on *Judge Judy*. Finally, going into the "My father is a judge or policeman or politician" routine is a good way to ensure you get royally fucked with.

STAY COMPOSED.

The anti-authority streak that made you a hero in seventh grade will not serve your best interests here. If you get treated rudely, don't take it personally. Put yourself in the officer's boots—he or she knows nothing about you and wants to get through today intact...so the adrenaline may be running a little high. If a cop's sarcastic tone makes you feel bad, you can always pour your heart out later in poetry writing class workshop. Even if the treatment you're getting is downright abusive, further irritating an already unstable person carrying a gun, nightstick, and handcuffs is not well advised. Grin and bear it—and lodge a complaint later with the local Internal Affairs office.

DON'T GROVEL.

It's human nature to suspect and maybe mistreat someone who's constantly cringing and apologizing. You think a cop hasn't heard it all before? Be a man, you worm.

WHY NOT ASK WHY?

If you have no idea what you have done, says Puller, you do have the right to ask. Again, your delivery will make a difference. Screeching "What did I do?!?" in an out-raged voice will earn you less sympathy points than a dignified "Officer, you've obviously singled me out. I'm not sure why. Maybe you could explain."

CHANGE YOUR ADDRESS.

Calling the cop "Sir" to show respect is not bad, according to Puller. "Officer" is better, though, since it encompasses both sexes and is always accurate. "Ponch," "Cuz," and "Motherfucker" are to be avoid-ed, and shouting "I smell Oscar Mayer!" is also a bad call.

THINK TWICE ABOUT THE PALM GREASE STORY.

Bribing is likely to backfire, so it's best to stay away (unless you're in Mexico). If you're determined to risk it, at least test the waters before you take the plunge: "You guys don't get paid much to be out at this hour, do you?" can't be prosecuted; "Would you let me off for 50 bucks?" can.

"That's the cologne. Want to try the aftershave?"

Freaky Foreign Laws

And you thought no beer after the seventh inning was a crappy law. As if jet lag and mystery sausages weren't enough reason to stay on U.S. soil, wait till you read about some of the wacky laws on the books *they practice* in other countries. Bon voyage!

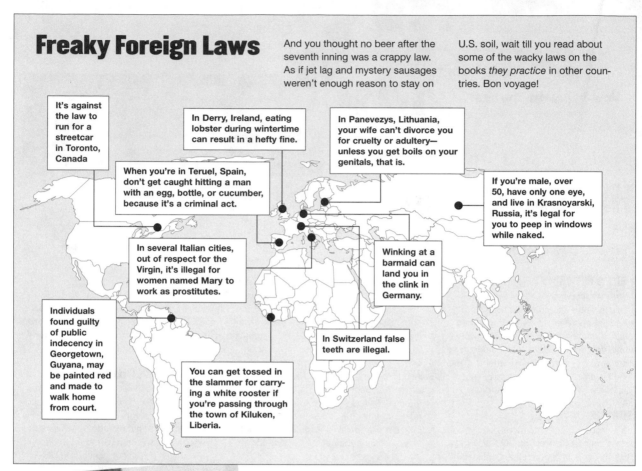

It's against the law to run for a streetcar in Toronto, Canada

In Derry, Ireland, eating lobster during wintertime can result in a hefty fine.

In Panevezys, Lithuania, your wife can't divorce you for cruelty or adultery— unless you get boils on your genitals, that is.

When you're in Teruel, Spain, don't get caught hitting a man with an egg, bottle, or cucumber, because it's a criminal act.

If you're male, over 50, have only one eye, and live in Krasnoyarski, Russia, it's legal for you to peep in windows while naked.

In several Italian cities, out of respect for the Virgin, it's illegal for women named Mary to work as prostitutes.

Winking at a barmaid can land you in the clink in Germany.

Individuals found guilty of public indecency in Georgetown, Guyana, may be painted red and made to walk home from court.

In Switzerland false teeth are illegal.

You can get tossed in the slammer for carrying a white rooster if you're passing through the town of Kiluken, Liberia.

Sniff Out a Liar

"Bubba need pie!"

Since their pants are almost never literally on fire, good liars can be hard to spot. We consulted *The Lie Detection Book* by detective William J. Majeski, and other sources, to discover the major symptoms of the two-faced, four-flushing, bunk-slinging humbug. Honest.

WANDERING EYES.
According to researchers, it's got something to do with the lobes of the brain. If your companion is looking up and to the left when he speaks, he's probably remembering something. But if his eyes shoot up and to the right, he's being, um, creative. (Yeah, we saw *The Negotiator* too...)

NERVOUS TICS.
Is a normally serene coworker doing a song and dance with a rhythm track of drumming fingers? Switch your bullshit detector to the "on" position. Similarly, if a Jittery Jimbo suddenly turns into a Tamed James, that new, smooth demeanor may accompany an equally smooth line he's feeding you.

DRAMATIC ORATION.
Beware the man who puts on an Oscar-worthy performance during conversation— overemphasizing points and making grand, sweeping gestures. He could be a frustrated thespian...or he could have your wife's bra in his back pocket.

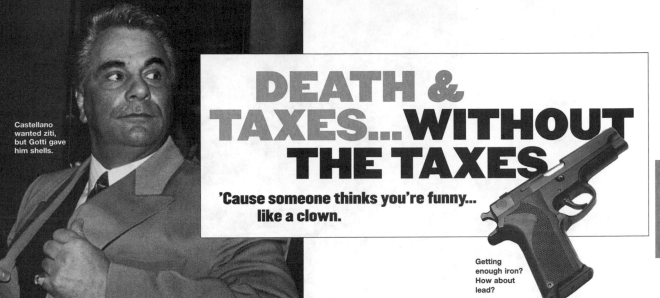

Castellano wanted ziti, but Gotti gave him shells.

DEATH & TAXES...WITHOUT THE TAXES

'Cause someone thinks you're funny... like a clown.

Getting enough iron? How about lead?

Survive a Mob Hit

Here's how to keep your shoes outta the concrete and your horse's head where they belong.

Tip #1: Don't drop your guard in your home neighborhood.
"In a mob hit you're most likely to be killed in familiar surroundings by the people you trust the most," says ABC News mob guru John Miller. A good example is "Big Paul" Castellano, former honcho of the Gambino family, who was gunned down outside of his favorite Manhattan eatery, Sparks Steak House. Gotti's boys had guns under their trenchcoats; Big Paul never made it to the table.

Tip #2: Keep your hands free.
Charles Dion "Deanie" O'Banion, feared leader of New York's North Siders gang in 1924, ran a flower shop. He got his when three hit men, with a thuggish sense of irony, ordered a custom-made funeral wreath. Closing the deal at Deanie's place, one of the men stepped forward to shake Deanie's gun hand, thus pinning it while his partners plugged the feared florist in each cheek, twice in the throat and twice in the chest. To this day this is referred to as the handshake murder. Next time you're approached by three goons, try tipping an imaginary hat instead.

Tip #3: Never call "shotgun"—you might get your wish.
This one's an old mob trick: A group of

guys pile into a car, leaving the shotgun seat open—then, when you sit down, the guy directly behind you does you in. "When the front seat is open and everyone's sitting in the back with a big smile," Miller says, "it's time to say 'Guys, I'm gonna take a taxi.'" Even though this technique's been exposed in movies like *The Godfather* and *GoodFellas,* made men keep falling for it: In fact, according to court reports, this is how Sammy "The Bull" Gravano got his first victim.

Tip #4: Start your car *very* carefully.
A marked man can thwart some car bombs—the Ignition-connected kind—with a $300–$600 remote-control car starter. But other bombs have fuses that can be attached to the tailpipe, which heat up and blow after the car's been running a few minutes, warns Miller. "It might be a good idea to start the car, then wait," he advises. If you're on somebody's bad side, you'll need to prepare for remote-controlled bombs too.

Tip #5: Come in from the cold.
Don't be afraid to ask the experts, says our man Miller. "The best information about who's going to get whacked comes from the FBI. They constantly warn mobsters, who all too often dismiss the information as trickery, but in almost every case the FBI has advised, people get killed because they didn't listen." So be a wise guy, *capiche?*

"Tonight, you sleep with the penne."

How To Shake a Tail

"Get the hell out of the passing lane, Cowlings!"

So what if everyone thinks you're a paranoid nut? They're not the ones with the problem: This is the third time you've seen that guy lurking across the street in as many days. If you suspect a shadow, there are some simple actions you can take to get "clean." David Whipple, executive director of the Association of Former Intelligence Officers, tells how professionals evade surveillance.

STEP ONE: Assess the threat.
Are you very wealthy? Do you have a sensitive job? A suspicious spouse? Have you recently fired a hostile employee? Broken up with a psycho girl? Screwed over any international terrorists? Any of these circumstances may lead to your being placed under surveillance.

STEP TWO: Confirm your suspicions.
Here are three professional techniques used to detect surveillance.
Mirroring.
As you're walking around town, stop in front of a large store window and observe everyone behind you. Take special notice of people not moving and with their backs turned to you.

Doubling back.
1. Walk briskly along an uncrowded street. Just as you approach a corner, snap your fingers as if you've forgotten

something, and quickly turn and walk in the opposite direction. See if anybody stops suddenly or looks alarmed.
2. Then make a mental note of everybody who passes you by. At the corner look over your shoulder to see if any of these people also did an about-face.

The KGB special.
Run to a bus stop as a bus is pulling up. Watch to see if anybody else arrives in haste, but don't board the bus. If someone is trailing, he'll be compelled to either get on the bus, in which case you've shaken him for the moment, or he'll blow his cover.

STEP THREE: Determine the tail's professionalism.
Private investigators will use a tail with the same physical attributes (age, strength, gender, race) as their subject. This allows the tail to go inconspicuously wherever the subject goes: If the subject is male, he can be followed into a strip club; if female, into a bridal shop; and so forth. Government agencies tend to use the best-trained and hardest-to-detect surveillance teams.

STEP FOUR: Take countermeasures.
Run an SDR (security detection route, a.k.a. sierra dog romeo) the day before. Make your way to your destination using a predetermined and complex course,

employing the diversionary actions explained above to expose any operatives. Try to include areas that are wide-open and deserted, always walk against traffic to foil vehicle activity, and make sure to first pass your eventual destination, then double back.

Disguises are not recommended. People have more physical characteristics than can be hidden properly, and it's usually to your advantage to act as if all were normal. But removing and ditching a colored jacket and a hat midway through an SDR may help you elude Big Brother.

Enlist a friend to follow you at a distance. During the SDR, it should become obvious to him if someone is tracking your moves. He in turn can follow your tail back to where he came from and identify him and, perhaps, his intentions.

Once you've identified your tail, start carrying a camera. The next time you spot the guy, approach him and snap his picture. Now you've got the edge: He knows his cover is blown and will fear being reported to the police, or, worse, incurring personal recrimination.

AFTER MEMORIZING ALL INFORMATION, EAT THIS PAGE.

Dump a Dead Body

It was an accident; yeah, that's it, an accident. You were helping your, er, friend here clean his pistol and...oh hell, who are you kidding? You've got a body on your hands and no "connections" that'll help you dump it. And who better to look to as experts in body hiding than those good "family" men?

A WATERY GRAVE. According to officer Rick Porrello, author of two books on the Mafia, when hiding a body, water is probably your best bet—the deeper the better. There's no smell; the body breaks up quickly; and if you do everything right, there's a good chance no one will ever find your handiwork. Plus, it's fun! (OK, we're just kidding about that last part.)

"Make sure to weigh the body down," says Porrello. "Buoyancy is going to be created by the gases that develop, and you don't want your stiff to become a body bobber." Lead weights tied securely to the stiff should work great.

AN OUTTA THE WAY PLACE. If you opt for a non-water burial, Porrello notes that "you've gotta make sure you don't dump or bury him in an area that's slated for future construction," à la *GoodFellas*. Hello, national park.

HANDS OFF! Another mobster favorite: Cut off the head and hands so the body can't be identified. What you decide to do with the head and hands is your problem. Hairy meat pies with a side of pinkies, anyone?

LIME TIME. Finally, if you're going to bury a body, don't forget to bring a bag of quicklime, which accelerates decomposition and kills the stink. Just pour a generous amount of the mixture—available at most hardware stores—over the body, then finish the burial. No muss, no fuss.

Talk Someone off a Ledge
When screaming "Jump! Jump!" just doesn't work...

You're there in your office, working away, when out on your window ledge appears that squirrelly guy from accounts payable—the one with the halitosis and the creeping dandruff. At first it seems like no big deal, but then you realize, *My God, my car's parked down there!* Time to take action.

■ Understand the odds.
"A person who's climbed out on a ledge and hasn't jumped still has the will to live," says John F. Pollinger, a former negotiator and currently the commander for the Emergency Services Unit in Middletown Township, New Jersey. "People intent on suicide do not hesitate."

■ Take it easy.
"The first 45 minutes are the most emotionally volatile," says Pollinger, "for both you and the guy on the ledge." So don't climb out there or try to grab him and haul him in. Instead focus on slowing the situation down, and use calming phrases like "I'm listening" and "I understand."

■ Talk like a Clinton.
In other words slow, soft, and reassuring. "Maintain your calm in order to maintain a calming influence," says Pollinger. Take a deep breath and listen to your vocal inflection. If you bug out he'll do a backflip faster than you can say "Greg Louganis."

■ Don't be an armchair shrink.
Saying something like, "Think of your wife and kids," is probably not the right move if his old lady just split to Algiers with the pool boy. Likewise telling an atheist that "God doesn't want you to do this" is a surefire way to make him take the Nestea Plunge. So learn about the person before you make suggestions. "The person is going to want to tell you why he's there," says Pollinger. "Find out what's making him tick, and avoid that topic." Ask instead about something that gives him joy in life: Maybe his favorite team has a shot at the playoffs; if so, focus on that. Unless he's a Bengals fan, in which case the poor soul might as well take the plunge.

The *Maxim* Macho Challenge

Hey, you in the comfy chair! Is your testosterone level wimpy, respectable, or freakishly high? Take our quiz—and see how macho you really are.

We admit it: the whole macho thing can get pretty exhausting. Swaggering requires advanced muscle tone. Orgies take a ton of planning. And who has time to rassle 'gators and gnaw bloody slabs of moose meat when there are bills to pay, crucial X-*Files* reruns to watch, and all that dirty laundry to rearrange? On the other hand, who wants to be a *total* wuss? So where do you stand, mister? To help you rate yourself on the universal scale of machismo, we've created this extra-hearty *MAXIM* Quiz. Check off all of the macho life experiences that apply to you, add up your points, then face the raw and sweaty truth.

WORK

Have you ever:

Quit a job? (**score 2**)

Gotten your ass fired? (3)

Fired someone's ass? (4)

Been paid for risking your life? (4)

Been paid for sex? (6)

Scored a book, record, or movie deal? (10)

Served as your company's emergency fire warden? (**minus 4**)

Total

SEX

Have you had sex with:

A teacher? (**score 1**)

A hooker? (2)

Anyone remotely Swedish? (5)

A porn star? (10; **50 if Traci Lords**)

A lesbian? (20)

A fruit or vegetable? (**minus 10**)

Total

SPORTS

Have you ever:

Won your office NCAA pool? (1)

Cheered your pro team—any sport—to a championship? (2)

(Cubs and Red Sox fans may claim exemption)

Scored a game-winning touchdown? (3)

Hit a grand slam-homer? (4)

Nailed a hole in one? (10)

Rolled Yahtzee? (0)

BONUS BOX

Score 1 point for each pro-sport stadium or arena nationwide in which you've seen a game

Total

ADVENTURE

Have you ever:

Chopped down a tree? (1)

Smoked a Cuban cigar in Cuba? (2)

Driven an 18-wheeler? (2)

Sky-dived, hang-glided, or bungee-jumped? (2)

Flown a plane, piloted a ship, or operated a tank? (4)

Gotten a tattoo? (5; **20 if self-administered**)

Had it removed? (**minus 10**)

Eaten a mammal you killed yourself? (7)

Spent a night in jail? (7)

Shot a grueling set of rapids? (7)

Lived off the land for 48 hours? (8)

Lived off pizza for 48 hours? (8.5)

Climbed a significant peak?

(**1 for every 5,000 feet**)

Been shot or stabbed? (10)

Written your name on the Great Wall of China? (12)

Total

MORE SEX

Have you ever:

Slept with the mother of a friend? (2)

Slept with a friend of your mother's? (2)

Been blown by a baby-sitter? (5)

Talked your way into a threesome? (10)

Had sex with Cindy Crawford? (45)

Talked your way into a threesome with Cindy Crawford and a French-Swedish baby-sitter? (**YOU WIN!**)

Total

BRAWLING

Have you ever:

Been tossed out of a bar? (1)

Been tossed out of a strip club? (2)

Defended a buddy with your fists? (2)

Fought over a woman? (3)

Had a woman fight over you? (10)

Stopped a crime in progress? (5)

Broken someone's nose? (6)

Broken someone's limb? (7)

Performed the *Rocky* cheer while jogging? (**minus 5**)

Total

DIET

Have you ever tasted:

Dirt? (**score 1**)
Caviar? (**2**)
Frog's legs? (**2**)
Haggis? (**3**)
A tequila worm? (**5**)
Alligator? (**6**)
General Foods International
Coffee? (**minus 3**)

BONUS BOX
In the last six months, score:
(**1**) for each tequila shot
(**1**) for each martini
(**minus 5**) for each strawberry daiquiri

Total

SKILLS

Have you mastered:

Turkey carving? (**score 1**)
The art of telling dirty jokes? (**2**)
Burping on cue? (**3**)
Knife throwing? (**3**)
Judo, karate, or kickboxing? (**3**)
Tai chi (**minus 3**)
At least three awe-inspiring pool-
hall tricks? (**4**)
A dancing style that's in no way
reminiscent of Al Gore's? (**5**)
The machete? (**7**)
Moose gutting? (**10**)
Origami—the Japanese art of
paper folding? (**minus 5**)

Total

BALLS OF STEEL

Have you ever:

Dined and dashed? (**score 1**)
Had sex in public? (**2**)
Joined the Mile High club? (**2**)
Hot-wired a car? (**2**)

Hung up on a lawyer? (**2**)
Come face-to-face with a wild
animal? (**3**)
Gone to work stoned? (**4**)
Stared into a gun barrel? (**5**)
Defused a bomb? (**8**)
Dumped a psycho chick? (**10**)
Been buried alive? (**10**)
Performed in a porn movie? (**15**)
Tried to start "The Wave"? (**minus 5**)

Total

MISCELLANEOUS

Have you ever:

Drunk directly from the milk
carton? (**1**)
Chewed tobacco? (**1**)
Picked up a gigantic bar tab? (**1**)
Wailed on an electric guitar? (**1**)
Shaved your head? (**1**)
Grown a beard? (**1**)
Ordered beer in another
language? (**1**)
Groped silicone breasts? (**1;
minus 20 if they're your own**)
Lost that gut? (**1**)
Triumphantly reacquired that gut? (**1**)
Arm-wrestled to square a dispute? (**1**)
Opened a beer bottle with your
teeth? (**1**)
Acquired a scar? (**2**)
Run the table in a pool game? (**2**)
Watched *Brian's Song* without
crying? (**2**)
Driven across the country? (**2**)
Seen every James Bond movie
(even that crappy one with
George Lazenby)? (**2**)
Had a lesbian ask you for sex
tips? (**2**)
Owned a motorcycle or all-terrain
vehicle? (**2**)
Ridden a horse at full gallop? (**2**)

Stayed sloshed for 24 hours? (**1**)
Woken up with no idea of where
you are and how you got there? (**2**)
Run a marathon? (**3**)
Tossed a keg? (**3**)
Avenged your good name? (**4**)
Blown $1,000 at the craps table? (**5**)
Worn sequined paramilitaristic out-
fits while basking in the love of
Romanian children? (**minus 30**)

Total

Your Score

SIMP:

Less than 30 points. It may be time to
dial 1-800-PILLAGE. No one's going to confuse
you with the Terminator, Mr. Civilized. And
while we understand the value of restraint
(especially during a tense game of Yahtzee),
just remember: Nice guys finish last. If you're
interested in self-improvement, *Maxim* will be
offering a special "How to Trash a Hotel
Room" seminar in the new year. Look for
details in an upcoming issue.

STUD:

Between 30 and 100 points. 'Atta
boy! Though operating safely within the legal
limits of machismo, you are certainly no
stranger to mayhem, raw fear, and debauchery. You have better things to do than be
buried alive, yet remain a hearty and well-
rounded rascal. We'd be proud to have you
break our limbs anytime.

SUPERSTUD:

Between 100 and 150 points. Du-ude!
You are unusually macho. This is an important responsibility. Understand that you are
now expected to save lives, have sex with
entire sororities, and eat massive amounts
of repellent foods. We'd also like you to
captain our softball team and open this bitch
of a pickle jar. Thanks, man.

SUPERFREAK:

Over 150 points. Your testosterone level is
dangerously high. Frankly, you're scaring us.

HANDYMAN EDGE

"How bout a little phillips head?"

For when Bob Vila's not around to save your sorry ass.

The pyramids, the Roman aqueducts, and the wood-paneled den: Since time immemorial, men have wanted to build things, fix things, and make 'em run. We've distilled the secrets of the ages for you into one handy guide. Now get to work.

Must-Have Starter Kit

There are some basics every handyman needs to be, well, handy. But how do you get started without breaking the bank? Here's a complete set for less than $300.

TOOLBOX. A plastic or metal kit with trays for smaller tools, nails, and screws. **$10**

HAMMER. Get a classic curved-claw 16-ounce jobber. But get a fiberglass handle—it's sturdier than wood, and it won't vibrate and wreck your wrists like metal. **$10**

SCREWDRIVER. Get a single magnetic baby with interchangeable tips. Yes, interchangeable tips. It may sound cheap, but they work. **$10**

TAPE MEASURE. A 16- or 25-footer should be plenty long enough. Metal, not plastic, so it will hold up. **$9**

PLIERS. You should get standard pliers for light jobs, small needlenose pliers for fishing her earring out of the drain; a set of Channellocks, whose angular mouths will give you mucho leverage; and a 10" crescent wrench for home plumbing. Now how much would you pay? **$5–$10 each**

SOCKET SET. Unless you're going to open your own shop, a socket set can replace a whole set of wrenches for only **$20.**

HACKSAW. Buy one all-purpose blade in the 16–18 tpi (teeth-per-inch) range. Good for metal, wood, and disposing of bodies. Just don't let anyone find that femur in your crawl space. **$8**

POWER TOOLS. First buy a cordless drill with attachments for screwing (yeah!) and sanding. Then get a good circular saw. **Drill: $90; Saw: $50**

ODDS AND ENDS. Get a razor knife, nails and screws, chalk line, electrical tape, duct tape, WD-40, pencils, safety glasses, caulking gun, and good pair of work gloves. **Around $35**

Now bump it up by $55 by adding a pair of jeans that shows the crack of your ass when you lean over to measure something.

Clearing Clogs

Because Bubbilicious only holds for so long.

Sraight up, with a twist, please.

Not everyone builds an extension on their house, but everyone has to deal with a clog now and then. Here's how to handle the situation without putting some plumber's kid through college:

GET A GOOD PLUNGER. Make sure it's a real heavy-duty number with a thick, reinforced cup and a firm grip. They're a few dollars more than those flimsy, red-eraser jobs, but they give you plenty of suction, and they won't wear out. Keep it near your toilet for quick action should the shit water start moving up instead of down. (Plus, it's a documented fact that the older men get, the more often they clog up the toilet, so you better be prepared.)

SNAKE IT. Buy a drain auger, or plumber's snake. This is a long flexible cable—like the kind they used on flexible lamps, only made tougher. A 25-foot model will do, and it's only between $10 and $20 (www.ehow.com). If toilets are your thing (and aren't they for all of us?), get a closet auger, for about the same price, which is specially angled to get through a toilet's piping.

PERFECT PLUNGING.
Water, water everywhere...and it smells like poo!

SINKS
1. Remove the sink strainer or plug from the drain.

2. Make a seal before you start by partially filling the sink (or tub) with water. Now pop the plunger down on the drain, and work it up and down a few times, hard, before ripping it away. If necessary, stuff a rag in the overflow hole, usually found at the ridge of the sink or near the opening lever on the tub.

3. Remove plunger and give sink a chance to drain.

4. Try using a chemical de-clogging agent (no, don't eat it, Waldo), and then attempt the above steps once again.

If the above fails and you still refuse to call a plumber, it's time to attack those pipes on your own. Here's what you do:

1. First get a pipe wrench and remove the sink trap. This is the bolt at the very bottom of the U-curved pipe underneath your sink. Now get your feet out of the way while a quart of foul, black sludge spills all over your floor. OK, next time put a bucket there. Start feeding cable from your auger into the pipe until you feel resistance. This is the alien, er, clog.

2. Pull out a foot and a half of cable, and tighten the screw on the front of the auger—that locks it into place. Crank the handle clockwise as you push it forward, driving it farther into the pipe. Repeat. If the cable catches, turn the crank counter-clockwise, as you pull back. When you've pushed it out of the way as far as you can, put the pipes back and turn on the hot water to see if it drains.

It won't always drain right away—loose debris can settle in and clog it a little. But if you keep plunging with hot water, the system should clear.

TUBS.
The easiest way to prevent clogs is to dump a few quarts of hot water with baking soda into the drain once a week. But if it's plugged, unscrew the drain pop-up button. Wires and shit connected to the stopper will come out.

Then feed the cable auger into the hole where the button, not the drain hole, was. You should feel resistance almost

immediately, but that's just a trap that lies beneath the tube.

Keep cranking until you push through.

TOILETS.
Most clogs here are right in the up-curving trap in the fixture itself. Before you start messing with whatever's in there—get yourself a stiff drink. When you're ready insert your plunger into the toilet, making sure the rubber-plastic dome of the plunger is fully sealed over the drain opening. Plunge with forceful strokes, using your new industrial-strength plunger. If the shit water is steadily rising, plunge as if your life depends on it (especially if you're at your girlfriend's parents' house and they have a new rug covering the bathroom floor).

If frantic plunging proves fruitless, it's time to attack that stubborn sum'bitch with your auger. By now you should be well versed using this contraption, so you don't need us to repeat the instructions again.

However, be sure to wear gloves, a smock, and goggles while executing this delicate technique, and, most importantly, don't let any women see you.

You can also use drain chemicals to unclog your toilet, but make sure the label says it is safe to use on porcelain before you fool around with that stuff.

END RUNNING TOILETS
If your toilet is constantly "running," we're here to help.

The key components that will cause your toilet to run are the stopper, valve seat, and chain assembly.

Open up the tank on the back of the toilet and listen. If you can see or hear water coming from the ball cock—a valve attached to the float—the valve may need to be cleaned or replaced. The chain or wire attached to the valve may be tangled or out of whack, preventing the stopper from coming down flush (sorry) with the valve seat. In that case bend or untangle. That was ridiculously easy, wasn't it? You should go into this line of work.

Rules of Thumb

Unless you're Mr. Roper, you can't get away with wearing a tape measure hooked onto your belt everywhere you go. Here's how to use handy, everyday items to guess-timate measurements.

To measure: a yard
Use: four regular (#10) envelopes; five new, unsharpened pencils; or six greenbacks laid end to end (and watch that nobody swipes them)

To measure: a foot
Use: two bills, three small paper clips unfolded all the way, or four open matchbooks

To measure: an inch
Use: a quarter, or half the height of a business card (fold it over)

To measure: a centimeter
Use: your passport—to leave the U.S.A., because no one in this country gives a shit about the metric system

1"

2 bills = 1'

1 yard = 4 #10 envelopes

Ultimate Pest-Control Guide

Sure, you wanna live and let live. But sometimes you gotta kick ass. When your house or apartment gets overrun with critters, try these easy "homegrown" ways to make 'em scat.

ANTS.
Wash countertops, cabinets, and floor with a half-and-half mixture of vinegar and water. If you find a hole where ants are entering the house, squeeze the juice of a lemon into it.

FLEAS.
Vacuum everything in sight, seal the bag, and throw it in your neighbor's yard. Mixing one teaspoon vinegar to one quart water (per 40 pounds of pet weight) in your pet's drinking water will help deter the fleas.

FLIES.
Sprinkle dry soap into garbage cans after they've been washed. Allow it to dry. Scratch the skin of an orange and leave the fruit out in the garbage. Scratching it releases more citrus scent in to the air—the little buggers hate it. And clean that lump of shit off your countertop; that's where they lay their eggs.

MOTHS.
Run clothes through a warm dryer to kill eggs.

ROACHES.
Close off gaps around pipes and electric wires where they enter house, seal food bags, don't leave pet food out, and don't leave dirty dishes out in the sink. Mix equal parts baking soda and powdered sugar, and spread around infested area. Boric acid is also an effective roach deterrent.

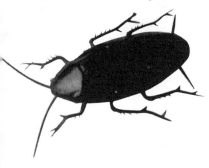

" Hi there! We're looking for a clip, you got one?

BEAM THERE, DONE THAT

Raise the Roof, Ya'll!

A home is where your heart is. It's also a place where shit can't rain down on you from the sky. To keep this vital "protect-you-from-falling-shit" function working, you need to keep your roof in good repair.

Dammit. Shut that window!

■ Update your will.
Just in case you take a nosedive off the top of your castle.

■ Get your ladder set up safely.
The distance from the base to the wall should be one-quarter of the ladder's length. Too close, and you'll fall backward, waving your arms in the air like Wile E. Coyote. Too far away, and you're more likely to slide—*rat-a-tat-tat*—down the side of the house, just as if you're starring in a *Three Stooges* classic.

■ Find the problem.
To check the health of asphalt shingles, peel one back on a section of the sunniest side of the roof. If it snaps like kindling instead of flexing nicely, it's replacement time. Note: The steeper the slope, the longer it will last. Also, when grains start appearing in your gutter, replace fast. That's a sure sign that the roof is crumbling and on its last legs. OK, it's only a couple of shingles that need fixing. Let's go for it.

■ Fix torn shingles.
Spread a layer of roofing cement under the torn layer. Reposition torn parts, and then tack them in place with roofing nails on either side. Spread roofing cement over the crack. Cover the nail heads with a dab of cement, too.

■ Replace damaged shingles.
Each shingle is held by two sets of nails: one under the shingle above and one six inches farther back. Raise the tabs overlapping, and take out the nearest nail set. Try to get the set farther up, but if it won't come, tear it out, taking care not to rip the roofing felt below. Cut the top corners off the replacement shingle to help you slide it in easier.

"If I had a hammer, I'd...oh, you know. Hammer stuff."

Do this before the rainy season, on a hot day if possible, when shingles are more pliable. Nail the sucker in place.

■ Lay down flat roof patches.
Sweep gravel aside and cut out problem area with a razor knife. Cut a matching patch of asphalt shingle. Spread plastic roofing cement inside the cutout area. Lap cement over areas. Spread some on a pita with tomato-smoked turkey—mm-mm! Lay the patch down, and pound galvanized roofing nails all around the edges. Cut a second patch that overlaps the first by two inches for that extra belt-and-suspenders security. Spread cement three inches around the first patch. Nail the second patch in place and cover with roofing cement. Cover rest of roof with cement, just to be sure.

■ Clean up.
To remove roofing cement from your tools, use a rag soaked in paint thinner or kerosene. To get it off your hands and face, use vegetable oil—which works slower, but is gentler on your tender, girlish skin. Mmm, vegetable oil...

Troubleshoot Your Appliances

You can ignore that mortar-size hole in the wall. But when the fridge is busted, or the washer's on the fritz, that spells real trouble. We're talking warm beer and dirty underwear, which may be your reality even when your appliances are working just fine. Here's how to troubleshoot some major and minor snafus.

STOVE/OVEN

Problem: It won't start.
Many electric ranges with timer clocks must have them set to MAN before the oven will work. Or the oven selector switch might be set to TIMED BAKE instead of BAKE, which means the oven won't come on if the clock's not running.

Problem: Top range won't heat.
Check top elements for poor connection. Make sure they're firmly inserted. If the plug ends are burned from arcing, replace them as well as the receptacle they come in. Also check the pilot lights. If you don't smell any gas down there, the connection may be off, or you may be out of gas.

REFRIGERATOR

Problem: Leaky door
Close door over a dollar bill, and see if you can slide it out easily. If you can it's busted somewhere. Check around the gasket (the big gray rubber thing that makes the door go, "woosh," when you open it) for cuts. You can seal these up with a silicone caulk. For major damage, you can either buy a new gasket seal from the hardware store, or try to buy a piece of a gasket salvaged from a scrapped refrigerator.

Problem: Constant noise
Check coils either behind or under the refrigerator. They may be covered with gunk, or the cooling fan may be broken. Clean the coils, but if the fan is out, call the refrigerator repairman, exposed butt-crack and all.

Problem: A weird squealing noise from the freezer compartment.
Either the cat got stuck in the fridge again, or, more likely, this means the evaporator has gone out (on most models). This can be fixed, but you should have an expert check it out.

DRYER

Problem: Takes too long to dry.
Check entire vent system—hoses and all—for lint. This can often happen when dryer vents up through the roof. If the vent is clear, you may need a new element coil.

WASHING MACHINE

Problem: Clothes don't rinse.
Could be a kinked drain hose—this happens after you move the unit. Check behind the sucker to make sure.

Problem: Machine gets stalled in rinse cycle.
Check that both water-supply faucets are fully open. The machine feeds hot and cold water into the drum at different times and will stall while waiting for water to come if the friggin' faucet isn't on.

DISHWASHER

Problem: Dishwasher soap cakes up and doesn't dissolve.
It's probably because you're using old soap. Don't buy the four-gallon vat of the shit at your local Costco, cheapo. And try the liquid or gel variety instead of the powder.

Problem: Doesn't clean well.
Clean the food screen in the bottom, as well as the little holes in the spinner.

"Hey Moe! Hand me a screwdriver."

SPORTIN' WOOD!

Everything you just gotta know about lumber.

Before you paint, sand, or prime, you've got to know what you're dealing with. Use this guide and you won't (no, must... resist... pun...) get lost in the woods. (Damn!)

DOUGLAS FIR

A strong, average-weight soft wood. Splinters easily. Used for plywood and for studs in walls, not finishing.

BIRCH

Hard, strong wood. Excellent for finish. Light in color with fine grain and smooth texture. Used for interior trim, doors, plywood, desktops, and toothpicks.

TEAK

Lightweight, with a deep grain. Dark-brown color. Used for furniture, drawers, cabinets, and on boats and decks. Expensive.

PHILIPPINE MAHOGANY

Open grain and coarse texture. Medium hardness. Varies in color from dark reddish-brown to light tan. Used for medium-priced furniture.

OAK

Heavy and strong. Striking grain pattern, with shiny light "flakes" from indentations in the wood.

WHITE PINE

Soft and light, with an even texture. Cream-colored with light resin canals. Used for trim and shelving. Knotty grains are used for wood paneling. Works well with hand or machine tools.

BALSA

Light-colored porous wood found on a kid's airplane stuck on a roof near you.

Finishing That Wood

Staining and top-coating a piece of wood makes it look like real, adult home furnishing, and not like that college shit you've been stuck with for the last six years. Plus, it's easy.

1 Start by cleaning the surface of the wood and allowing it to dry thoroughly.

2 Give the wood a fine sanding to avoid surface fuzz. Sand in the direction of the grain. For most woods, use medium sandpaper, no finer than 150-grit (or 150 grains per inch; higher numbers mean finer paper). For oak try 120-grit. Make sure wood-fill (used to cover nicks or holes) is sanded well; don't leave any schmutz.

3 Mix stain thoroughly—up to five minutes—to dissolve pigment settled at the bottom of the can. Chill and garnish with olive and swizzle stick—no, wait, ignore that part. That comes later.

4 Apply stain across the grain with a clean 10-square-inch cloth or rag, completely saturated for a smooth, even coat. A foam brush also works well. Consider doing a test mark on the bottom to check color against wood. Start with corners and uneven areas, then spread the rest of the stain onto the flat spots. When finished wipe away any excess, using a clean rag.

5 While one coat may suffice, applying a topcoat will deepen the finish. With topcoat do one small area at a time, and apply with the grain. Wipe off excess immediately. Allow coating to dry completely, then sand with a very fine (#400 or #600) wet/dry sandpaper to remove fuzz.

6 Feel for fuzz. Make sure the piece is clean and dry before you apply any additional coats. If you have an uneven sheen, apply additional coats, and sand in places. Four coats is good for water-resistance. When you're done get into a shower, before the stuff makes you look like an Oompa-Loompa.

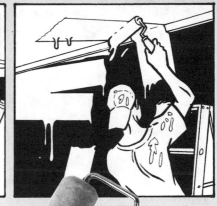

BRUSH GROOVE

Paint Like a Pro
The no-fail guide to frosting your walls like an old master.

The following tips, gleaned from painting professionals, can help you do the job faster, cheaper, and better. So throw on some old clothes...oh, we see you're already dressed for the occasion...

PREPARATION
Taking the time to prep a room can save hours and sweat, and will give you much better results. Use a paint scraper to remove peeling paint, and fill cracks and holes with Spackle. Sand smooth any spackled areas. Tape off anything you don't want with Royal Blue #5618 painter's tape, and start with the proper primer/sealer (ask your paint store) to ensure your new coat will adhere properly. You might even save a coat of paint.

All carefully plucked from Dom DeLuises's back.

PAINT
Spend a few extra bucks to get a quality paint (check the label—you're looking for 100 percent acrylic for better adhesion, and at least 35 to 45 percent solids by volume for spreadability) from a reputable manufacturer like Benjamin Moore. Use oil-based paint to cover wood or in situations requiring extreme durability (e.g., a kitchen); use latex for all other interior painting. Choose a glossy finish for bright areas that get a lot of use (kitchens, bathrooms), a eggshell finish for normal-use interior walls, and semi-gloss eggshell for trims and moldings.

TOOLS
The standard set for an interior job includes a nine-inch roller, a two-inch trim brush, a one-and-a-half-inch angled brush, and a three-inch straight-edge brush. Use synthetic-bristle (nylon or polyester will do) brushes and sleeves for latex paints, and natural-bristle (we're pretty sure it's either made of pig hair or Bette Midler's, if there's a difference) for oil-based paints. Quality brushes, such as Purdy's, have split ends, flexible tips, and bristles that are attached to the handle using epoxy cement rather than glue. The best rollers (for example, Purdy or All-Pro) offer a heavy-gauge -steel frame, a good-quality sleeve, and the ability to accommodate extensions and shields.

"We're reaady for you in makeup, Ms. Rivers."

TECHNIQUE
If you're painting an entire room, start with the ceiling and work your way down—you'll stay out of your own way, plus drips won't be a problems when "cutting in" one color up against a higher one. Use the roller wherever you can—it's smoother, quicker, and saves paint; use a brush for moldings, corners, and anywhere a roller won't fit. Paint in long strokes, go back and check for drips, and use at least two coats, ideally with a light sanding (100-grit paper or finer) in between.

CLEANUP
Synthetic brushes and rollers can be cleaned with water, but natural-bristle tools (used with oil-based paints, remember) require a soak in paint thinner. Wrap band to help keep bristles from frazzling all over. Crack open a brew and inspect your fine workmanship.

"Yo! I said step!"

Well, I need a good hobby. I certainly can't masturbate.

Grassy Knolls

Win the turf wars and make your neighbors green with envy.

It's the unwritten code of the 'burbs: If the inside of your house looks like crap, it's her fault. But if the lawn looks like crap, it's proof you're not a real man.

■ **Fertilize in late summer or early fall.** Do it earlier and you'll get a Chia Pet–like surge of growth, but it won't last, because intense growth depletes plants' energy and makes them less resistant to stresses such as disease (and your backyard keg party).

■ **Buy the more expensive fertilizer.** "The best fertilizers cost more than twice as much, but they contain nitrogen that releases slowly, so you only need to fertilize once a year," as opposed to three times a year, says Mike Henry, environmental horticulture advisor with the University of California at Berkeley. Also check the label to make sure that you're getting the most nitrogen per pound.

■ **Do not hand-toss the fertilizer pellets**. You'll end up with patches of dead grass that'll make you the laughingstock of the block party. Borrow a push spreader from Flanders next door, and go over the whole lawn twice, in different directions. Water your lawn immediately after fertilizing so pellets wash into the soil.
■ **Water in the morning.** This is when

evaporation is minimal. Leave the sprinkler on for at least 20 minutes, until the ground is soaked. In most of the country, water only once or twice a week. This forces grass roots to go deeper into the soil in search of more water, which makes for a healthier lawn, says Michael Gaffney, horticulturist for the Professional Lawn Care Association of America. Otherwise short-rooted weeds will take over your yard. If you're not watering often enough, your grass will look blue and won't spring back right away when it's walked on.

■ **Mow off only a third of the grass blade, or you'll weaken the grass.** Adjust your mower based on the height of your lawn, then stick to the appropriate schedule—probably once a week.

■ **Don't haul away the clippings if they're short.** They'll decompose and release vital nutrients, like nitrogen, back into the soil. If you have longer clippings, get them outta there.

■ **Keep your mower sharp.** Dull blades shred, rather than slice, the tops of the grass blades, making your lawn look gray or brown. Take your mower to a nearby dealership, who will sharpen your blades for around $20.

Double Your Car's Lifespan

Now that you have it, here's some quick no-brainer tips to help you keep the thing going.

AIR FILTER

Check every: two months
Replace when it's dirty, or every 15,000–30,000 miles. It's easy to reach, right under the big metal "lid" at the top of the engine in some cars, or in a rectangular box at the front end of the air duct hose in others.

BATTERY

Check every: 3,000–4,000 miles
Make sure the cables are attached securely and show no corrosion. If you're driving a Flintstone-era car, make sure the pterodactyl is properly fed and has a sure, easy footing on his treadmill.

BRAKE FLUID

Check every: 3,000–4,000 miles
Wipe the dirt off the reservoir lid, remove the lid, and just give 'er a gander. If you need fluid, add up to the mark and have the system checked for leaks. Especially if your psycho ex-girlfriend has been spotted in the area, looking disheveled and slightly greasy.

TRANSMISSION FLUID

Check every: 3,000–4,000 miles
Do this when the engine is warm and running. (Make sure the parking brake is on, nimrod—you wanna kill somebody?) For optimum protection, change the fluid and filter every 30,000 miles (unless you have a new vehicle that is filled with Dexron III ATF, which is supposed to be good for 100,000 miles).

"How do you spell that?"

CAR CARE

Squeezing the Lemon for Everything It's Worth!

Cold Wheels:
Start your car when it's freezing outside.

For a car to start, gasoline and air must meet, combine, vaporize, and ignite. And it's that last part—vaporizing and igniting—that gets fouled up when Mother Nature goes all frigid.

If your car is over a decade old...
It's the carburetor. When cars with carburetors don't start, there's something very specific you can do. According to Rick O'Brien, a technician at McKenney's Service Center in the South Portland, Maine, tundra, "It's a matter of stepping on the gas pedal one-half to two-thirds of the way down. This closes the choke [which ensures a rich air-fuel mixture that ignites faster] and pumps some gas into the manifold. Then step off the pedal before you turn the key."

If you have a newer car with fuel-injection...
The computer system mixes gas and air according to exact atmospheric readings. So, if you're still having trouble starting in the cold, it's your own fault! There's nothing you can do except get the damned thing tuned up, which you should have done in the first place.

Fuel to burn...
"The higher the octane in the fuel, the harder it will be to vaporize the gas to start the car," O'Brien offers as another warning for the snowbound. So don't necessarily fill up with the gas the manufacturer recommends. You're not always doing your car a favor with high-test 94.

Meanwhile try not to freeze your gonads off.

Checking a Used Car

Some fast tips on spot-checking a used car—before you get screwed by a mechanic:

■ **Look down each side**. Panels that are a slightly different shade or a little off-kilter means the car's been in an accident.

■ **Check for rust underneath doors and around wheel openings.** Put a small magnet up to any repaired surface. If it doesn't stick, a mechanic might have repaired the thing with cheap-o putty, which means trouble down the line.

■ **Check the seats and carpeting for stains, or a telltale moldy smell.** It means there might be a rain leak. If there's a red splotch and a chalk drawing of a guy's silhouette in the back, that's doubly bad.

■ **Check underneath the car for coolant drips.**

■ **Turn the ignition and make sure the "check engine" sign flashes.** If it doesn't, it could mean it was disconnected to cover up an emissions problem.

■ **While driving on a level road, loosen your grip on the wheel to see if the car veers.** The car should drive straight, without pulling to one side. Swerving means it might have sustained body damage in a crash, or at least that the tires need to be realigned.

■ **Speed up in low gear to 15 miles per hour.** When you're done release the accelerator, let the speed drop to 5 mph, and floor it. This is to check for an oil-burning engine. A cloud of blue smoke is bad. Lots of white smoke is a serious lemon sign. A few wisps on a cool, damp day is all you should get.

Call Carfax (888-801-2202).

They'll give you a report on the car's entire registration history. This will let you know about serious accidents, as well as what the car's real mileage should be.

DATING EDGE

Date the Temp

Look at their title...it's right there... temporary (duh!).

It's stated quite plainly in the Ten Commandments of Work: Thou shalt not date thy office-mate. Inter-desk liaisons create conflict-of-interest hassles and come with huge risks: Think of the mess when one of you inevitably dumps the other...unless, of course, the girl's a temp.

"The temp is one of the best dating scams going," claims Sparky (not his real nickname, thank God), a TV producer who hooked up with a two-week freelancer he's still seeing. Temporary replacement work- ers—the wandering gypsies of the working world—tend to be young, eager, and used to shabby, contemptuous treatment (so you'll look like a prince). Best of all they're in and out of your office with no messy strings attached. Here's advice on finess- ing the part-time lover, from veteran temp- daters and Dr. Judy Kuriansky, author of *The Complete Idiot's Guide to Dating.*

BE DISCREET.

Keep a low profile at all times—even outside the workplace—or you risk tripping coworkers' alarm systems. One gentleman, now living with former part-time help, wouldn't dish with us even though he'd changed jobs more than a year earlier. He was instinctively following Dr. Judy's prime directive: "Keep your mouth shut." An intact reputation as the friendly guy in the next cubicle will protect your career...and, incidentally, help put your next temp target at ease.

KEEP YOUR DISTANCE.

"Proximity does get the pleasure chemicals going," admits Dr. Judy, "but try to make sure you're not dealing with that person every day. A different area or even a different floor works better." Why? Because a clandestine office affair can easily be exposed by the tiniest public show of affection—which is hard to resist if you're two desks away. The upshot: Hit on the new girl upstairs in accounts payable before making a move on your boss' interim secretary.

STAY AWAY FROM INTERNS.

Extreme youth, beauty, inexperience, and a naive willingness to join you for drinks may be irresistible, but one misstep and you'll be branded a ruthless coyote. Even if you're not actually breaking any statutes, interns should be handled—actually, not handled—with care. One worker took an intern out to the opera; a few months later, he learned that the next round of interns had been warned by someone about the sleazy guy who was going to try to date them all. Then there was this other intern in D.C. who had a thing for pasty older men and...you know the rest.

DELAY YOUR PLEASURE.

Patience is all-powerful, Grasshopper: Unless the feeding frenzy for the new temp is overwhelming, don't pounce on your first sighting. "If you can get her on her way out, you're set," opines Sparky. "When Karen started, the first thing I found out was when she was leaving." Making your move on her last day plays the temp advantage to the hilt: You avoid interoffice mayhem completely, and if it doesn't work out, your problem has already disappeared.

BEWARE OF BOOMERANGS.

"After I hooked up with Karen, she came back about three weeks later," cautions Sparky. "We had to keep it under wraps for a month." But Sparky was fortunate: They were a congenial match. But you may not be so lucky. Even worse for the failed affair, some temps become permanent fixtures—so watch out. "My general advice," says Dr. Judy, "is, be really, really careful in the office."

Score at a Wedding

You've got a smokin' tux, a cool buzz, and five hours to make your move.

"At least somebody will get some after the party."

When you get past the slimy prime rib and the chicken-dancing old ladies, weddings provide better scoring opps than a singles bar. Dancing is mandatory, drinking is strongly encouraged, and consummation is on everyone's mind. To secure the pick of the bridesmaids, just follow our guide to playing your advantages to the hilt.

1. Advantage: You're pre-approved. Someone invited you to this gig—and armed with the bride and/or groom's seal of approval, you can expect the women you meet at a reception to trust you right off the bat.

Strategy: Play up your relationship to the person who invited you. Not "We killed small children together in 'Nam—what a bonding experience," but "Jim's a great guy —we've known each other since college."

2. Advantage: You look *mahvelous.* Single guys know: The tuxedo, not the dog, is man's best friend. The penguin suit—a *rental,* for Chrissakes—takes off 15 pounds, adds 50 IQ points, and doubles your income. What straight woman wouldn't fall for it? You're Prince Charming before you even open your mouth.

Strategy: Charm the pants off her. Bring honor to your outfit by being Mr. Chivalry. Ostentatiously bring someone's elderly aunt a plate of food. Dance with the obnoxious, fat little flower girl. Every woman in the joint will melt like butter.

3. Advantage: She's starved for attention. She's sure to have dropped major hours and bucks on her outfit and hair, but she's well aware her look can't hold a candle to the gloriously decked-out bride...and she can't even hate her, because it's her best friend.

Strategy: Compliment the crap out of her. She lights up the room, she must work out every day, she's the only bridesmaid who makes that atrocious dress look good. Feel free to err on the cornball side—weddings put even the most cynical women in a gushy mood.

4. Advantage: You clearly support marriage. You must support the idea of weddings, or you wouldn't be here. By extension you're not averse to commitment. By hopeful stretch of the imagination, you're clearly Good Husband Material.

Strategy: Ladle it on thick. Demonstrate your staying power in whatever pathetic way possible. Mention your dog, a grade-school ex you're still friendly with, the fact that you've belonged to the Columbia Record and Tape Club for years. No drunken sobbing, no rousing choruses of "Another One Bites the Dust."

5. Advantage: She's feeling self-conscious. For women it's awkward to be single at a wedding: Everyone's talking about marriage, old friends keep asking whatever happened to their last boyfriend, and even the bride's whipping bouquets at them.

Strategy: Give her a pseudo-boyfriend. Skip the formalities and pretend you've been dating for months: Drink what she's drinking, act as her protector ("Stay away from the chicken fingers"), and dance all those goofy wedding songs with her. By the time you escort her to the after-party, she'll be yours...'til Monday do you part.

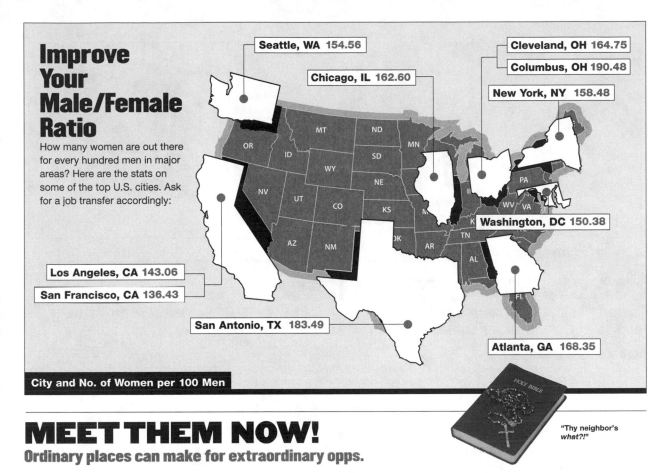

Improve Your Male/Female Ratio

How many women are out there for every hundred men in major areas? Here are the stats on some of the top U.S. cities. Ask for a job transfer accordingly:

Seattle, WA 154.56

Chicago, IL 162.60

Cleveland, OH 164.75

Columbus, OH 190.48

New York, NY 158.48

Washington, DC 150.38

Los Angeles, CA 143.06

San Francisco, CA 136.43

San Antonio, TX 183.49

Atlanta, GA 168.35

City and No. of Women per 100 Men

"Thy neighbor's what?!"

MEET THEM NOW!

Ordinary places can make for extraordinary opps.

Sex writers Ron Louis and David Copeland, authors of *How to Succeed With Women,* came up with a couple of places that don't involve drinking all night or doing your laundry nine times in a row. Hey, we figure you can get into that on your own time.

ANIMAL SHELTER. "There are about eight women to every man," says one former volunteer. Add that to the fact that a cute dog can do a better job of getting you laid than Iceberg Slim, and you've got a recipe for one hell of a good time with man's best friend.

CHURCH. "Many churches like to promote dating within their communities," our experts report, which means you just have to look up a few picnics on the bulletin board and you're in. But do these people actually have sex? "Like bunnies," says one interviewee. Hey, it worked for Jimmy Swaggart. Best thing to do is pretend you're just discovering your spiritual side. You're lonely, you're scared, you need some help getting in touch.

NEO-HIPPIE GATHERINGS. They're a certain type to be sure, but the good thing about women who attend Renaissance Fairs, belong to the Rainbow People, or go out to the Burning Man Festival is that they believe in sharing the love. And the love should be shared, Sugar.

OUTDOOR MUSIC FESTIVALS. They're romantic, laid-back, and there's a lot of jostling around before the show. Ask her for a beer from their cooler—and if she doesn't say yes to anything else, you'll still be ahead.

COOKING UTENSIL SECTION OF ANY STORE. This is not the place to look for youngsters, Louis and Copeland write. But you're apt to find a randy divorcee or two who are looking to let off some steam...and can whip up mad pasta to boot.

HOTEL BARS. Women are in business—you knew that. Business people travel—you knew that too. Traveling businesspeople hook up like rabbits dropping X—why didn't you put any of this together before?

EQUESTRIAN EVENTS. No, we're not talking about the bettin' track. At major universities, they have horse shows and obstacle races, and shit like that. The coeds there are all former horse girls. We shouldn't have to explain the whole deal about horse girls.

UPSCALE MEN'S CLUBS. "Find an upscale topless club in any city," says Frank, a former bouncer in just such a club. "Then find the nearest place you can get a beer 24 hours a day. It can be a bar or an all-night diner. At 3 A.M. the girls have to get out of the club—and they usually go somewhere to unwind." Trust us. We've seen it happen.

INTERSPECIES COMMUNICATION

Crack the Female Code

Sometimes the best course of action is to wait for her to "tell" you what to do. Right next to a 12-digit salary, communication is the key to a successful relationship.

READ HER BODY LANGUAGE.

You've read the books. You've watched the videos. You think you can decipher female body language, but whenever you meet a woman, you may as well have learned Esperanto. What are you missing? "Nonverbal communication is not a language," cautions psychologist Ron Riggio. "The meaning of a particular cue varies, depending on individual factors, situational factors, etc." In other words, you have to play it by ear. Here are a couple' of clues to cues you can use.

EXTRA SMILEAGE.

Sure, she's smiling at you, but what kind of smile is it? A researcher who studies smiling offers this tip: "In a genuine smile, you will see crow's-feet wrinkles appear at the outer edges of the eyes. This indicates that the person is enjoying herself." As will relaxed body movements that mirror her smile, showing that she really did find your joke funny. Otherwise, as with so many things, your target could be faking it and be actually pissed off about something you just said. Don't fixate on the mouth; check out the whole package.

SKIN TRADE.

Gabriel Ra'am, a nonverbal communications consultant and author of *Men and Women Beyond Words,* says a good rule of thumb is how much thumb she shows you. If she makes motions that reveal the palm of the hand, or she "uncrosses her legs, then recrosses, showing part of the thigh," she's opening herself up. A behavior deemed universal among interested women is the tilting or turning of the head just enough to expose the neck. Obviously, if she turns 180 degrees, the back of her neck is all you'll get.

CONFLICTING SIGNALS.

Ra'am recommends watching fingers, eyelids, and lips. "When one of these twitches or shakes during conversation, there may be a problem with what is being said." Additionally, if you're engrossed in what you feel is a meaningful conversation and she stares off into space, back up a step or two. Other danger signs are excessive self-touching and/or arm or leg crossing, or lips pressed together. Basically, if she looks restless, uncomfortable, or downright pissed, she probably is. Time for you to chill out a bit.

HAIR PLAY.

It's often said that a hair-toucher wants to be a you-toucher—though it all depends on what she's doing with it. Ra'am says women who are interested in a particular man will "play with [their hair], pushing it away from the face," especially in a seductive manner. But if she's holding it against her face or in front of her eyes, say Monica Moore and Tim Perper, two psychologists who have researched flirtation behavior, she may be trying to slow things down—for good.

UNHAPPY FEET.

"Try watching her feet," adds Dr. Jack Dovidio, a specialist in nonverbal communication. "If she shows impatience or is oriented toward the door, she wants out, no matter how pleasant she appears." On the other hand, if she has started to slip her foot out of her shoe in a suggestive manner, your prospects look good. And if she has slipped her feet out of her shoes and is running her toes up your thigh, then for God's sake, put the fucking magazine down and get in the game!

SIDES MATTER.

One sign everyone agrees on is isopraxism, or following your lead. "Doing the same thing is a powerful bonding agent in courtship," says Dr. David Givens, author of *Love Signals.* "When people show rapport with each other, they swivel their upper bodies toward each other and align their shoulders in parallel." See if she's on your wavelength. "When the man shifts position, is it followed and reciprocated?" Then you've got isopraxism. If nothing else, at least your vocabulary is improving.

Extras

■ If she smiles, showing both upper and lower teeth, with a relaxed face—it means she's comfortable around you.

■ If she raises or lowers the volume of her voice to match yours—called mirroring—it's her way of flashing you the all-clear signal. It's said we do this to show people that we mean them no harm.

■ If she rubs her face or cheek while talking to you, it means she's thinking about you and her relating in some way. If you're in the Ozarks, she could mean it quite literally...but it's not illegal.

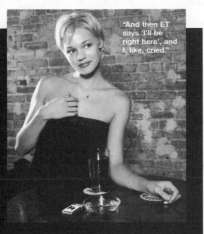

"And then ET says 'I'll be right here', and I, like, cried."

■ Her skin tone becomes red around you. This is either a blush response, which means she's excited, or she has a severe rash.

Use Your Body

"Barry say relax"

Slow down, Spaz. We don't mean that way. (This ain't the Sex chapter, Romeo).

All the time you're out in the field, you need to use your voice, eye contact, and body language to help, not undercut, you. Here are the secrets to making everything work like a well-oiled machine.

LOWER AND SLOWER. According to relationship consultant Janet "The Love Coach" O'Neal, that is the key to having a warm, inviting voice. Most of us—especially when we get excited—tend to speak more quickly and raise our voice pitch. It conveys nervousness, lack of confidence, and powerlessness. Everything you don't want. So practice slowing it down and speaking at the low end of your comfortable range. And, according to vocal experts, smiling does really help you sound better—it changes the shape of your face and lets the sound out more mellifluously.

ENGAGE. While a person's talking, keep your eyes locked on them, says O'Neal, and you'll give them the impression that they're the only person in the world. It makes you, not them, more charming in

the long run. To keep from looking like you're staring in a scary Charles Manson kind of way, though, make a mental triangle between their eyes and the tip of their nose. Focus on the middle of that triangle and you won't freak them out.

KEEP YOUR MITTS CLEAN. According to O'Neal, this is a part of the body women often notice...especially the way it feels against their skin. We're not going to spell this out for you, but you should use a little moisturizer and keep your nails trimmed.

READ SIGNALS. You know how to do this now, remember? Next time you're at a party, O'Neal advises, observe a group of people across the room. Notice whether people are turned toward the speaker or have their arms, legs, and feet tilted slightly away. Also notice whether people have open or closed-up postures. Start observing this all the time, until you can pick these signals up easily and instinctively. The prize? Instant feedback from any woman you're trying to chat up.

Scope the Territory

Before you engage the enemy, know the battleground.

■ **Never approach two women sitting together.** No matter how much she likes you, the cute one won't leave her girlfriend stranded at the bar. And she won't give you her number until she's gotten her friend's approval.

■ **Always approach small groups of women.** It's easier to pry one loose, and you can play on their competitiveness.

■ **Always approach a woman talking to a male bartender.** She's out to meet guys, but she's too shy to approach fellow customers. And he's stuck there till closing time.

■ **Always bring cigarettes (even if you don't smoke).** Leave them sitting out so girls can bum them from you. Plus, it attracts the right kind of woman: If she's willing to risk getting cancer, chances are she's willing to risk getting an STD.

■ **Always pick a central location.** Find the one spot in the bar most conducive to seeing and being seen.

■ **Always buy a bottle of champagne for your table.** Offer a glass to any woman who walks by. Tell her that in Paris it's considered impolite to turn down champagne.

■ **Always have a good bar trick.** The best ones include large bills (yours) and some good reason for you to touch her.

■ **Never dress in uniform.** The clichéd guy-after-work look is a blue shirt and khakis. You need to find a different one. This ain't a Dockers commercial.

MAKE IT HAPPEN

"If she attempts to choke herself, that's a bad sign."

Learn the Right Lines

Can you ever be sure that any one line is better than another?

Yes, according to a study by University of Louisville psychologist Michael Cunningham, Ph.D. In bars throughout the suburbs of Chicago, Cunningham's guinea pigs approached women with a variety of lines.

Here are the highs and lows, with their success rates. Success, for his study, was just if a conversation started, not if she did the guy right there and then.

WINNERS:
- "I feel a little embarrassed about this, but I'd like to meet you."—82%
- "What do you think of the band?"—70%
- "Hi."—55%

LOSERS:
- "Bet I can outdrink you."—20%
- "You remind me of someone I used to date."—18%

NOTE: In our own research, we've found that even though "bet I can outdrink you" only works 20% of the time, when it does work it works really well. Just wanted to share that with you.

Flirt Right and Reel Her In

"Show her you're a master baiter."

Flirting isn't just the first step toward seducing a particular woman. It's a way of behaving toward all women you run across—fun and playful, but definitely sexual—that raises your general odds of having them tumble into your lap (so to speak). Here's how to make flirting work like a lobster trap that's out there, constantly collecting nature's booty for you.

CREATIVELY MISINTERPRET.
You're leaving the parking garage when you see some lovely thing up ahead collecting tickets? You ask, "Are you the parking goddess?" if you've got balls. Or simply "How big a cut do they let you keep?" It's funny, and it's a way of seeing her surroundings that she's never thought of before. It's either an ice-breaker, or a way of making her remember you the next time you come by.

"WHAT'S THE STORY?"
That's what you ask her—about her necklace, her car, an interesting sweater. It's nonthreatening, but it's open-ended enough that you two can start talking.

CUT IT SHORT.
You have to stop while it's still fun and leave her wanting a little more. As charming as you are, you're going to run out of shit to say about her crummy poodle. Don't let her be there when you do. Just figure out how to make sure you'll see her again, if you're interested. Or use the good vibe to land someone else, if you're not.

GOOD-BYE COMPLIMENT.
This is where you push the envelope just a little bit more than you normally would. You can tell her she looks lovely and it doesn't put her on the spot because you're leaving right after. And it makes it more of a real compliment and less of a cheesy come-on.

PLAN YOUR RETURN.
Find a reason to go back in a few days so you don't look stalkerish. Continue whatever shtick worked the last time, but make it a little more subdued. Then go for the kill. Ask her to an event (preferably a party or an outing), something semi-public that's a little bit romance and a little bit just fun. You, my friend, have cleared a path.

"You mean none o' y'all know how to work a deep fryer?"

Women Answer Your Questions

All the important ones anyway. We asked several women (really) about certain dating do's and don'ts. Read and learn.

■ When should we call you after a date?

Not the next day, but the second day after. Don't call before, but don't try to blow me off to look cool. It is definitely not going to work.—*Georgia, 25*

■ Sex on the first date. How can we get there?

There's no strategy. Women know when you're on your way to pick them up whether they will have sex with you. There's very little you can do to change that, so relax and take the date for what it's worth.—*Marcy, 27*

■ Should we pay?

Absolutely. I used to feel differently. I would have paid every other time, but now I'm not that generous. Look, *The Rules* was right about one thing. The guy must chase, and that includes paying. I would say half my friends feel that way.—*Kay, 22*

It's a nice flirtatious gesture on the first date. Don't make a big show of it, though. That's really bad.—*Frances, 22*

■ Opening doors, getting chairs, etc. Cute or Neanderthal?

I think it's sweet, as long as it's done in moderation—natural, no darting in front of me. Holding chairs out is dumb. So is diving for everything first. If he tries to carry every damn thing I pick up, I'm going to deck him.—*Suzanne, 26*

■ Talking about past loves. OK or horribly wrong?

I can see situations where it would be OK, but in general stear clear. But if she asks, don't be evasive. —*Brenda, 21*

■ What's the worst thing you can do?

Call me the same day after the date. It's downright creepy. —*Jill, 20*

Speaking negatively about people. Ex-girlfriends especially. —*Paula, 24*

■ How long do you take to decide if a guy is worthy?

I decide probably in the first hour. But I will go on three dates if I don't like the guy, just to make sure. I can't remember ever changing my mind, though. —*Charlie, 26*

The first time I have a conversation with him, I know. And afterward, I might change my mind about him as a person, but the romance—or lack of—won't change. Ever. It's nothing you can pin down. —*Anna, 29*

Know What Works

Ironman Magazine did a survey of women's turn-ons and turn offs. Although it's a muscle mag, it covered what they like and don't like about the whole package.

Here's the lowdown on what you've got going for you—and where you really need to improve. Get cracking.

What are the physical attributes that most attract women?

Broad shoulders:	40%
Muscular arms:	35%
Flat stomach:	20%
Tight butt:	5%

What are the general characteristics that attract women?

Sense of humor:	50%
Good body:	29%
Kindness:	20%
Money:	1%

(OK, we know the money one is bullshit.)

What one thing makes me weak in the knees?

Top answers, in order of preference: smile, sense of humor, body

Tight rippling abs...	
Turn me on:	70%
Don't matter:	30%

General looks that get sexual attention:

Khaki pants, polo shirt, short hair, athletic:	45%
Jeans, T-shirt, clean-cut, muscular:	40%
Harley, tattoo, long hair:	0%
Propeller beanie, jockstrap, "Hello Kitty" backpack:	0%

Date a Woman Who Doesn't Speak English

You are, how you say? King of America? How nice...

Even in your neighborhood tavern, the biggest obstacle to meeting women is the language barrier: A few minutes into a conversation with the beauty at the end of the bar, you say something less than clever and she loses interest. Maybe what you need is a woman who doesn't understand anything you say—a woman whose concept of charming is a guy who has all his teeth. Here are a few pointers to keep in mind when it's time to show your foreign lady fair that the international language ain't Esperanto.

Whether they're from Switzerland or Swaziland, what women want is a self-confident man, and the best way to project this confidence is to have a steady gaze. "Hold the eye contact for longer than usual, glance away quickly, then look back again," says dating expert Pamela Regan,

Ph.D. Of course, try not to overdo it: "Don't just stare at a woman unblinkingly," Regan adds, "because she'll think you're nuts."

CLOTHES MAKE THE MAN.

"When there's a language barrier, the single most important thing a man can do is look good," Regan says. "People who say appearances don't count are bullshitting you." (Hear that, Mom?) "Buy something with a nice texture that women will like to stroke," says Lever. Because, hey, if she'll stroke your suit...Also wear nice shoes and make sure they're polished. "This indicates that you're hip and can afford more than one pair."

GRIN AND BEAR IT.

Smile at her and see if she responds, says relationship authority Janet Lever, Ph.D. If she smiles back, you can assume she's interested. If you've gotten the

green light, indicate nonverbally to her what you're really looking for. Touch a part of your body, say your neck or your hair, while you look at her; this tells her you're sensual. But go easy: "If you start fondling yourself, that's a big turn off," says Regan. That's why she's an expert.

SPIN THE BOTTLE.

If you haven't already been escorted away by *la policía,* buy her a drink. Point to the libation you're holding, as if to say, "May I get you a cocktail?" But be subtle. "Flashing a wad of cash says, 'I can buy you like a hooker,'" Regan warns. If nothing seems to be working, consider the possibility that she's playing hard to get. "Many people in cosmopolitan areas of the world today do speak English," says Lever.

YOU LOOK DESPERATE

Nine sure signs you've been studying up on George Costanza's courtship rituals.

You got dumped. You feel desperate. And females can smell it a mile away. Rabbi Shmuley Boteach and a gaggle of single women give you the signs that'll give you away:

■ You hold her hand on the first date. "That's like saying, 'We're a couple,' to the world before we've even seen each other naked!" says Karen, 32.

■ You bring your baggage. You're so used to being with someone who knows you're on lithium that you automatically babble on about the raise you didn't get and that pesky bipolar thing.

■ You talk about your ex. "This will make her feel that either you're comparing her or you haven't moved on," says the rabbi. (If it's the latter, he suggests you talk to a member of the clergy.)

■ You over-call. "I like a reliable guy who calls when he says he will," says 23-year-old Safiyya. "But if he pages me, or E-mails me before I've even had a chance to call him back, he looks like a creepy stalker."

■ You suck up her time. A new relationship needs room to breathe. "Don't ask for too many dates or she'll think you're demanding," the rabbi says.

■ You say things such as "My friend Bivens, you'll love him" within minutes of meeting her. When is she going to meet this Bivens? How do you know if she'll love him? Or if she'll even stick around long enough to find out?

■ You let her pay. You were so used to going splitsky with your last girlfriend that you let a new girl pony up for dinner on the first date. "She's pretending she wants to pay," admits Katy, 30, "but the truth is, she'll think you're cheap if you let her."

■ You pick her up without a plan. "You know what this reads?" says 27-year-old Christina. "'I have no idea what I'm doing; please take care of me.' I can't be bothered."

■ You send her flowers after the first date. Think those buds you sent her smell pretty? Sniff, sniff: Smells like you haven't gotten lucky in a while.

The Palm Read

When you want to impress the girl with your sensitivity, but there's not a puppy in sight, nothing does the trick like palm reading.

The crux of Gypsy science, palm reading, is easy—the three lines cutting horizontally across a woman's palm tell you all you need to know about her. Just grasp her hand firmly in one of yours and stroke it smoothly with your fingers as you work your wizardry.

Wait...in whose pocket?

THE LIFE LINE, THE ONE FARTHEST FROM THE FINGERS, STARTS HALFWAY BETWEEN HER THUMB AND INDEX FINGER, AND ARCS DOWNWARD, TOWARD THE WRIST.
The closer it stays to the mound of the thumb, the more of a homebody she is; veering away into the palm hints at an adventurous spirit (maybe she'll try that thing with the bungee cords you read about once).

THE HEART LINE IS THE UPPERMOST OF THE THREE, CLOSEST TO THE FINGERS.
If it starts near her index finger, tell her she's spiritual and difficult to please; if it starts under her middle finger, she's calm and mellow. A straight heart line indicates she's in control of her emotions; a curved one means she's hard to predict and sensual.

JUST BELOW THE HEART LINE, YOU'LL FIND THE HEAD LINE.
If it's short and straight, the woman is ambitious and focused; if it's long and arching, extending almost to the pinkie side of her palm, it shows a supersensitive nature—she's subject to overpowering passions. (Jump her now.)

A BREAK IN THE LIFE LINE MEANS THAT A DRAMATIC EVENT WILL DRASTICALLY CHANGE HER LIFE.
At what age? The line, long or short, represents her total lifespan, so if the break is, for example, a third of the way in from the life line's thumb-index "birth" end, she should expect a radical life-changing occurrence around age 30. Can interruptions in this line be used to predict animalistic, life-changing sex in the extremely near future? Just use your own discretion.

Marriage Lines

Heart Line

Head Line

Life Line

Line of Mercury

Line of Apollo

Line of Saturn

Travel Lines

The Hand

DATING EDGE

PLAN YOUR FIRST DATE
So you can get somewhere, dammit!

The key, according to sexperts Louis and Copeland, is to realize the importance of the initial, priming dates. Priming dates are short and to the point. They're lunch dates or dates for a cup of coffee somewhere public. You don't just hang out—what you do is get to know enough about each other to pique some interest and see where it leads. It's disarming, friendly, and shows you can be interested in them even if it doesn't mean immediate booty. A company called It's Just Lunch!, operating in 30 cities nationwide, will set up a series of these kinds of dates for you. The cost is steep—between $725 and $1,000—but it's a great way of meeting a hell of a lot more women than if you brown bag it again. Call their main office in Chicago at (312) 644-9999, for more information.

The most important thing during a priming date is to get a woman thinking romantically about you. Here are tips to pulling this off:

■ Pick a time and place that truly works for you.
You also have to consider what you'll do if she doesn't show or she's late. You should have somewhere to be, or something to do, so it doesn't sap your confidence. And it should be a time of day when you're alert and at your best.

■ Put the romance in.
Ask her questions that have a lot of romantic potential but are very carefully structured, so she doesn't freak. Each question should have: an excuse ("I was talking to a friend about whether there's love at first sight"), a description to pull her in ("You know, chemistry, when you feel a rush just from meeting someone new"), and the actual question, ("How do you know when it's working?").

■ Don't overdo it.
If you think she might be put off answering questions about her love life early on, you should get her talking about how women and men are, in general. This is a cool, no-pressure way you two can talk about how you feel.

■ Plan to stay from 30 to 75 minutes.
No more. You need to get her interested, but leave her wanting a little more.

■ Touch her at least five times, and touch her hand once.
These should be quick, nonintrusive little touches. You lead her to her seat, you brush her arm to make a point. It gets her comfortable with you. Just keep gauging her reaction to make sure she's not put off by it.

■ Compliment her three times.
And find something original—preferably something she obviously cares about. Shoes. Women put a hell of a lot more into buying shoes than men can imagine. Be the one guy in her life who notices.

■ Look at her body.
Once, very quickly, sweep your eyes down from hers and then back up. It should be quick and subtle, and you have to return to her eyes to show you're not ashamed and you're not ogling her like a stripper. But it lets her know you two aren't going to be pals.

■ Kiss her?
You have to be careful: Unless there's some obvious chemistry going on, you could blow it. And you definitely shouldn't go for it if you leave her in your meeting place. But if it's a little more private—say, you're walking her back to her car—and you have a little chemistry going, give her a peck. If she suddenly seems ready to jump your bones, by all means go for it. But probably what you're going to do is get out of there and wait until the next step before you do more. But if you took the risk, and it went well, you've piqued her interest.

Steal This Girl

What's her man got to do with you? Follow our no-fail blueprint for commandeering someone else's girlfriend. It's nasty business, but it's a dog-eat-dog-and-get-bitches world.

STEP #1: CASE THE JOINT. Without becoming a stalker, get close to this girl—join her pottery class, hang out at her health club, befriend her roommate—and worm your way into her confidence by any means necessary.

STEP #2: SHOW HER YOUR STUFF. In your one-on-one talks with her, find excuses to talk about your strengths and Dickhead's shortcomings. Use backhanded compliments, like: "I really envy Joe's ability to make ends meet on his salary. Personally, I just don't think I could do it."

STEP #3: START SABOTAGING YOUR RIVAL. If you've planted the seeds of doubt, tension will start to grow between Dipshit and his girlfriend. He will be looking for answers—and you, his gal's new chum, will be in a prime position to besiege him with crummy advice. Tell him she hates public displays of affection; claim the surprise trip he's planning will only scare her off...you get the idea. As you comb the romance out of their relationship, keep asking her, "What's wrong? You seem down lately..."

STEP #4: BE THERE FOR HER. As your advice to him sours things again and again, at some point The Dork King's going to get wise and stop listening to you. Suddenly your relationship with her—the deep conversations, the long walks, yadda yadda yadda—will start bugging him worse than inflamed hemorrhoids on a six-month cattle drive. He'll tell her to stop seeing you, she'll accuse him of being an overprotective meathead, and she'll gravitate to you, the only guy who understands her.

STEP #5: FINISH HIM OFF. For the coup de grâce: Become the most sensitive son of a bitch she ever laid eyes on, especially when they fight. The more she obsesses about what's wrong with her current guy, the sooner she'll realize she needs a guy more like—hey, what are you doing Friday night?

Date Insurance

You're doing fine. Now make sure you seal the deal.

According to Louis and Copeland, this is where you make your move. Plan it right and it's next stop, Nookieville—population, you and her. Here's what to do:

SPEND TIME. A seduction date has to be long—four hours at least—to close the deal. With the priming date, you want to give her a little taste and make her feel like she's spent enough time to sleep with you without being a slut.

SURPRISE HER. You need to take her someplace she hasn't been before—and it should have an element of secrecy and surprise. The secrecy and surprise part is to trigger the little-kid-at-Christmas feeling in her, which makes everything fun and playful. Taking her somewhere different forces the two of you to spend time bonding as you discover new things.

PAY. You know this already. If you're the type of guy who ends up paying more than he should, wining and dining women, then figure out how much the date will cost you, and plan it out so you can stick to it without making a scene. That way you don't look cheap, but you have a feeling of confidence and control.

SHOW YOU WERE LISTENING. This date should have elements of stuff she likes, stuff she may have told you about on the initial dates. A small, quirky, inexpensive gift that you picked up, because it reminded you of her, is the perfect, low-key way to romance her. But it can't be generic or she will blow you out of the water.

TOUCH HER SIX TIMES. Hold her hand, brush up against her. Whatever she seems comfortable with. But don't go anywhere private—her ass, breasts, etc., are off-limits.

PLAN THE ITINERARY. And have one backup in case of rain, fire, flood, or any other acts of God. The idea is that, as the date is ending, you two will be someplace sexy and inviting—where the mood will be right to spend time kissing—maybe more. We know you can handle it. We'll just leave the porch light on, sport.

The 20-Minute Detail

Turn your busted wreck into a carriage of seduction in four lazy steps.

Working late? Got a date? Women say they can tell a lot about a man from his car, and you don't want yours saying, "Hi, I'm the Vermin King." So, if your car's a mess, use this emergency detailing strategy, prescribed by Jeff Jeppesen of Classy Cars in Huntington Beach, California.

1. On the way home pull into a self-service car wash and swipe the interior with the high-powered vacuum. Pay extra attention to the passenger area, where she'll be placing her pretty new pumps.

2. Using the "spot-free rinse" option, hose down the car with the hand sprayer. Put some of this water on a towel and rub down the windshield and windows, inside and out. Then lather the car with soapy water, and rinse again.

3. Take another towel and wipe the car from the roof down. Hit the tires with some tire dressing.

4. Race home. Concentrate your efforts on the areas of the car she'll actually be looking at, such as the hood. If you can spare five minutes, throw on a coat of quick-drying wax, then wipe it off. Next, use a warm, damp towel to attack the passenger-side windows and side-view mirror. Skip your side.

"Sit on it? All right, for a quarter you can."

The Ultimate Weapon

We feel the need...the need for Speed Seduction.

A new no-fail method of seducing women faster than you can sign a hotel register. It's called Speed Seduction, and it's the brainchild of former loveless geek Ross Jeffries. Back when he was desperate, Jeffries was reading every dating manual he could get his mitts on when he came across information on Neuro-Linguistic Programming, a theory of influencing people by manipulating your language patterns like Bill Clinton in a deposition. We've gone through his material and pulled together some pretty neat tricks. Look him up on www.seduction.com if you want the full course.

"So I'm on the fourth green, and... am I boring you?"

MAKE THE CONNECTION. One of the main tricks is to make a woman experience a mental state, and then link it to yourself. Ask her questions that start with phrases like "Have you ever..." or "Can you remember the first time you ever..." These questions don't have to be overtly sexual—they just have to get her thinking about a good, exhilarating time...just as if she were having sex. Start talking about amusement park rides, for instance. Then work sentences that have hypnotic commands embedded in them, such as "Do you remember what it feels to DO THAT, because WITH ME, NOW, it's just like..." You see, you've got her thinking about being in an aroused state—which makes her actually experience it. And you're making her connect it to you.

GETTING READY FOR A DATE. Your own language influences how much confidence you have when going after babes. When you talk about the thing in war terms—"I got shot down," "I'm going to storm the beaches tonight," etc., you subliminally set yourself up for a love life that looks like the first 30 minutes of *Saving Private Ryan*.

DON'T ASK, DON'T TELL. Never ask a woman for anything. Literally. If you phrase everything as a statement, you will set yourself up as more of a challenge. One simple way is to walk up to a woman and say, "Excuse me for interrupting, but I had to pay you a compliment..." Then pause. Wait until she says, "What?" And then go ahead with whatever gem you've thought up. In a subtle way, you've just made her ask you for flattery...Sneaky, huh?

PHONE HER IN. Another way to make her come to you is to leave a message when you don't think she'll be home, asking for a date. Wait for her to blow you off. Then, after a few days, call her again and leave another message, identifying yourself, then saying, "I thought I'd give it one last shot at getting a chance to talk. If I've learned anything, it's that beauty is common... but people with great energy (or attitude or real connection, or whatever you think sounds brainy and deep) are rare and worth getting to know. I think that understanding goes both ways. So if you can find your own reasons to call me..." This works for a number of reasons: The "one last shot "language makes her think you're a commodity that might be disappearing. And the "beauty is common" crap is purposefully vague, so she might think you're paying her a compliment...but you could just as easily be saying you're the special one, and she'd better jump on you. Finally, by telling her that stuff about "finding her own reasons," you're making her think she's in charge of this. She'll bite.

GET THE NUMBER. Don't. Instead, you should say, at the end of your small-talk phase, "So what steps would we have to take to make sure we can continue this another time?" If you do it right, you will make her start thinking about how and where to see you again instead of passively giving you digits. And, hey, she just might forgo the phone and ask you over to her place right on the spot.

RELATIONSHIP EDGE

"Never trust a punk-rock accountant."

Get Yourself Committed

Relationships are great. No, really. At least they *can* be if you handle yours like a stand-up guy. You'll get a good friend to help you handle the headaches, plus crazy sex in weird places. A one-night stand won't do this for you without charging—and no kissing allowed—but it's yours for the taking once you take the high road. But how do you maximize all these good times and great kicks without the tearful fights, guilty feelings, and bad blood you hear about? Maintenance. Learn how to fight right, and what to give and what to hold onto when you negotiate. Most of all you've got to make her feel special and give her respect without looking like a whipped puppy in the process.

Fortunately, you have us. We've come from the mountain with all the heartwarming, yet sneaky, shit you need to know to keep you both happy.

How to Buy Her Flowers

Introduce her to your buds...

We might as well get this one out of the way right off the bat. Face it, you're gonna be buying *a lot* of flowers. On paper it seems simple: Just dial 1-800-FLOWERS, ask for "something nice for 50 bucks," and voilà, squeals of delight from your beloved. Unfortunately, women read deep meaning into your most casual words and deeds: A random bouquet sends a random message, and yours could elicit anything from "Oh, so he thinks I'm tacky!" to "Whoa—looks like he's marriage-minded after all!" To fend off disaster, we quizzed Denise Lee, consultant to the Society of American Florists, for the lowdown on saying it with flowers.

■ **Find a regular florist.**
Just as a trusted bartender knows exactly what you need after a rough day at work, your florist, if you see him or her regularly, will soon be able to nail your perfect bouquet for any occasion.

■ **Describe your babe.**
"Using adjectives such as *romantic, exotic, or fun* helps us select flowers that express your feelings," adds Danny Fowler, manager of McPhail Florist and Greenhouse in Austin, Texas.

■ **Go with what's fresh.**
Your reign as Prince Charming will be short-

Romantic Gift Ideas— Corny Yet Effective

Sometimes flowers scream "easy way out," which is when you need to rise above and beyond her lowly expectations of you. Here are some slick alternatives to blindside her (romantically speaking) and keep the magic alive.

"Call 1-800-whupped."

lived if the goods wilt en route. Of course this is a bit tough to control if you're ordering over the phone or the on the Internet, which is why finding a regular florist you know and trust is a great idea.

■ Personalize the note.
Don't just scribble "I love you" or "Happy birthday, Baby" on the teeny card. Write something private only she will understand.

■ Don't go overboard.
Too much too soon—say two dozen roses after a first date—indicates that you're desperate or overeager. Again, communicate with your florist about what message you want to convey. Spend $30 to $40 for an occasion.

■ Good choices:
Tulips, roses (all except yellow, which mean infidelity to some people), freesias, irises, flowering cherry branches, wild flowers (if you're the free-spirited bohemian type).

■ Bad choices:
Lilies (especially the phallic calla lily), carnations (funereal and cheap), mums (too grandmothery), plain daisies (too generic), sun flowers or pussy willows (too messy), any potted plant (too sensible), too much baby's breathe (looks like you're padding), anything dyed a hue not found in nature.

Get a blank puzzle, available at any craft store. Write some secret message or riddle, that, when she decodes it, will give the name of a favorite hotel or restaurant where you'll be waiting for her. Send her the pieces one by one.

"Stop staring at me!"

Call the International Star Registry at (800)282-3333 (www.starregistry.com), and have a star named after her.
It's relatively cheap, at $91, which includes a framed certificate ($48 for unframed), and it comes with a sky-chart listing of latitude and longitude so you can find her star in the sky. Just make sure to pick one that's visible from her hemisphere, Copernicus.

I love you

"Now can I stop sleeping on the couch?"

For gifts, think small and many, rather than big important stuff just for birthdays and national holidays. Instead of spending scads of money investing in flowers, buy a small colored notepad and a good quality pen. Write simple notes—just an "I love you" will do it—and leave them around every few days where she'll find them and realize how lucky she is to have such a thoughtful, romantic guy.

Try a romantic scavenger hunt. Send her on a fun expedition, going from smoky bar to smoky bar,

collecting love notes and strange messages from a few of your friends she doesn't know. One guy did this using an espionage theme—his friends dressed up, met his girlfriend in different places throughout their town, and gave her a little spy-type gift everywhere she went. It was cheap, yet thoughtful, and she was floored.

Set up a slide show of pictures of your past together. Sit her down, crack open a bottle of wine, and narrate. If you have trouble with public speaking, put a tape together to go with it, complete with the gym-class-health-film-type "beep" for when it's time to advance.

There's always chutes and ladders. "Kids games," swears a friend of ours who's managed to maintain a two-year relationship and is soon to be married, "They are sweet, thoughtful, and will bring out her fun and playful side." His advice is to get four or five friends together and set up a game of Capture the Flag with suction-cup dart guns or water pistols.

Chutes and Ladders

Quarters: Another childhood favorite..

"Remember that time I hurled on your Mom?"

"Hang on, Hon! I'm gonna lift up the safety bar and kill us, OK?

Riding Her Moods

Buckle your seat belt—rough roads ahead.

Variety is the spice of life, and women don't want plain vanilla sex all the time any more than you do. The key to adventure without weirding them out? Take advantage of the feelings they're always yammering on about. Here are some typical mood-specific sex variations, with the lowdown on what's in it for you.

THE ADRENALINE BOP.

You had a close call on the off-ramp, the plane hit some turbulence, or maybe that mole on your neck looked asymmetrical. Heart pounding, hairs standing on end... you get the picture.

Bonus for you:
She'll be giving it her all, bless her!

ROOM SERVICING.

Ah, hotel sex: Something about a sparkling clean room with a spotless tub in the next room drives a gal over the edge. Plus, she's on vacation, so she'll be up for adventure.

Bonus for you:
A king-size bed with the TV remote bolted to the nightstand.

THE EARLY RISER.

She's still groggy and not as turned-on as you are, but pull this off (think dreamy groping, lots of turning about) and you'll reaffirm that you want her even without makeup and toothpaste.

Bonus for you:
If you're really good, she'll make you breakfast!

STAR STRUCKER.

After two hours of watching Brad Pitt, Tom Cruise, or Antonio Banderas, she's unbuckling your belt before you hit the bed.

Bonus for you:
Picture Sandra Bullock, Cameron Diaz, or Michelle Pfeiffer with perfect impunity. (But don't shout out the name.)

THE NOONER.

A blissful midday desktop quickie squeezed between lunch and her 3:30. Fast and daring for when she's frazzled.

Bonus for you: No "hold me" issues—she's gotta run.

GRUDGE SEX.

You're mad, she's mad, clothes are flying...and how she can still scream at you with her tongue down your throat is a mystery.

Bonus for you:
You never realized how cute it is when she grunts like a mad woman!

MAKE-UP SEX.

No matter how down-and-dirty your fight was, ladies translate the act of love as a signal that all is forgiven (but it helps if you stroke her like a rosary bead).

Bonus for you:
No more whinin'!

THE STRESSBUSTER.

She worked a seven-day week and just needs a release, period.

Bonus for you:
When you're finished you can rollover and say goodnight. Or, go park yourself in front of the tube with a six pack and a pizza while she sleeps her troubles away.

DON'T SPEAK!

How To Listen To Her

Uh-huh...yeah...uh-huh...

We know, we know...but we never said this relationship stuff was easy. According to Ron Louis and David Copeland, romance gurus and authors of *How to Succeed With Women,* there's a whole science to this. And it's a hell of a lot more complicated than just clamming up. We've crunched it down and thrown in a few of our own tips.

STEP 1: Turn off the TV. The guys overlooked this statement, but we thought it was worth mentioning. Turn that fucker off. *Don't turn it on mute and think you can get away with it.* Not even if she's calling you on the phone to tell you something. "They know," says one *Maxim* staffer who tried it. "They always know, because you can never time the 'Uh, huhs' just right. And then it gets ugly."

STEP 2: Listen. Just let her vent. That's what she wants. She doesn't want you to quickly fix it, and she doesn't want to answer a barrage of questions and have a *Meet the Press*–style debate where you trap her with something she said days earlier. She has emotions she needs to get out of her system, and the quicker and more thoroughly you let her clean house, the easier it's going to be to wrap this up. *And we're not just talking about bad feelings either.* She could be excited about something, and if you don't let her share—man, you've just shot your blow job in the foot, haven't you?

STEP 3: Repeat back what you just heard. "So you're saying that yammer, yammer, yammer..." when it's a crisis. "Wow, I can't believe that blah, blah, blah," when it's an exciting anecdote. Clarify that you understand what she tells you. Demonstrate you care. By doing this you put yourself on her side—which is where the sex is.

STEP 4: Thank her. If this is heavy emotional stuff she's telling you, it's probably hard for her to bring up. She's risking something just by talking to you. "It really must have been hard to say that," you tell her. "Thank you." Yes, it's corny and you might be pissed at what you've just heard. But first you have to put her at ease and show you care.

STEP 5: Continue to listen. By showing her she can talk, you may have opened floodgates. This may take awhile. You probably have to go to the bathroom. Don't excuse yourself. Next time stop her right before she speaks, plead bladder, and get back to her. We should have told you this first. But if you're reading this while she's talking to you, you kind of missed the point anyway. Good luck, genius.

STEP 6: Promise and apologize first. Get it out of the way. We don't

mean cave. But anything you think you've done wrong that she's brought up, clear it away first before you think about arguing back. Shows you're fair-minded and not out to "win."

STEP 7: Let it go? Maybe, maybe not. When in doubt we recommend that you back down. (You're saving karma for when she says something that's truly ridiculous and you can't cave without losing your balls forever.) Then you get quiet, wait for her to get completely quiet, and say it like this: "I just feel that W. It's important to me that X. How are we going to make sure that Y and Z happen?" W is your demand in the short term: "*SportsCenter* makes my day complete." X is your broader, more historical desire: "I have sports television a few times a week." Y is a restatement of what she wants: "Your cats get fed." Z is a restatement of what you want: "I can watch TV." By phrasing it like this, you speak in emotional, nonthreatening language. You put your desires on the same level with hers. And then you group the two of you together against this dilemma.

STEP 8: Compliment her. When all is winding down, tell her how strong and insightful she is, not that you appreciate her talent for hammering away at a guy until all resistance is gone.

Daddy Dearest
Become pals with her old man, or else.

"OK, yes, I thought *Caddyshack 2* was funny."

You'd think bonding with your gal's dad would be easy. After all he's a guy, you're a guy—what more do you need? Yes, but don't forget: *You're now indisputably sleeping with his daughter.* Here's how to smooth things over:

■ When you're dating:
Look for common, traditional points of male bonding—sports, business, lawn-mower repair—suggests Colorado psychologist Dr. Elan Spector. But don't talk about sex—ever. And not just sex with you-know-who, either. Dad's unlikely to enjoy hearing all about what you and your old buddy from high school got into after you tied one on at a Las Vegas convention, even if it was years ago. Only discuss women's attractiveness in sexually neutral terms ("Yeah, I suppose Uma's pretty"); don't get into body specs.

■ When you're living with her:
Give the guy his dignity and don't force him to acknowledge that you two are shacking up. Insisting he drop by for a meal or joking about how tough she is to live with when she's got PMS will just rub his nose in it and force him to picture the two of you knocking uglies. Instead be diplomatic. When he calls, say, "I'll see if she's in her room," even though you both know who else sleeps there.

■ When wedding bells are ringing:
Since he's on the verge of losing his darling to you forever, expect more antagonism than usual. On the other hand, men are notoriously unwelcome during the organization of a wedding, so seize the opportunity to share the doghouse with Dad. A joint exile in the garage will bridge the communication gap—grab some beers and some tools and have at it.

■ After you're married:
Involve him in your life as much as you can stand. Play to his strengths: If he's handy, ask for help in retiling the bathroom; if he's an accountant, let him do your taxes. You'll get free help, he'll feel useful—and it will help ease any lingering resentment over your hostile takeover of his little girl's heart.

DEALING WITH PMS
Which she seems to think stands for "Penis Means Stupid."

It's almost that time of the month again, and while it has its pluses—you've managed to avoid fatherhood again—the sudden rush of hormones involved can cause trouble for both of you. Mainly, it seems, for you. If she's not weeping softly over a Hallmark commercial, she's threatening your privates with cropping shears because you left the toilet seat up again. Don't panic: Here are a few things you can do to ease her discomfort—and simultaneously make her think you're all sensitive and crap.

GIVE HER A TUMMY RUB. Have her lie on her back on the bed. Using moderate pressure, massage her abdomen in a clockwise motion, eventually moving in smaller circles that are concentrated over her uterus (about an inch above her pubic bone). Congestion in the uterus can cause cramping from her waist to her thighs. Massaging this area helps the blood circulate, which gives her relief.

MASSAGE HER LOWER BACK. Ask her to roll over and lie on her stomach. (For bonus points place a warm towel beneath her: The heat and massage together will improve her circulation.) Using deep pressure, work your way from her waist down to her coccyx, gently pushing your thumbs into every nook and cranny along the way.

PRACTICE THE ANCIENT ART OF ACUPRESSURE. With your thumb and first two fingers, grab about two inches above her ankle and hold for a minute or so. This triggers a pressure point along her body's meridian, allowing her chi, or life force, to...oh, hell, we don't believe it, either. Just tell her you saw this stuff on the Lifetime channel and she'll lie in traffic for you.

OFFER HER SEXUAL HEALING. The friction from intercourse creates soothing heat, which loosens clots and softens the cervix, helping it open and allow more blood flow. And when you get her to the Big O, her body will release cortisone and endorphins, both natural painkillers. Hey, she can't argue with science. (Then again, when she's PMS-ing, she can pretty much argue with anything...)

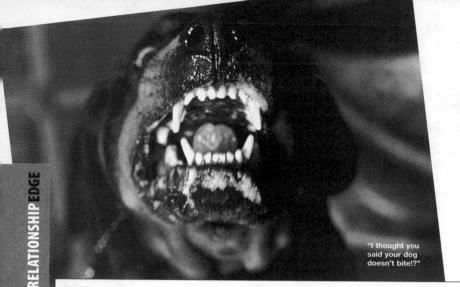

"I thought you said your dog doesn't bite!?"

Kids and Animals

Make friends…even with the ones that aren't housebroken.

They're a gal's final test of your worthiness—get past these li'l' nippers and you're home free. You've gotten past her friends and family, but now inevitably you're going to run into her final bullshit detectors: the kids and dogs of her little world. Here our experts evaluate common strategies for handling 'em:

■ Move in slowly?
Kids: Yes　　**Dogs:** Yes

"Be cool and friendly," says Dr. Anita Gurian, senior psychologist at the NYU Child Study Center. "Children have different temperaments, and many don't like having their space invaded." With dogs, according to Jim Keenan, of Keen Dog Training, the trick is to use positive "calming signals" like letting him smell the back of your hand before making eye contact (the part people screw up).

■ Get down on their level?
Kids: Yes　　**Dogs:** No

Make sure you're at eye level with a child, suggests Gurian. This might mean crouching down if necessary. But dogs don't like it when you hover or bend over them, advises Keenan. "It's best to let them approach you."

■ Do some homework?
Kids: Yes　　**Dogs:** No

Ask your gal pal what her child's interests are beforehand, and you'll have something to talk about with Junior. He'll be amazed at how cool you are, and she'll appreciate the effort. Dogs, on the other hand, all love pretty much the same things: the satisfying crunch of a mailman's leg bones; a declawed cat on a rope; the rich, heady aroma of another dog's ass.

■ Try bribery?
Kids: Yes　　**Dogs:** Yes

"Treats are the quickest way to a dog's heart," admits Keenan, and kids aren't much different. It also gives you the chance to impress your lady friend with your desirable boy scout qualities (you're kind, courteous, generous, etc.) In fact it wouldn't hurt to bring her something too—remember, you want to score big with everyone. A rawhide bone or squeaky toy earns you big points with the mutt, while a game that enables a child to amuse himself will double as a distraction to let you make the moves on your gal.

■ Play the "got your nose" game?
Kids: Yes　　**Dogs:** No

Kids under six will usually enjoy this if they're comfortable with you, but it's a definite no-no with the pooch, unless you want to play the "Got your fucking fingers!" game, too.

SLEEPING TOGETHER
Yeah, you think you've got this covered. Think again, Casanova.

As opposed to doing the wild thing, sleeping in the same bed for the long term takes a lot of getting used to. Here's how to get into a groove that works for both of you.

1. Five and a half hours of good solid sleep is better than seven hours of fragmented sleep. And naps, even for as little as 15 minutes, can make a difference. If you have a big sleep debt, consider the benefits of going into the bedroom for a couple hours and just getting some horizontal sack time.

2. Exercising six hours before bedtime is optimal, because after you're done, your body temperature—which has just peaked—gradually lowers to a point that starts shutting you down and getting you sleepy. If you're dealing with a new person in your bed, start running in the early evenings and it won't be such a problem.

3. Invest in a white-noise machine. Either that or get soft music that does not require any brainpower to listen to (Enya has based an entire career on this). The reason is that noises your bedmate might make—snorting, grunting, calling out another man's name—have little peaks in them. It's the peaks, not the noise itself, that keep you alert and up. White noise levels off those peaks.

4. If one of you is a night person and the other is a morning person, you should establish rules that whoever is up should be away, in the living room watching TV, or in the kitchen with coffee and a paper.

Stop Those Snot-Trumpet Solos

Tired of sounding like a hibernating bear at night? We're here to help.

If you saw logs like an ADD-addled lumberjack, your girlfriend just might knife you in your sleep. Here are some tips to keep the log sawing to a minimum:

SPOON HER AND SLEEP ON YOUR SIDE.
Dozing on your back lets your throat muscles and tongue relax, narrowing your airway so that inhaling causes your tonsils, soft palate, and uvula to vibrate. In other words you're snoring through no fault of your own and pissing the crap out of the gal next to you. Some experts suggest stuffing a tennis ball into a sock and pinning this onto the back of your shirt so it will be painful to lie on your back. Some experts are a little weird.

SKIP THE NACHO CHEESE. Eating or drinking dairy products within two hours before bedtime will increase the production of mucus in your throat and block your air passage further.

TURN DOWN LAST CALL. Alcohol, drugs, and sleeping medications before bed relax the musculature of the throat (among other things), increasing the likelihood you'll snore.

DON'T GET FAT. Those Egg McMuffins may go down easy, but they leave their mark over time, adding excess flab around your neck and around the tissues in your throat.

VISIT THE DENTIST.
There are two basic types of dental mouthpieces designed to help snorers: One holds the tongue forward, whereas the other brings the lower jaw forward during sleep. Both keep your airway open. Try not to drool on her neck.

CONSIDER DRASTIC MEASURES.
If none of these tactics work, talk to your doc about long-term options such as a nasal mask, which provides continuous air pressure, or laser surgery, which is done to remove or shrink extra skin in your airway.

The Six Commandments of Living Together

The flowers and games worked well—maybe too well. If you're ready to take it to the next level, do it right.

1 Thou shalt make space for both of you. Try to have space in a place that each person can call their own. Don't be a fanatic about it, but you both need a place to be alone. Also there will be an added need for you two to take time off to be alone—you're not chained at the ankle. Don't act like it.

2 Thou shalt let her decorate. Lord knows you never thought you'd live anywhere with frilly curtains or shelf paper or figurines. Actually, with one badly hung shelf, you can break all the figurines and make it look like an accident. But for everything else, you need to allow her to add her touches to the place or she won't invest in it. And remember this, the more you agree with her choices—"that wallpaper looks great, honey"—the more veto power you'll have when there's something you truly hate, or truly want to hang that she won't like, like the Buffy poster you've had for five years.

3 Thou shalt set house rules. Bills, cleaning, lights out, having friends over—all the nitty-gritty stuff you'd have to discuss with any roommate, and the stuff they have fights about on *The Real World* and then kick somebody out over. What makes you think you won't have to deal with this stuff just because you and your roomie also happen to be doing the box-spring boogie? Sit down and hammer it out early—*before* there's an argument. That way you'll be able to discuss things while you're still cool-headed, before she finds out what you do with your dirty underwear.

4 Thou shalt talk about your feelings. You've just taken the relationship to a new level, but you're still not married—which means what you have is in a particularly vulnerable state. Make sure you don't keep issues to yourself when you should vent a little. This time in your life is supposed to help you two figure out whether you should make it legal or move into different states. Like it or not this means it's time to confront what it is about her that bugs the shit out of you.

5 Thou shalt keep the romance rocking. You still need to date, even though you can get sex with just a Blockbuster movie and some pizza. That's because it will get stale, friend, and you two will start treating each other like a married couple. You'll never touch each other and she'll end up sleeping with the delivery boy. Don't let yourself get lulled into complacency just because you've got matching addresses.

6 Thou shalt face the clock. Her biological clock. You don't need to start talking marriage seriously, yet. But in about two years, you're going to have a discussion. In three you'll have a request or maybe even an ultimatum. Add one year to these deadlines if you live in a large, liberal city. Take two years away if her parents express extreme disapproval for shacking. Add one if you two get a puppy.

Negotiate Better Now

Talk yourself down from the ledge.

Getting what you want from a relationship requires subtlety, wit, and a willingness to eat it once in a while.

You want: Poker night out with the guys
The issue: She might feel you don't like spending time with her.
You give: One dinner out, a long walk together, a movie she likes, and a big, long chatty gabfest over coffee later.

You want: Forgiveness for forgetting her birthday
The issue: She's not on your mind at all.
You give: A poem she wrote to you years ago, framed.

You want: A choreless, uneventful, sit-on-your-ass-and-watch-TV weekend
The issue: Her desire for you as an intelligent, active, manly man might be diminished by seeing you in your underwear, scratching at your belly while glued to *The Jerry Springer Show*.
You give: A session at the gym, where you teach her a few new exercises and spot her while you both try to break personal best bench-press records.

You want: For her to make you a nice dinner and give you a back rub
The issue: It's all about you, isn't it?
You give: Flattery. "I just had veal scampi in a restaurant after work the other day," you say, "But it was nothing like when you made it." Then you tug at that crick in your neck that's been pretty bad lately.

"Oh well. I guess it's all over."

Urge Her to Slim Down

Because, yes, her ass does look big in that miniskirt.

Tread softly, gentlemen: We are in dangerous territory here. She's twice the girl she was when you met her, and you ain't talking spiritually. While it's true that there's indeed more cushion for the pushin', dating fat girls, as the saying goes, is like riding a moped: fun...until your friends see you on it.

Since the three most important words you can tell a woman are "You're not fat," you've got to encourage her to do what's in her best interest health-wise in a way that won't get you hit—after all, she's now bigger than you are! So

don't say something like "Boy, honey! You better watch out or pretty soon the seesaw's gonna be all yours." Instead, according to "Dr. Romance" columnist, Tina B. Tessina, you need to pick a time when you're not fighting. "Start by saying something such as, 'I don't know how to talk to you about this without you getting upset, but I need to talk about it, so please help me here.' Usually if you ask for help to start with, it doesn't feel like so much of an attack," says Tessina. "And it doesn't put the other person on the defensive so much."

Make Your Girlfriend Think Her Cat's Death Was an Accident

Hey, shit happens.

WHAT HAPPENED:
Two seconds after your girlfriend leaves for the airport, you kick the cat out the door, despite your girlfriend's previous warnings not to let him outside. Later that morning, you discover ol' Boots has lost a nasty brawl with a raccoon, which explains those awful noises that kept waking you.

What you tell her:
Death by curiosity. You cleverly rip a hole in the screen door, then claim that Boots must have clawed it open to go after that pesky raccoon. "Your boy sure had spunk!"

WHAT HAPPENED:
When Mittens hacks up hair balls all over your suede jacket *just out of spite,* you spoon a liberal dose of rat poison into a dish of cream and call for kitty. A few agonized minutes later, your dry-cleaning woes are a thing of the past.

What you tell her:
Heart attack. "I guess it was just his time. No one knows why these things happen. I mean, he was almost five weeks old. That's, like, a hundred in cat years."

WHAT HAPPENED:
Backing out of the driveway, you hear a sickening crunch. So you drive back and forth over it until the crunching stops.

What you tell her:
It was a mob hit. There had been several mysterious phone calls, which Tiger insisted on taking in private. Then came the package—a fish wrapped in newspaper. Ordinarily, you'd think a cat would be glad to get something like

that. But not this time. The last thing you remember was a black sedan speeding away from the house.

WHAT HAPPENED:
Awakened at 3 A.M. by the horny little bastard's obscene caterwauling, you pick up the cat and toss it out onto the porch. But in your semi-somnambulent state, you forget that you live in a high-rise apartment building. Your underhand pitch sends Fluffy hurtling 23 stories to a messy death.

What you tell her:
Suicide. The cat had seemed depressed, but you were unable to comfort it. Tell her, "I guess he just missed you so much, honey—you shouldn't have deserted him," cleverly shifting the guilt onto your broken-hearted gal pal.

WHAT HAPPENED:
You feel the need to practice your golf swing. You don't have any balls.

What you tell her:
"Boots? Boots is dead, baby, Boots is dead. Hey, look at this nice shiny diamond ring I have for you."

Cat Scratch Fever

Dogs are easy. Welcome to hell.

You've invited her to live with you. But it's not just "her." It's "them." Deal with her feline entourage and cat-proof your place (because we wouldn't want any accidents, now would we?)

RECLINER CHAIRS.
Cats hide beneath these things, in the housing of the reclining mechanism. You go to lie back and watch some sports, and the next thing you know you and your hysterical girlfriend are rushing the cat to the intensive care unit.

DRYER.
We shouldn't have to explain this.

DRAPERY AND BLIND CORDS.
Always keep them pulled up. Otherwise a cat who starts playing with one of those babies could string himself up like a western outlaw.

BAGS WITH HANDLES.
Cats love to play with the handles but can become caught and choke themselves.

STOVE TOPS.
Get burner covers. Or learn pussy-flambé recipes.

Don't worry! He still has 101 uses.

Is Your Relationship Normal?

"OK, Honey. Time for your piercing."

■ 71% of Americans have only one sexual partner in the course of a year; 12% have none; 3% have five or more.

■ 53% had one sex partner in the last five years.

■ About 40% of married people and over half of people living together have sex twice a week. 25% of singles living alone have sex that often.

■ 88% of married people reported enjoying "great sexual pleasure" from their relationship. 85% reported "great emotional satisfaction." That other 12% to 15% didn't want to talk to anyone about it, because who listens to them anyway?

■ 15% of wives reported they have had an affair at least once. 24.5% of husbands have. The figures shoot way up for men in their 50s (37%) but drop to 12.4% for women that age.

■ 75% of men, but just 29% of women, report they always have an orgasm during sex. A frightening 4% of women and 1% of men claim they've never gotten there. The

entire 1% group constitutes the staff of *FHM,* we believe.

■ Sex lasts between 15 minutes and an hour for most, with 20% of men and 15% of women reporting that they spend more than an hour.

■ Here's a scary fact: Married men are five times more likely than single men to spend 15 minutes or less for sex.

■ Top four turn-ons for most Americans: 1. Vaginal intercourse; 2. Watching your mate undress; 3. Receiving oral sex; 4. Giving oral sex. (We'd like to add 5: receiving oral sex again.)

■ 60% of men and 40% of women masturbated in the last year. Among couples living together, though, that number increases to 85% of men and 45% of women.

■ Here are stats on problems people reported in the past year: Pain during sex (men, 8.1%; women, 14.4%); lack of interest (men, 15.8%; women, 33.4%); unable to keep erection (men, 10.4%; women, 100%...what did you think?)

BLOCKHEADED VIDEO
How to avoid video-rental blunders

More relationships have ended at the video store than we can count. She's got her mitts on *The Bridges of Madison County,* you're trying to talk her into a classic Jackie Chan flick, and things are getting tense. Here's some compromise-worthy choices.

GUY FILMS YOU CAN SELL

TERMINATOR 2: JUDGMENT DAY
What to say: Linda Hamilton is the strongest female lead to come out of Hollywood since Marlene Dietrich.
Clinch it: As a matter of fact, I always thought she looked like you. *[Feel her bicep]* You've been working out more, haven't you, hon?

Avoid saying: Chicks with guns get me hot. Sweaty chicks with guns get me really hot.

JACKIE BROWN
What to say: It's really the story of a middle-aged single woman, doing what she can to survive, who finds love along the way.
Clinch it: I hope we have the same chemistry they do when we're older.
Avoid saying: Bridget Fonda is stoned and braless throughout the film. Can I get an *Amen!*

DIRTY HARRY
What to say: Harry Callahan has a subtle vulnerability throughout the film

that you don't see much in Eastwood characters. He's tough, but he's crying on the inside.
Clinch it: Not many people could pick it up, but I bet you'll see it.
Avoid saying: Do you feel lucky, punk? Huh, do ya?!

BOUND
What to say: Two women scheme together to double-cross a manipulative, uncaring husband. Along the way they discover they love each other.
Clinch it: Women are endlessly complicated and fascinating, aren't they? God, what are you thinking?
Avoid saying: Let's watch it with your sister.

Chick Flicks You'll Like

ELIZABETH

Queen Elizabeth I is an inspiring figure, someone your girlfriend will look up to. But what's great is that her court was a nest of spies—you really get a sense for how much dirt these people dealt on one another. Not only that, but everybody sleeps with everybody else, and some French dude gets completely found out and humiliated as a cross-dressing freak.

CONTACT

It's headed up by a brave female scientist, which scores feminist points. But it's still a good old-fashioned sci-fi that will appeal to the Carl Sagan–loving geek in you.

THELMA & LOUISE

Sure, it's an empowering movie about the beautiful and wonderful friendship between two women who yadda, yadda, yadda. But it's got guns, car chases, and plenty of killing and mayhem. Also it stars Harvey Keitel and Michael Madsen from *Reservoir Dogs,* and to top it off, it's directed by Ridley Scott, who's famous for giving Rutger Hauer the only good work he's done in his life, *Blade Runner.*

CHASING AMY

It's got plenty of relationship talks and gritty honesty, and it's ultimately about women having the freedom to choose their own lives. But what it's really about is lesbians and comic books.

Love is a Battlefield
Whether you're the dumper or the dumpee, here's all the classified info you need to win the war.

Can't work things out? When you gotta go, you gotta go. We got Lee Covington, author of *How to Dump Your Wife,* to adapt her strategy for the tricky girlfriend *sayonara.*

■ **Be a man.** Even though her shrieking laugh makes you want to pull a double Van Gogh, she's still a sweetie, right? Don't let her charm distract you from your plans. "Choose an exact date that you're going to break up so you don't waffle," says Covington. "And don't keep going back and sleeping with her once you've called it off." Damn...

■ **Be a gentleman.** Break up on neutral territory (if you do it somewhere public, she's less likely to heave a potted plant at your head), and don't ask for your Clash CD back. You should discreetly reclaim anything of real value before the breakup (and sneak *her* things back, so she doesn't have a reason to call or drop by when you're wooing your new, improved babe).

■ **Be brief.** "Give away as little information as possible," Covington warns. "Remember, she's going to chew on everything you've said," so don't blather on and on or later she'll interpret the energy you

put in to the explanation as a sign that you really *do* still like her. Scary, isn't it?

■ **Keep it simple.** Obviously you'll have to respond in some way when she shouts, "Why? Why are you doing this to me?!" Recognize that there's no good answer to this question. You're rejecting her, so *everything* is going to come out bad. Covington advises against the "It's not you; it's me" cliché: "Remember, she watched *Seinfeld,* too." Instead present it as a *fait accompli:* "We just don't fit well together." Resist the urge to say you want to remain friends, even if you really do, says Covington. "Women hate that, because it *always* sounds phony."

■ **Prepare to be the bad guy.** When a woman dumps a man, her girlfriends cheer and take her out for margaritas, and even her guy friends chime in with "You were too good for him." But when a man dumps a woman—even if she ruined his credit rating or made him watch *Touched by an Angel* every week—these same people will call him a heartless lout, a commitment-phobe, and an enemy of family values. Take it all on the chin. "It's better to be strong and break it off now," says Covington, "before you need to buy my book."

The Truth Behind Those Damn Magazine Quizzes

We think they're bullshit. But just wait until you score low on the "Is He Mr. Right?" quiz and you're sent packing. Remember this:

■ **The writers aren't experts.**
These people aren't mental health professionals. They're freelance hacks or magazine editors, every one of them. And take it from us: When it comes to credibility, that's one step below *crack whore.*

■ **The experts aren't experts.**
The head shrinkers they use are either a) friends of the magazine who are known for their complete willingness to make oversim-

plified pronouncements on shit they don't know about, b) people with books they want plugged, or c) interns they couldn't find another use for.

■ **The scoring is random.**
After the writer interviews a source, he or she makes up a question for each point or symptom that the head shrinker had. And they pull the point values right out of their ass.

Breaking Up, Part 1: Extreme Measures

The kinder, gentler approach didn't work? Try these more drastic methods for dumping your girlie, courtesy of our friends at *Stuff* Magazine.

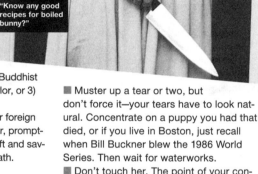

"Know any good recipes for boiled bunny?"

CONFIDE IN ONE OF HER FRIENDS.

Why deliver the bad news yourself when you can get a patsy to do it for you? We suggest calling one of her good friends—we'll name her Patsy. Invite Patsy out for a cup of coffee; tell her that it's "urgent that you talk to her." Once you're together, bite your lower lip, rub your eyes, and say, "Patsy, I didn't know who else to turn to." Then, rather than recite a litany of problems you're having with your girlfriend, let her do the work for you. Say, "I feel terrible that I'm feeling this way, but Lisa and I have been having serious problems. You know her better than anyone. What should I do?" Then sit back and pretend to listen as she launches into a diatribe of the inner workings of her friend's mind. Whatever you do, make it seem as if you're hanging on her every word. Finally, bow your head and mumble, "I'm scared, Patsy—really scared. I think we should be apart for a while. Will you talk to her for me?" Delighted at the prospect of playing mediator, she'll gladly agree.

DISAPPEAR FROM HER LIFE.

Nothing—not even the infamous raised toilet seat—pisses a woman off as much as a guy who quits calling her back. "For a man to simply not call is not only inexcusable; it's incomprehensible to a woman," explains Drew Pinsky, cohost of MTV's *Lovelines.* Unfortunately for her, this technique—affectionately known as the fade—is also the easiest and most convenient way to break the ties that bind.

A typical fade involves at least one of the following: refusing to answer the phone, instructing your secretary to screen your calls, changing gym memberships, and spending more time at the office. Though effective, these methods lack style, however,

being a bastard is one thing but being a boring bastard is unforgivable. If you prefer to be remembered as an underhanded snake, try one of these slick moves:

■ Hire a woman with a deep, sexy voice to leave this message on your machine: "[Your name] is temporarily indisposed right now. If he has any energy left, he'll send you a fax."

■ Forward incoming calls to: 1) a Buddhist temple, 2) a "midriff" massage parlor, or 3) the county jail.

■ Blow up the embassy of a major foreign power. This should start a land war, prompting Congress to reinstitute the draft and saving you from a fate worse than death.

TELL HER THAT YOU LOVE SOMEONE ELSE.

Here's another bizarre difference between men and women: If a woman were to tell you that she's dumping your sorry ass 'cause she's found her real soul mate, you'd probably consider: a) murder, or b) the priesthood. But if you tell *her* you're leaving because you've fallen in love with someone else, this is somehow tolerable. Why? Because in her eyes, it's not entirely your fault. Love is a cosmic thing, after all, and if the universe wants it this way, then so be it. How to execute this strategy:

■ Fall in love with another woman. If this proves difficult, proceed to the next step.

■ Pretend to have fallen in love with another woman. Keep it brief. The more you divulge, the more she'll catch the loopholes in your story.

■ Muster up a tear or two, but don't force it—your tears have to look natural. Concentrate on a puppy you had that died, or if you live in Boston, just recall when Bill Buckner blew the 1986 World Series. Then wait for waterworks.

■ Don't touch her. The point of your confession is to symbolize the wide, barren emotional chasm that is now between you.

MAKE HER CHEAT ON YOU.

Contrary to their saintly image, 54 percent of women have reported cheating on their partners. And since there is no better reason to break up with a woman than infidelity, use these pointers to force her hand.

■ Take up smoking cloves.

■ Refuse to close the bathroom door, especially when disposing of solid waste.

■ Grunt, "Ugh!" every time you thrust your pelvis.

■ Routinely tell her that you want to: a) crash-land the alien, b) wet-dock the "nub-marine," or c) take the pigskin bus to Tunatown. Continue to use these juvenile phrases until they cease to be funny.

Breaking Up, Part 2: How to Know When You're About to Be Dumped.

It's lunchtime at Rosie O'Donnell's!

Never get blindsided again. We begged, pleaded, and threw a hissy fit to get 100 women to reveal the sure signs that they are gonna give their guy the boot.

■ **She encourages you to go out with your drinking buddies.** A sudden appreciation for those guys she affectionately calls alcoholic Cro-Magnon men can mean that she wants to give you the slip but just doesn't know how. Her brilliant solution? Practically forcing you to go out, get drunk, and screw...someone else. That way she gets to break up with you, but *you're* still the bad guy. Crafty, eh?

■ **She lets you win an argument.** Women's mags have brainwashed ladies into thinking that arguing is healthy for a relationship. But if her mantra is "You're right; I'm wrong," put on your goggles 'cause you're about to get waxed. Total submission means she doesn't give a rat's ass about you or your relationship anymore.

■ **She stops faking it.** You've noticed that she's suddenly correcting your technique on stuff you've done with no complaints for five months: "Higher, lower, softer!" You can prevent this humiliating experience from ever happening by following the Granny Panties principle: If she's wearing them, don't bother taking them off. They are obviously being worn to repel you—another sure sign that you'll soon be put out to pasture.

■ **She stops laughing at your jokes.** Used to be that she couldn't get enough of your impressions of Regis Philbin. But lately your comic gems are met with blank stares, eye-rolling, and the occasional "My god, you're an idiot." Well, we hate to tell you this, but you're really not a laugh riot—never were. She was drunk on love, and when she sobered up, you went back to being the same old unfunny guy you've always been. Sorry.

■ **She starts banging the copy boy at work—and tells you all about it.** Please don't make us explain this one to you.

RELATIONSHIP EDGE

100 Women Tell You How to Dump 'Em

Just in case you think we're being mean-spirited, we asked the same 100 women about their preferred methods of getting eighty-sixed. In other words, break her heart like this and you're less likely to lose an appendage.

ACT MORBIDLY DEPRESSED.
Our panel voted unanimously against the surprise breakup, so if you're going to part ways, you need to set the mood first. Mope around for a few days, looking as if you're on the verge of suicide. This will goad her into asking what's wrong. At that point mournfully reply, "I don't know, it's just...Julie, this isn't working for me anymore."

STARE HER DOWN.
Once you've brought up the subject, don't *ever* take your eyes off her. She needs to feel like this is the most gut-wrenching, difficult thing you've ever done, and eye contact will achieve that effect.

TALK ABOUT "WE," NOT "ME."
Saying something like, "I'm unhappy with the relationship," will immediately put her on the defensive and make her feel as if it's all her fault, says our panel. But saying, "We're having problems," makes it seem as if you're not just concerned about your own selfish needs, but the health of the relationship.

DO IT CLEANLY AND CLEARLY.
"Mean is bad, but blunt is fine," says Lynn Harris, author of *Breakup Girl to the Rescue: A Superhero's Guide to Love, and Lack Thereof.* "Don't try to avoid hurting her; just spare her feelings as much as possible. Give her enough information to where she has a good idea what you're thinking, but don't tell her everything." In other words refrain from comments like, "You're boring" or "You remind me of my Uncle Fred."

TELL HER THAT SHE'S TOO COMPLEX FOR YOU.
According to our female panel, every woman secretly yearns to be told that she's too "colorful" and "untamable" so she can console herself knowing that she's just too much woman for her own good.

NEVER TELL HER, "IT'S NOT YOU—IT'S ME."
This age-old lie not only has the distinction of being vague and mushy but also completely lacks in any originality. It registers .02 on a woman's give-a-shit scale.

Are You Over Her?

Take this quiz and find out.

1. You hear you and your ex's favorite song in a public place. Do you:
a) Cry.
b) Yell for the DJ to "turn this crap off!"
c) Cry, but only to get sympathy sex from the hot blonde on the next stool.

2. You find her hair on a pillow. What do you do with it?
a) Find a murder scene and plant the hair in a pool of blood.
b) Put it under your pillow.
c) Eat some ribs and use it to floss your teeth.

3. You run into her sister at the mall. Do you:
a) Tell her to pass the message on that you're sorry.
b) Tell her to get lost.
c) Ask her out on a date, then stand her up in favor of a hot night of weed and Thunderbird.

4. What would you do if you saw her current boyfriend at the mall?
a) Defensively explain that you're heading to Victoria's Secret to buy underwear for the stripper you've been dating.
b) Smack him in the face and call him a bitch.
c) Slap him a high five and ask if she still speaks Italian when her vulva is rubbed.

5. You get an invitation to her wedding. Do you:
a) Rent *The Graduate.*
b) RSVP "Fuck no...never, never, never."
c) Go to the wedding and tell her dad it's a shame he wasted all this good booze on such a cheap whore.

6. She says she still loves you. Do you:

a) Say you love her too.
b) Tell her to call back after *Jeopardy* is over.
c) Ask her to prove it by scrubbing your toilet with her teeth.

7. In a pinch she asks you to watch her cat while she goes out of town. Do you:
a) Agree, then, using the cat, vicariously "patch up your relationship."
b) Agree, then forget to feed the cat for about three weeks.
c) Tell her you don't have the time but that you do know a great kennel by the name of Hunan Chinese Buffet.

8. She invites you over for a conciliatory "Let's be friends" dinner. You:
a) Spend $100 on a bottle of wine in a desperate attempt to win her back.
b) Tell her you'd rather eat a baboon's puckered asshole.
c) Accept, then bring over your special beer chili, a 12-pack of Pabst Blue Ribbon, and a copy of your high school football team's highlight reel.

9. What celeb most reminds you of your ex?
a) She's not like anyone else in the world.
b) Jessica Alba, Heather Graham, and Shannen Elizabeth combined.
c) Sue from *Survivor.*

10. She calls you and tells you she's becoming a lesbian. What do you tell her?
a) All lesbians are evil, and she'll never go to heaven if she doesn't get back together with you.
b) She'll probably scare her new partner straight.
c) "You mean you weren't one already?"

If you guessed mostly A's, you're codependent. Your sense of identity is completely intertwined with having her, and you've got a better shot at pissing mercury than successfully moving on.
If you guessed mostly B's, you're borderline psychotic. While there is a small danger that you might act out your insecurities in

some violent act, it's just as likely you'll spend the next three months worshipping an altar to her memory before finding someone else to cling to.
If you guessed mostly C's, you're over her completely and can get on with the important business of finding other relationships to screw up.

Dumping-Her Dilemmas

Answers to your most burning breakup quandaries.

■ **Should you keep in touch with your ex-girlfriend's father?**
Fortunately, this difficult question can be answered using this handy formula, devised by *Stuff* mathematicians:

Dad's average yearly income x Number of country clubs to which he belongs ÷ Number of weapons in the house (including kitchen knives only if father has an assault charge on his record) *or* Number of years father served in Vietnam = If the result is more than $200,000, stay in touch.

■ **Is Ex Sex OK?** Yes.

How to Tell if a Woman is Checking You Out

Waste no time, you're back on the prowl.

Don't ogle her back, don't ask, don't use those stupid backward mirror sunglasses you got in your cereal box when you were a kid. Instead just look at your watch. The action will make her subconsciously want to look at her watch too—she might not even really check the time, just glance down and then up. And you got her—the rest is, of course, up to you.

Buying the Rock

Size is everything.

You've made it through the worst. Time to go pro.

Diamonds are a girl's best friend—and a guy's worst enemy. When a regular Joe like you shows up in a diamond store, the dealer knows that 1) you're there because you have to be, 2) you've got thousands to spend, and 3) you're a chump.

TRICK: The diamond is actually cubic zirconium, or bottle glass, or smells vaguely of Cracker Jacks.

TIP: Insist on the pedigree. These days "a lasered number should be inscribed on your stone," says Jay Ehrenwald, GG, ASA, at the International Gemological Institute. "That number must match the number on the accompanying certificate."

TRICK: The jewelry store's bright lights disguise the fact that a stone's been cut poorly and doesn't have any sparkle.

TIP: A correctly cut stone's 58 facets are mathematically designed to reflect back as much light as possible—a dull stone means the diamond's been cut incorrectly, and light's leaking out on the sides. Ask to see your target stone on the counter next to three or four other stones of similar size (smaller stones can falsely appear brighter). If you don't get knocked out by the sparkle, send 'er back.

TRICK: They disguise a stone's poor color by displaying it next to duller stones so you won't notice.

TIP: Open a sugar packet and compare—the brilliant white of the sugar should reveal any yellowness in the rock. Also don't let them use their own "color rating"—get the stone's color in the standardized GIA grading system. According to *Survival Skills for the Modern Man* by Donn M. Davis, you can settle for lower grades G through I if your ring is going to be yellow gold but should spring for D (colorless—the most expensive grade) through F if the ring's platinum or white gold.

TRICK: The stone contains microscopic flaws the dealer doesn't bother to point out.

TIP: The official GIA certificate will detail all such "inclusions" and "occlusions"; make the dealer show them to you under magnification. If you've somehow bamboozled a supermodel into marrying you and have to spring for a flawless stone, you can use the medieval test for perfection: Drop the diamond into a glass of water; a perfect rock will become invisible.

TRICK: A dealer hedges on what the real carat weight is, telling you the diamond "spreads" to a full carat, or some other BS.

TIP: Don't fall for it. According to *Weddings for Dummies* (IDG Books Worldwide), combinations of small diamonds in arrangements aren't worth the greater carat weight they supposedly "spread" to. Get the real damn carat weight of the stone you're interested in. Then find out what you should be paying for it at the International Gemmological Institute Web site (www.igiworldwide.com), where you can have them do an independent assessment for a fee that starts at $35. That way you don't light more $1,000 dollar bills on fire than you absolutely have to.

Stop Screwing Up Your Anniversary

Forgotten birthdays and anniversaries can cause hurt feelings and painful kicks to the groin. Fortunately, you no longer have to rely on your booze-marinated brain cells to warn you about such nuisances.

■ **www.candor.com/reminder.** Ah, simplicity. Merely enter your E-mail address, the date you want the reminder sent, and the reminder itself. Now crack a tall boy and say good-bye to all your cares.

■ **www.magicmemory.com.** Forget anniversaries and holidays—this Limey site

has preset reminders for every category under the sun and then some, down to household chores (fridge, cooker, plumbing) and pets (fur trimming, claw cutting). Bonus: Laugh at the silly British spellings and terms ("tyres", "life assurance"). Ha!

■ **www.iping.com.** The cream of the reminder-service crop in our book, iPing.com delivers reminders in the form of phone calls ("pings"), which you set up on their Web site in advance. Home, work, or cellular numbers may be pinged, and you can choose between having an automated voice read

your typed message, pre-recording your own dulcet tones, or using a novelty messages from the iPing archive. Best of all it's free, leaving you extra green to spend on whoopee cushions, sea monkeys, x-ray specs, and the like for your best gal.

For the technologically challenged, try A&M Answering service at (337) 265-3000 to arrange your wake-up calls. You have to shell out, but it's cheaper than getting fired because your boss didn't consider "I kept hitting the snooze button" to be a delightfully endearing excuse. What?!? No phone either? You're shit out of luck, pal, unless you've got the guts to try one of those ancient "calendar" or "daily planner" systems...

SURVIVAL EDGE

IF YOU CAN'T MAKE IT HERE...

Endure the wild with nothing but pure balls. And this chapter.

As any outdoorsman knows, nature is majestic, dark, and deep...but it'll eat you for lunch if you don't show it respect. Whether you're fishing, have gotten lost in the woods, or have just kicked through the window of your downed 747 somewhere in the Rockies, it helps to be prepared. This chapter shows you how to handle tricky situations without having to cook and eat your trusty, but tasty, friends.

NICE BOX!

Lightweight Lifesaver

Bare essentials you can carry everywhere you go.

Sure, you could pack a steamer trunkful of every camping and first-aid doodad they sell in the L. L. Bean catalog...and you'd get felled by a hernia trying to lug the motherfucker through the woods. This stuff comes in handy no matter where you are but is compact enough to stow in a jacket pocket.

BOX:

A medium- to large-size pipe-tobacco tin works best. Fill it with the items listed below, and seal it with electrical tape to make it water-resistant. Pack any extra space with cotton wool to keep the contents from rattling around. You can use the cotton for lighting a fire or for sticking in your ears to keep the bugs from laying eggs in your ear canal. Polish the inside of the lid to make it reflective so it can be used for signaling planes and rangers, and for checking out those cool new welts on your forehead from sleeping face down in a nest of fire ants.

Fill the box with the following items for the ultimate survival pack:

■ Matches
Forget waterproof—too bulky. Take the ordinary strike-anywhere kind, snap them in half to save space, and dip the heads in candle wax to ward off dampness.

■ Candle
Shaved short and square to fit. Can help you light a fire without your using every last match. Use a tallow candle if possible—you can use it for cooking later, or can even eat it in an emergency. Yum.

■ Flint
Get a welder's flint striker for a few bucks at any hardware store. It's simple, hardy, and throws sparks like a Grucci sprinkler.

■ Magnifying glass

For starting fires, searching for splinters and stings, and making bugs pop open for cheap laughs. Get the small, fold-in-a-leather-envelope kind.

■ Needles and thread

Include one small needle for tiny jobs and one large-eyed needle for sinews and coarse threads, for when you need to make long johns out of Gentle Ben.

■ Hooks and line

Include as much line as possible—and make the hooks small, not large, so you can catch a wider range of fish and even birds!

■ Brass wire

Two to three feet should do it. When you find one of God's creatures out there, this will help you snare it by the shank so you can turn it into a meal. A guitar string will do.

■ Flexible saw

Not the big, clunky hacksaw kind, but the thin, ultraflexible kind sold in camping shops. Take off the large ring handles to save space. You can use wooden toggles later.

■ The one drug you need

If you really want to save space, get potassium permanganate, a sort of all-in-one wonder drug. Add it to water and mix until bright pink to sterilize it. Add more for a deeper pink shade and it makes a good antiseptic. Add until it becomes full red to treat fungal diseases like athlete's foot. Now, if you could only smoke it.

■ Condoms

They're not just for fucking anymore. Each one of these babies holds two pints of water, and is a hell of a lot less bulky than an extra canteen (and more fun to lob at unsuspecting friends). Just don't get the lubricated kind or your morning coffee will taste like your momma's behind.

■ Also

Get two X-ACTO blades of different sizes (just the blades: you can fit them onto a wooden handle if needed), and get butterfly sutures for the tough stuff.

That's Not a Knife...

"is this the Moskowitz bris?"

You need a knife. A good one, mind you—this is going to be your workhorse. If it has a toothpick in it, you might as well give it to your little sister. A folding knife is good if it has a good locked position, and a one-piece wooden handle for a no-slip grip that won't blister your hand.

Consider investing in a Parang, a Malayan multipurpose knife that can handle tough jobs faster than you can say "Ginsu." The knife, shown here, has three different cutting surfaces along its curved edge: One is a fine edge used for skinning: another does your chop and hack work: while the third is for your most delicate carving jobs. Note: Never hold the sheath on the blade side when drawing the knife; it's sharp enough to cut right through the sheath...as well as your fingers.

SHARPEN A KNIFE

Speaking of sharp...you can sharpen a knife on sandstone, quartz, or granite, as long as the stone is smooth and wet. Hold the handle in your right hand, and carefully press the blade against the sharpening surface with the fingertips of your left, making sure the sharp edge of the blade is facing away from you. Move the blade in a clockwise circular motion, maintaining steady pressure with your left hand. Also, make sure to keep the angle of the blade to the rock constant and to keep the rock wet. Reduce pressure for a finer edge. Now, go out and gut something.

1. Move in clockwise direction

2. Keep wet

3. Gut something!

Find Your Way Home
When you don't have breadcrumbs.

"We're almost home—your house is only 3 inches from here."

Getting lost is no kinda fun—just ask any German tourist in Florida. Whether you have a map or not, you need to know which direction you're headed at all times. Here are the easiest ways to figure out which way is up when you're caught without a compass.

STICK METHOD:
On a clear, sunny day, jam a three-foot stick or pole into the ground, so it sticks straight up. Mark the tip of the shadow, and wait 15 minutes. Then mark the tip of the shadow again. Connect the dots and you have a good east-west line. The first mark is east. You can take it from there.

We wouldn't be lost if you didn't insist on making breaded chicken.

WATCH METHOD:
If you're In the Northern Hemisphere, hold your watch flat, with the hour hand pointing at the sun. The midpoint between the hour hand and the 12 mark is North. If you're in the Southern Hemisphere, do the same thing, only point the 12 mark at the sun. If you have a digital watch, turn the face over, use it to pound a stick into the ground, and follow the method described above.

PLANTS:
In the Northern Hemisphere, plants have more flowers, moss, and other growth on the south side. In the Southern Hemisphere, it's the opposite. If trees have been chopped down, the rings on the sid pointing toward the equator will be more widely spaced. If you don't know which side of the equator you're on, you've got bigger problems than any book will solve. Lie down, wait for predators to descend, and let natural selection take its course.

STARS (SEE BELOW):
First find the Big Dipper (A). As you can see, it is above Orion (B), and to one side of Cassiopeia (C). The two lower stars of the Dipper, Dubhe (D), and Merak (E), point right to the North Star (F), midway between the Dipper and Cassiopeia.

Note: Don't confuse the Big Dipper with the Big Coke Spoon (G), which points directly toward Darryl Strawberry's house.

"Great. We found the steel plate in your head. Now what?"

Predict the Weather: A Crash Course

Now that you know which way to go, find out whether Mother Nature's gonna let you make it there. If you've got a TV out in the bush, then allow us to call you a pussy. If you're roughing it without Al Roker, use our guide:

TEMPERATURE

■ According to *The Old Farmer's Almanac,* the coats of woolly bear caterpillars are good predictors of future climate. Six or more reddish-brown segments mean colder weather's on the way.

■ When plants in the bindweed family (like the morning glory) stay open, the weather is likely to stay warm.

■ Summer fog usually predicts a hot day (unless you're in San Francisco, where it's friggin' foggy and cold on most days).

■ A good "old-saw" method for figuring out current temperature Fahrenheit: Count how many times a single cricket chirps in a 14-second period, and add 40.

RAIN

■ The smell of vegetation becomes more distinct before it rains, as plants open to receive the moisture.

■ Another old saw: *Red sky at night, shepherd's delight; red sky in the morning, shepherd's warning.* The thinking behind this limp verse is that a red sky at night signifies decreased air moisture, and thus no rain or snow is approaching. Conversely, the opposite is true in the morning.

■ Over the long term, if you notice a pattern of rain falling after there's been a wind from a particular direction, you can generally rely on the pattern to repeat itself.

STORMS

■ Cats and dogs often become restless before a thunderstorm. Wolves, extra sensitive to the low pressure, may actually howl in pain. If your girlfriend's antsy, it could mean a storm. Just kidding.

■ If you're having a cup of java out in the wilderness, look inside. High air pressure, which means fair weather, will push down on the center of the coffee's surface. You'll see bubbles clustered in the middle. But low pressure—bad stuff's coming—pushes the bubbles to the side.

■ Also watch smoke from your campfire. If it rises steadily, the weather is nice and fine. But if it swirls or starts to dip down, a storm is coming.

■ Better yet, if you have a working TV, tune it to Channel 2 and turn the brightness all the way down. Tornados create electrical interference on this channel, so if the picture suddenly brightens, it means one of those tall boys is within 20 miles. Of course if you have a working TV, that means you're probably not "really" out in the woods after all. It just means your medication has worn off and you're having those "camping with Judy Garland" fantasies again. Avoid Toto (he's venomous, remember?), and call the night nurse.

■ Approaching bad weather will tighten curly hairs (yes, even those) on humans and animals, shrink rope, and increase tension on guitar strings (listen for the pitch to rise). While it's foggy you'll get condensation but not rain—but if the wind rises and blows away the mist, you may expect a downpour. Look outside your home or office window. If you see any part of the city of Seattle, the weather will be shit that day.

"Honey? You done typing your manifesto?"

Setting Up Camp: The Top Tips

If you've made it this far, you're ready to build your temporary outdoor dream house. But before you pitch a tent, Grizzly Adams, check around. Avoid camping in places like these and you'll stay warm, dry, and safe:

■ **Exposed hilltops.** Move down a hill on the lee side to avoid the wind.

■ **Low in valleys or hollows.** These are moisture and frost accumulation zones.

■ **Spurs leading down to water.** These are common routes for animals to get to their water sources.

■ **Terraces on hills.** In areas that get a lot of rain, these get damp quick.

■ **Too close to lakes, ponds, or rivers.** This is bug heaven here. Plus, the sound of running water could drown out the sounds of something furry and mean coming your way.

■ **Near a single tree in a field.** These are to lightning what trailers are to tornadoes.

Note: When tenting up make sure you keep the opening away from the fire and upwind of it so you get the warmth but not the smoke.

STORM A BREWIN'?

Look up at the sky, rub your chin in a wily-old-sage manner, and make your weather prediction with *Maxim's* cloud chart.

Sodom... Gomorrah! He shoots, He scores!

STRATUS: They form a uniform layer below 1,650 feet and look like fog. Can produce a drizzle. When they cloak the morning sky, a fine day follows.

CIRROSTRATUS: High, thin lines of cloud in a uniform sheet through which you might see the sun or moon with a halo round it. Forecast: Rain or snow.

NIMBOSTRATUS: Very dark and low sheets of cloud. Expect rain or snow within four hours.

CUMULUS: Chunks of cauliflower. If small with lots of blue sky between, you've got fair weather. If large and gray, prepare for a celestial golden shower.

STRATOCUMULUS: Low rolling mass like a blanket of cobblestones. Not usually associated with rain.

ALTOCUMULUS: Slightly less defined and higher version of stratocumulus. Again, rain unlikely.

CIRRUS: Thin wispy clouds scattered about the sky. Known as mares tails, these are seen in fine weather.

ALTOSTRATUS: A gray uniform sheet. Can produce light rain.

CIRROCUMULUS: High cloud pattern that looks like ripples of sand. Known as "mackerel sky," it denotes good weather.

CUMULONIMBUS: Dark, fluffy, towering bastard with anvil-shaped top. Start gathering pairs of animals.

An easy rule of thumb when you've forgotten everything else about clouds is this: The higher the clouds, the finer the weather. Also when you're at sea, look for cumulus clouds. If they appear in an otherwise clear sky, it indicates land is below them.

No Tent? No Problem!

Either you didn't pack right or you're a Rambo wannabe on the run from the law.

You don't have a tent, and you want shelter in the woods. If you were a Boy Scout, you'd probably know how to build a teepee, a log cabin, or some shit out of a couple of tree trunks and twine. But why not try building something you can finish before next year? The following "homemade" tents can be made with a few supplies, and a minimum of fuss and bother.

TREE SHELTER. Find a large branch that hangs to the ground, or a small tree that has toppled over in the woods. Angle it upward, and tie the base to the trunk of a large tree at a point a few feet off the ground. The branch or small tree should slope downward, making a lean-to. Cut twigs and leaves out of the inside, clearing out a space for you to hole up with your peanut butter, assault rifle, and back issues of *Hustler*. Use the branches, as well as other twigs and leaves, to weave through the covering. Patch up spots to (hopefully) keep the rain out.

NATURAL HOLLOW. Find a ditch, depression, or other hollow in the ground. Dig the hole out deeper, making sure it is properly drained. You can use a fallen tree or a short wall of stones on the edge of the ditch as a "wall" that provides a windbreak. Lay a few strong branches across the hollow and windbreak, and follow with a log laid crossways for extra weight. Make sure the pitch of the roof is steep enough to allow rain to drain off.

SHELTER SHEET. Using a waterproof poncho, some twine, stones, and two trees, you can build a small pup tent in a snap. If your fabric is closely woven, but not waterproof, make sure the angle of the tent is steep enough to let the water roll off. Even better is to use two different layers of fabric, tied at different points on the trees. Note: Don't allow the inner and outer layers to touch each other or it will draw the water through.

CAVE. We know what you're thinking: "This is an easy way to get eaten, trapped, or covered in bat dung." And you're right. But many of these babies make for pretty good living. First pick a cave above a valley—these stay the driest. Build a fire outside to smoke most critters out. And when they come out, get out of their way, for God's sake! Check for loose rock inside the thing, to make sure there won't be any rock falls, then cover the ground with dry plants and pine branches to keep the place insulated. Also when you set up camp, build the fire in the back of the cave—smoke will climb the walls and exit the mouth, leaving you clean, dry, and un-asphyxiated.

"OK, weenies are done!"

Make Fire
Remember, only you can cause forest fires.

Starting a fire by rubbing two sticks together really is possible—even when one of them isn't a match. But try literally rubbing two sticks together and you'll end up with nothing but fir and ire. Here's the definitive nothin'-but-your-wits method.

THE SUPPLIES
■ **Platform:** a level surface on which the fire can be built, like a dry rock or a well-cleared patch of earth.
■ **Brace:** a flat piece of wood as thick as your wrist. Scrape out a notch in the center with a knife or a sharp rock.
■ **Bow:** a curved stick about two feet long, loosely "strung" with some sort of thong, such as your shoelace.
■ **Drill:** a.k.a. another stick, half an inch thick and maybe a foot long, sturdy and sharpened at each end.

■ **Socket:** a palm-size chunk of wood with a notch carved in the middle—like a computer mouse with the ball removed.
■ **Tinder:** very small items that will light from a single spark—a wad of extremely dry, dead grass; cedar or birch bark ground into dust; a finely shredded business card. Stack the material loosely so air can circulate within it.
■ **Kindling:** sticks thinner than pencils that you hope the small tinder flames will ignite. The best kindling can be found at the ends of dead, dry branches.
■ **Fuel:** more sticks, increasing in size—as thick as a thumb, then David Spade's neck, then your wrist—to keep that fire a-blazin'.

THE TECHNIQUE
■ Gather enough tinder, kindling, and fuel for three fires; this'll make it easier to go

Get Wood

When breaking up kindling to make a fire, here are two no-fail rules:

1 When using a flexible saw, cut so the tree or branch opens up rather than closes. If you don't the saw will jam up.

2 To break a long branch that's too thick for you to break on your own, lodge it in the crotch of a tree's branches and use the crotch like a lever; the dead wood will snap before the living fulcrum when enough pressure is applied.

Build a Potty
Do you shit in the woods?

For a deep latrine, dig a hole about four feet deep by one and a half feet wide. Surround the sides with rocks and earth to make a nice seat, then cover with logs laid side by side, leaving a hole to do your business. You can seal the cracks between the logs by covering them with wood ash.

This will also keep the flies away. Make a lid out of a large flat leaf held down with rocks. However, don't use disinfectant—that will kill the "useful" bacteria that breaks down your shit, and will make it smell worse. Instead cover your feces with earth and add more water to promote the growth of the bacteria. Feces will be done decomposing when toothpick a inserted in the center comes out clean.

back a step if a fledgling fire falters. Collect the tinder last, as it tends to absorb moisture from the air.

■ Set the brace on the platform. Loop the string of your bow once or twice around the drill (it should be fairly tight). Stand one end of the drill in the notch in the brace, and cap the other end with the socket. Pressing down firmly on the socket with one hand, saw the bow back and forth with the other. The loop in the bowstring will cause the drill to, well, drill into the brace much faster than if you turned it manually. As you saw away, a splintery powder will form in the notch and should eventually begin to smoke.

■ When there's a lot of smoke, start fanning the mess with your hand until tiny coals appear beneath the powder; place the tinder gently on the coals and blow on it a bit until it ignites.

■ Slowly add kindling in a tepee formation until you've got a roaring mini-fire going, then gradually add larger pieces of fuel. Get on your knees and thank *Maxim* for saving your sorry ass, then roast and eat the Sherpa "guide" who got you into this mess in the first place.

COME 'N' GIT IT!

Claim your spot atop the food chain with hunting-and-gathering pointers guaranteed to help you avert starvation.

Holy Mackerel
How to snag the biggest, baddest fish with practically nothing.

First, some basic tips to help you along:

■ If it's hot and the water level is low, drop your line in the shade and in any deep pools. This is where the fish go to, you know, chill out.

■ If it's cold look for the opposite: shallow, sunlit places in the water.

"I work for scale"

■ When a river is in flood, fish go where the water is relatively still: a small tributary or a pool.

■ Fish like to take shelter under banks, below rocks, and under submerged logs.

■ Leave lines out overnight, and check them just before dawn. Some fish feed at night during a full moon—just like little scaly werewolves.

■ If a storm's brewing, get your fishing done pronto. Fishing is really bad after a heavy rain.

■ If you see lots of ring ripples in the

"Ugh! What's this? People?"

water, that means the fish are around, feeding on surface flies. Go get 'em. And if you see a school of small fish darting away, cast your line for a large predator fish that is looking for a snack.

■ Keep low to the ground when coming to the water's edge. The water's surface bends light like the mirror in a periscope, enabling the little critters to get a look over the bank and see your big dumb ass trying to catch them.

Catch a Fish Without a Pole

Want to look really cool?
Try these no-line, no-net methods.

"Need a loan? How 'bout a game of pool? Cards?"

BOTTLE TRAP: Take a plastic bottle—a two-liter soda bottle, for instance—cut the top off near the neck, and invert it. Push it into the water far enough so it naturally stays in place. This works just like a lobster trap—small fish swim in but can find their way out. And you've got yourself some sardines.

FISH TICKLING: An old poacher's trick. Scale the edges of a shallow stream where the banks cut in slightly. Lower your hands gently into the water, waiting for them to adjust to the temperature. Keeping your hands as close as you can to the bottom, slide them under the bank. Wiggle your fingers very slightly as you do this, so they will seem like grasses and other debris, floating gently with the water. Eventually you may touch the belly of a fish. Gently move your hand toward the bugger's gills (they usually swim upstream as they feed), and then grab him quickly and yank him out.

ATTRACTING FISH: You can use a mirror or other shiny material to flash light into the water, which will often attract fish. Make them come to you, or your net or trap. At night a torch or flashlight can do the same thing.

FISH DRUGS: Some plants can be mixed into a stream to drug or kill the fish without making the meat poisonous. This doesn't mean you can eat these plants yourself, nimrod. Also don't eat fish that were dead when you arrived, as that could mean disease or pollution. Here are two such plants that are found in North America:

■ Goat's rue: Growing on open ground, it is slightly hairy, with many narrow leaflets and long, flat seed pods. The roots and stems are very poisonous. Crush and add them to the water.

■ Soap plant: This grows in dry country in the western states. It has narrow leaves and white starlike flowers. Crush the root and throw into a pool of water.

Be the Lord of the Flies
Eat more insects than a gap-mouthed biker.

Lost without food anywhere? Try bugs! These guys are loaded with fat, protein, and carbs, and give you more nutrition per pound than vegetables.

The first rule is to look for them where they're going to be inactive. In the heat of the day, bugs will hide in the nooks and crannies of trees, underneath bark, and in some pods of plants. Look for them to come out to collect moisture when it rains. Avoid bugs that are brightly colored or feeding on carrion or dung. These can be poisonous or carry infection. Also don't eat grubs found on the undersides of leaves; they often secrete poisonous fluids, and they smell terrible.

Here are some preparation tips:

■ **Locusts, Crickets, and Grasshoppers.** Swat them individually, then remove wings, antennae, and leg spurs, which can irritate your digestive tract. You can eat them raw, but roasting them—placing them on a hot stone or in the embers of a fire—removes parasites and makes them taste kind of neat.

■ **Termites.** You can catch them a few at a time by finding a large nest and lowering a stick slowly down into it. The bigger termites will lock their jaws right onto the stick (and onto you if you're not careful). Termites can be boiled, fried, or roasted but are most nutritious when eaten raw.

Termites can also be used as mosquito repellent. Just break off a chunk of their dirt nest and put it in the coals of your fire. It will produce a fragrant smoke that the skeeters abhor.

■ **Bees and Wasps.** Create a smoky torch from a bundle of dried grass, and hold it near the entrance of the hive so the hive fills with smoke. Then seal off the entrance with clumps of mud, and the smoke will kill the bees. Dinnertime! Remove the stingers before you eat. Boiling or roasting bees will improve the flavor, and remember, don't waste the honey either.

■ **Slugs and Snails.** Starve them or dry them out for a few days so they will excrete all the toxins and waste in their system. Then put them into a saltwater solution to clear out their guts. Finally boil for about 10 minutes, adding herbs or garlic for flavor. Voilà! Escargots! Note: Avoid sea snails, especially in tropical waters. They are poisonous. The toxoglossa, for example, has a venomous stinger that will fuck you up faster than Roy Jones, Jr.

■ **Worms.** These babies are loaded with protein and amino acids. Squeeze them between your fingers to clear the muck out of them before eating. Or leave on a hot stone to dry out, and then grind into powder—good if you need them to keep.

Find Water Anywhere
Walk east till yer' hat floats.

"Wonderful! I must have the recipe."

Alcoholics don't have drinking problems—guys lost in the desert have drinking problems. You can survive without sleep for about a week, without food for around a month, and without sex for three to five years. Without water, though, you'll be dead in just a few days. Here's how to quench that thirst regardless of where you are.

IN THE MOUNTAINS:

As *How to Stay Alive in the Woods* (Simon & Schuster, 1998) points out, If you can remember that water flows downhill (duh!), you'll be OK. Look for where running water has carved grooves in the earth, and follow them downhill; you'll eventually hit water.

IN THE DESERT:

Look for a dry riverbed or a low point in a canyon, and start digging wherever you see darker, moist soil or a depression in the ground. If you're lucky water will seep into the hole, and all you'll have to do is sit back and wait. If this doesn't work and you happen to have a large sheet of clear plastic,

follow the directions in *The Backpacker's Field Manual* (Three Rivers Press, 1998) for building a solar still. Dig a hole, place a bucket in its center, and cover the hole with the plastic, weighting its edges with rocks to make a tight seal. Place a small rock on top of the plastic, directly over the bucket, forcing the plastic to sag slightly. Over the course of the day, sunlight will cause water in the soil to evaporate; it'll condense on the plastic and drip into the bucket.

ON THE BEACH:

Not the place you'd expect to find fresh water, huh? Don't worry—there's still hope. Head to just below the high-tide line, and dig a hole in the sand. When water starts to seep in, stop digging and let the bottom of the hole fill up. Since fresh water is lighter than salt water, it lies above it, and you can drink from your little basin.

AT SEA:

As the Ancient Mariner told us in high school, the ocean is the great thirst para-

dox: "Water, water, everywhere/Nor any drop to drink." Try drinking the salt water and you will become violently ill. Instead try to catch a fish. A huge percentage of a fish's body is fresh water—just cut into bite-size pieces and chew 'em like gum, then use the chewed-up bits to attract seabirds. Drinking the blood of one of these, though unspeakably gross, can keep you alive until the rescue boat comes.

NOTE:

It's important that whatever water you drink is clean: The smallest drop of contaminated water can leave you too sick to move. Avoid water that has not promoted the growth of plants around it or that has bloated, bug-eyed corpses floating in it—this stuff could kill you. Try to purify any groundwater with iodine (five to 10 drops per quart volume), or by boiling it for at least five minutes. If purification is impossible and you're close to dehydration, at least filter it through fabric before drinking.

"Hi. I'm Sandy."

Doctor in the Wild

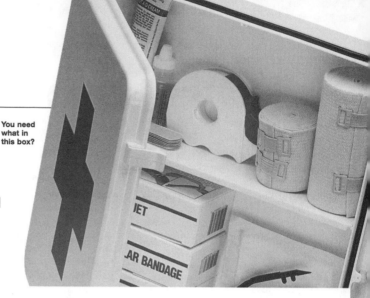

You need what in this box?

When you're out there in the shit, you're bound to break your foot off in a rabbit hole, scrape up a knee, or get clawed by a grizzly. Patching yourself up can be as easy as letting the buzzards pick at your putrid, rotting corpse.

BITES AND STINGS

When these little fuckers feast on your flesh, ward off trauma with ticks of the trade.

■ Bees:

Whether it's a wasp, hornet, or bee, its sting is usually benign. "Most people only have a local reaction to a sting," says Steve Sarles, Yellowstone National Park's emergency medical services coordinator. "Treat a bee sting as you would a minor wound—clean it." But if you're allergic, a bee sting can bring on anaphylactic shock: swelling and itching all over the body, hives, constricting of the throat, and possibly death. "More people in the U.S. die from bee stings than from snakebites," Sarles says. Having difficulty breathing? Seek help at the nearest hospital or ranger station. If you're allergic, you should carry an EpiPen ($54 at a drugstore): a syringe of epinephrine (similar to adrenaline), which counteracts anaphylactic shock. Don't get cocky if you've survived past bee stings—you may be allergic to, say, hornets or wasps.

■ Spiders:

Most aren't strong enough to break your skin, swears Jude McNally, managing director of the Arizona Poison and Drug Information Center. If you are bitten, clean the wound and elevate it. Beware two nasty arachnids: the black widow and brown recluse. With a recluse bite, expect localized pain within a few hours; the spot may blister or form a bull's-eye lesion. A widow bite will hurt like hell initially, then may trigger all-over cramping. "Surprisingly," McNally adds, "you can eat a black widow and not get sick, because our stomach acids destroy the toxins." (Note to idiots: Kill it first.) The good news: With either you'll get mighty sick, but you probably won't die unless you're a feeb.

■ Ticks:

To avoid tick bites, wear pants tucked into boots, according to John J. Hanley, acting director of the Park Service's Office of Public Health. If one's already feasting? Hanley advises using tweezers to gently pull it out. Be careful to get the entire tick; the head can snap off, and remain under the skin and cause infection. Most of the ticks you'll see are dog ticks, which don't carry Lyme disease. Even if you are nailed by the much smaller deer tick (which can transmit Bambi's revenge), it takes 48 hours for the disease to incubate. Still, go see a doc. If you missed the crawling-and-burrowing stage but spot a bull's-eye rash, call in the medics: Either you've got Lyme disease or you're a dartboard.

BLISTERS

To prevent your flesh from rubbing off, break new boots in by soaking them in water and then rubbing with oils to make them supple. Blisters are often caused when your socks fall down after getting wet, so you should change them immediately after wading through a stream or pond. To treat blisters sterilize a needle and wash the area around them. Puncture the blister at one edge and gently press out the fluid. Tape or bandage into place.

OBJECTS IN THE EYE

Examine the eyeball and lower lid, pulling it down to check inside while the patient looks up. If there's nothing there and the problem is under the upper lid, you may be able to pull the upper lid down gently over lower lashes and let them brush it out. If the object is still there, remove with a wet corner of cloth, clean watercolor brush, or feather.

EARACHE

If this is not due to an infection, it is most likely the byproduct of wax buildup. Simply pour a few drops of edible oil into the ear to break up the wax, and plug with cotton wool.

SPRAIN

Caused by wrenching or tearing tissues connected with the joint. Bathe the affected area with cold water to reduce swelling. Wrap with bandages—not too tightly—then elevate the relevant limb and rest completely. If you sprain your leg and have to keep walking, keep your boot on—it will act as a splint by helping to immobile the joint. Also if you take the boot off, the swelling may make it impossible to get it back on again.

HEAT CRAMPS/HEAT EXHAUSTION

Muscle cramps are the first warning—they're due to depleted body salt brought on by excessive sweating and can occur without direct exposure to the sun. Other symptoms are shallow breathing, vomiting, and dizziness. In more serious cases, the patient's face can become pale and his skin cold—accompanied by a weak pulse. The patient might become delirious and even pass out. Treat by moving patient into the shade to rest and giving him water with a little bit of salt—only a pinch per pint.

HEATSTROKE

This is the most serious result of overexposure to the sun—and to Tom Arnold's mouth. The patient develops a temperature that shoots through the roof, his face becomes flushed, and his skin becomes dry and feverish even though he'll have stopped sweating. The pulse becomes fast and strong, and the patient gets a wicked headache and might either start throwing up or pass out. Lay patient in the shade with head and shoulders slightly raised. Take off outer clothing and wet underwear with tepid (not cold) water. When patient returns to consciousness , give him a drink. When his temperature returns to normal, replace his clothing and keep him warm to prevent a chill.

HYPOTHERMIA

Caused by heat drain on the body. Symptoms include irrational behavior (i.e., sudden bursts of energy followed by lethargy), slow responses, inattentiveness, loss of coordination, headaches, blurred vision, and abdominal pains. Prevent further heat loss, and replace wet clothing with dry. Do not strip completely—replace clothing one piece at a time. Insulate patient, apply heat, and give warm fluids and sugary foods.

WHAT NOT TO DO

Never rub snow on frostbite, put butter on a burn, or cut out or suck the poison from a snakebite. For frostbite, put extremities in cold water and gradually add hot water. Clean and carefully bandage burns. And for snakebite victims, send for help and keep these people as still as possible. Do any of this other shit and you'll have a frozen, buttered, or poisoned dead guy on your hands.

SET A BROKEN LEG

Your buddy's fallen before, but usually in a bar. Now he's sprawled in the wilderness, and his leg is more twisted than the Clintons' marriage. Without treatment his name could become Peg Leg or The Deceased. Fortunately, you know how to set things straight.

ASSESS. Unless you've packed the Palm VII x-ray peripheral, you'll have to play detective. A hairline fracture will cause moderate pain and swelling. If the bone is fractured completely, he'll have serious swelling and pain, and even misalignment. In an extreme case—compound fracture—the bone will punch its way through the skin. EMT Steve Raiten was hiking in New Jersey's Pine Barrens and saw his buddy "lying on the ground with a pool of blood on his jeans. Then I noticed his thigh was at an angle, like a boomerang."

PULL TRACTION. The real danger is not to the bone (duh—it's broken); it's the damage that bone fragments can inflict on soft tissue. You'll have to "pull traction"— physically move the leg back to its normal alignment. This was-n't easy for Steve: "Nerves, blood vessels, muscles—everything was scrambled in there. So I grabbed his ankle with one hand and his foot with the other, pulled toward me, and twisted, feeling the fragmented ends of the split femur grind against each other. At this point he shrieked like a banshee. But hey, a good set will relieve that pain quickly."

STABILIZE. You've handled the immediate problem; now prepare the leg for splinting. A broken leg will wobble like a Weeble, so it has to be continually supported until the splint is firmly in place. Stack packs or rocks on both sides of the leg while you gather material to make the splint.

SPLINT. A good splint has to hold the leg straight and immobilize joints around the break. Lay branches or your pack frame along the leg and wrap strips of cloth (bandages, belts, T-shirts, etc.) around the leg, and the supports, tying snugly above and below each joint. Assure your friend that bears usually won't eat an immobilized hiker, and run off to get help.

STAYIN' ALIVE

Richard Hatch, John Rambo, and Roy Scheider ain't shit. Here's how to really survive—when you don't have a camera crew lookin' out for your sorry ass.

Survive a Flood

If you're too dumb to move to higher ground, here's how to stay dry when the mighty Mississippi's really pissed off.

■ If you are in a solid building, stay where you are. Turn off gas and electricity, and prepare emergency food supplies. Keep all water containers sealed to prevent contamination. Move to higher floors, and even the roof, as it becomes necessary. If you must go to the roof, secure everyone to a chimney or other solid structure. Be prepared to fashion a raft out of furniture, but unless the water begins to actually wash the building away, or rise above it, stay where you are.

■ If you must drive or run to a safer location, do not attempt to cross any pools unless you are certain the water is no higher than the center of a car's wheels or your knees.

■ Even a few inches of floodwater can do damage—lay sandbags or plastic shopping bags filled with dirt along the bottoms of doorways and windows to keep the *agua* at bay. Get it? At bay! Ha, ha, ha! Oh, sorry about that. We know this is a bad time.

■ If you're trapped in a just-flooded area, a major risk is disease from the filth that has been churned up by Old Man River. Burn all animal corpses, and boil all your drinking water.

Sleep Out in a Snowstorm

You're stranded on the tundra, night's approaching, and temperatures are dropping faster than Cincinnati Bengals ticket sales. Here's how to survive a sub-zero night's sleep with little more than your wits and a wool blanket.

Step 1: Build a fire
Dig a trench in the earth the length of your torso (hip to shoulder), making it a foot wide and eight inches deep. Line the bottom with rocks, toss in some brush, and start a fire. Keep it ablaze for two hours, giving yourself ample time to roast some polar-bear shish kabobs and producing enough coals to make a toasty bed.

Step 2: Cover it up
Spread the coals evenly throughout the trench, and then cover them with four inches of soil. "If the hole has been dug correctly, you'll feel the heat through the ground in about an hour or so," says Dr. Ron Hood, founder of Hood's Woods Survival Education Center. If you follow his Two-Four-Eight Rule—a two-hour burn for the coals, four inches of dirt on top, an eight-inch-deep trench— you'll keep your keister warm without getting it scorched.

Step 3: Make your bed, then lie in it
That wool blanket might smell like a dog's ass, but it'll shed water and retain heat even if it gets damp, so suck it up and deal. Lay the blanket flat over the

Step 4: Wrap up tight
Lying diagonally with your head and feet at opposite corners, fold the bottom over your feet and pull the sides around, tucking in all corners, until you resemble a human burrito. Heat from the coals will rise through the dirt and get trapped in the blanket. Don't worry if a light snow begins to fall—that frosty layer will help you retain even more warmth. Finally, pull the top corner over your head and turn up your body's furnace; try dreaming that you're rolling around on the beaches of *Gilligan's Island* with Mary Ann. That way if you don't make it, at least you'll die with a smile on your face.

Survive an Avalanche

Because you want to live to have ski bunnies sign your various casts.

"There are no sure techniques for staying out of avalanches," says K2/Oakley ski star Seth Morrison, who gets swept away by one in the ski flick *Global Storming*. "Anything can happen." But what you can't avoid you can at least react to:

GRAB ON. If you're near a tree when the slope rips, grab the trunk and hold on. With luck the slide will soon wash over, giving you a chance to descend safely in its wake.

RUN. Chances are you won't have much luck outrunning a slide, but you may be able to surf it without being killed. "Run and get yourself into a safe zone," says Morrison. Look for a ridge or higher ground, though anywhere the snow isn't flowing heavily will serve your purposes nicely.

SWIM. "It's like being in the white water of surf," says filmmaker Todd Jones, who got flushed off a 40-foot cliff during the making of *The Continuum*. "I just leaned back and started treading water." Your gear is an anchor; ditch it if you can.

DIG. Though slides tend to freeze solid shortly after they stop moving, it's not unheard of for buried victims to dig themselves out. Before the slide stops, get your arms in front of your face so you can clear an air pocket. Once settled try drooling. If your spit goes down your chin, start digging above your head for the sky. If it goes up your nose, you're upside down and have a bit more of a problem.

MAKE YOURSELF EASY TO FIND. Get a probe pole or a digital avalanche transceiver like the Tracker DTS, which is easier to master and locate than standard beacons. Of course all this is useless unless your assistant has the same gear and knows how to use it. Maybe you should just stay in the bar with the ski bunnies and forget about trouncing around on the mountain.

Survive a Shark Attack
Ba-DUM...Ba-DUM...Bum...bum...bum...bum...

If you see two fins moving in perfect time, relax. It's probably the wing tips of a large ray, which often look like a pair of sharks doing a synchronized swim routine. If you start to hear two-note cello music, keep in mind the following:

■ **Don't make weak, fluttery movements.** If you see a shark near-by, head for the shore using strong fluid strokes that cause a minimal amount of splashing. Avoid schools of fish.

■ **Clump together.** A group of clothed individuals bunched together is scarier to a shark than a lone human.

■ **Don't pee, or anything else.** It's not just blood that attracts sharks; it's any bodily waste. If you must pee do it in short spurts and allow time for it to dissipate. If you throw up—this is really horrifying, but it may be your only hope —hold it in your mouth, and then swallow your vomit or throw it as far away as possible.

■ **If the shark tries to attack you, evade and fight.** Sharks cannot stop or turn quickly. A good swimmer can evade a single large shark by rapidly changing direction in the water. Also a blow to the nose, or the jab of a sharp stick, will sometimes make a shark flee.

■ **Stay calm** If you are bitten, try not to panic. The vast majority of shark attacks are hit-and-run incidents in which sharks mistake people for something they would normally eat, like a baby seal. If the shark has let you go, it probably won't come back, so head to safety pronto. If it has its teeth in you, grab its gill openings or poke it in the eye. Hopefully you can cause it enough discomfort so it lets you go. Note: Don't play possum; sharks are more afraid of a live human than a dead one.

Survive a Lightning Strike
Don't get fried outside.

■ Get away from any high point (duh!). But if you can't get low in time, try to get some dry material to sit on. A dry coil of climbing rope makes good insulation. Bend your head down, hug your knees to your chest, keep your feet off the ground, and draw in all extremities. Do not sit on anything wet.

■ If you have nothing that can insulate you, get on the ground as flat as you can.

■ If you feel a sudden tingling in your skin and a sensation of your hair standing on end, you have maybe a second to get down like P. Funk. Drop to your hands and knees first, and then quickly lie down. That way if the lightning hits you mid-fall, there's a chance that it will travel down through your arms to the ground and miss clench-

ing your heart and lungs like a pair of balloon animals.

■ A deep cave is a great place to be. But beware—stay at least 10 feet inside the cave, with four feet of space on either side of you. At the cave's mouth, or under overhanging rocks, lightning can sometimes spark into the gap.

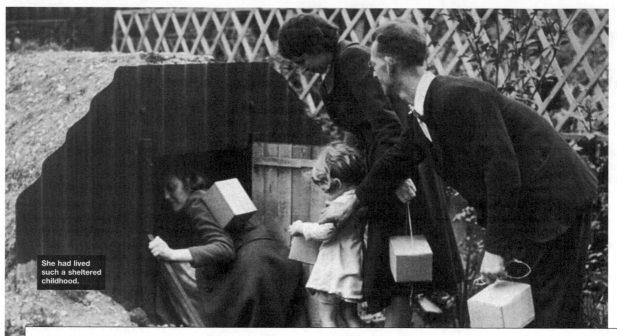

She had lived such a sheltered childhood.

Survive a Nuclear Attack

When the bombs drop apparently so should your pants. Keep the following in mind, and avoid becoming a member of the Fantastic Five.

■ The radioactivity you'll be exposed to in the first few hours following the flash can exceed the zap you'll get during the rest of the week. And the radioactivity you'll be exposed to in that week will exceed that of the rest of your lifetime. Get shelter immediately and your chances of living go way up.

■ When building or seeking a shelter, here's what needs to come between you and the bomb in order to shield you from 50 percent of the rads: 0.7 feet of iron and steel; 2 feet of brick; 2.2 feet of concrete; 3.3 feet of soil; 6.6 feet of ice; 8.8 feet of wood; 20.3 feet of snow.

■ Stay inside for 48 hours at the very minimum.

■ If caught out in the open, get to a shelter as fast as possible, take your clothes off, and bury them under a foot of soil at one end of the bottom of the shelter. This will minimize your contamination from heavier "particle" radiation. Scrape earth from the shelter bottom and rub it over the exposed parts of your body. Brush it off and throw the soil outside. Wipe skin with a clean cloth if possible—soap and water is best, but you may not have that luxury. Do not reuse discarded garments.

■ Boil and filter all water before drinking, except what you've taken with you. These sources of water are listed in order of how great a contamination hazard they are, from least to greatest:

1. Underground wells and springs.
2. Water in underground pipes/containers.
3. Snow taken from deep below the earth's surface.
4. Fast-flowing rivers.
5. Lakes, pools, ponds, or any other stagnant surface water (avoid this at all costs).

■ The safest canned foods to eat are soups, vegetables, and fruits.

■ Cured and processed meats are more apt to be contaminated with radiation than are fresh meats.

■ If you are foraging, eat root vegetables, and wash and peel them well before cooking.

■ If you are hunting for food, avoid birds and fish, although eggs are relatively safe to eat. Try to kill animals that live underground, like rabbits or moles. Wear plastic gloves when you skin and prepare them, to reduce contamination. Also do not eat any of the organs, or meat that is within one-eighth inch of the bone. This is where radiation is highest. Muscle and fat are the safest.

■ If you meet a hairy, heavily armed man with a cool car and an eerily intelligent shepherd dog, follow him. He is the chosen one, and he will lead you to a village where you can have anything you want. It's run by Tina Turner, and they even make electrical power out of pig shit! Welcome to the brave new world.

MAN IN THE BOAT

How to Build a Canoe

You and the boys planning a nice quiet river trip in hillbilly country? Then why not build your very own canoe? Here's how, according to Henri Vaillancourt, a New Hampshire native who has been turning trees into canoes for 35 years. "Building a canoe is not something that's done in an afternoon," warns Vaillancourt. "It's a demanding technological process that lends itself to a lot of artistry."

"This goes great with my puffy shirt."

Vaillancourt's 400-hour masterpieces are showcased in museums and will run you $8,000 on the street (er, river). Here's his cheap-ass, do-it-yourself-over-a-long-weekend 16-foot version:

STEP 1:
Hack down a cedar and split out two 16' planks roughly 11/2" wide, for gunwales (these run the length of the canoe). Use a curved knife to shave them to a slim 11/6" x 3/8", then bind the ends together, first bending them slightly. "Spruce root is used in traditional binding," says Vaillancourt.

STEP 2:
Next murder a maple or other hardwood, and split out five crossbars (they spread the gunwales and maintain the width of the canoe). "The middle crossbar should be 3' across," says Vaillancourt. "Then use matching pairs, one on each end, decreasing in size to the ends of the canoe. There's no exact measurement—it's all done by eye." Cut slots in the gunwales to fit the crossbars into.

STEP 3:
Bark is the most important element: If it's weak you'll sink. Find a straight birch tree about 18' tall that's free of knots and has strong bark about 1/8" thick. "Take a sample piece and bend it to see that it doesn't separate into layers," explains Vaillancourt. "It should feel like linoleum or leather—cut smooth." Slice the tree from end to end and gently remove the skin, trying very hard not to think about Jeffrey Dahmer.

STEP 4:
Lay the frame atop the bark. Trim the bark around it, leaving 1' extra. Cut indentations to within 1" of the gunwales. Fold flaps up; secure with stakes. Punch holes along the edge of each flap. Raise the frame parallel to the ground. Lash the bark to the gunwales with cane; sew the flaps together. "What's left should look something like a

bag," Vaillancourt says. Slather the inside with waterproofing rosin.

STEP 5:
You'll need 40 planks (8' x 2" x 1/8")—20 running from each end of the canoe, meeting at the middle—and 23 matching pairs of ribs (4' long for the middle, then decreasing in size to the ends of the canoe). Shave the ribs to 21/2" x 1/2", then soak them in boiling water for a few minutes so they're pliable, and bend into big C's. Work the skinny bastards in with a mallet (pretend you're styling Kate Moss for a photo shoot).

STEP 6:
Make an extra plank (same width and height as in step 5), cut two pieces to fit so they bend, and wedge vertically inside the bow and stern. Sew to the bark with cane; they firm up the structure and keep it running straight. Flip the canoe, seal the entire outside with rosin, and presto! You're up a creek. (Alternatively, scrounge $8,000 and buy a canoe from Vaillancourt at www.birchbarkcanoe.net.)

"Hey! That's my parking space."

Jeffrey Dahmer 101

Mm-m-m...tastes like chicken.

Remember *Alive!* the true story of the Uruguayan rugby team whose plane crashed in the Andes and who had to cannibalize their dead to survive? OK, so devouring human flesh isn't exactly mouthwatering, but if you ever found yourself forced to choose between starvation and cannibalism, wouldn't you want to know how to, uh, carve the animal? For just such situations, we've provided the following handy piece-by-piece guide on which parts of the human body are edible and which you're better off slipping to Rover, according to the book *Contingency Cannibalism: Superhardcore Survivalism's Dirty Little Secret* by Shiguro Takada (Paladin Press, $12). Just keep in mind that this guide is intended for extreme emergency survival situations only and not for fledgling psychopaths, Satan worshippers, or corrupt fast food managers. *Bon appétit!*

HANDS AND FEET Our source advocates passing on these too, unless you truly need to use every last scrap of meat. If you do, start with the palms, which apparently were considered goodies to the Aztecs. Also the feet can be boiled for soup stock (lucky diners may even get some corn in their portion).

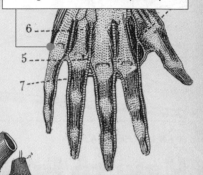

BLOOD Only if you've got fangs and speak Transylvanian, or your goal is to surpass your USDA-recommended daily allowance of germs.

ARMS AND LEGS Go ahead and munch away. Dark meat, anyone?

BRAIN Along with the spinal column, the brain is the tidbit most likely to give you a mad-cow-type illness. Finding a place to discard it should be a no-brainer, though.

HEART Though old-school warriors sometimes would feast on an enemy's pumper to magically acquire its possessor's strength, the disease potential makes this one a no-no nowadays (eat your heart out, Hannibal Lecter).

BELLY, chest, ribs, upper back/lower neck These are all kosher. Well, edible might be a better word to use.

ENTRAILS (liver, kidneys, intestines, stomach, etc.) High disease potential. Dispose of these, or use to string your tennis racket.

HEAD No, Reginald, we do not eat the head. The head is yucky, Reginald. Reginald! Put Grampa's head down at once!

BUTTOCKS By all means dig in. Tip: Referring to the upper thigh as "ham" will help your dinner guests get over the psychological barrier of eating someone's ass.

TESTICLES Delicacy or not, we're drawing the line here.

Preparation and Other Tips

■ Your NO GUTS, NO GLORY T-shirt may be neat, but the goal here is survival, and eating guts just increases the chances you'll croak from disease instead of starvation. So before you divvy up the body, slit the "donor's" stomach open vertically, remove the organs and bury them, rinse out the body cavity, and allow excess fluid to drain. Make sure to wipe your hands with a moist towelette.

■ Packaging up and labeling the pieces will ensure that no one ends up eating the flesh and blood of their flesh and blood.

■ If you're stranded in an icy climate, freeze your meat. If not, look for a cool, dry place to store it. If you're a fly wait for it to rot in the sun and lay some eggs in it.

■ If rescued get a good PR guy and hit the talk-show circuit.

"Okay, Frank, we got the demo tape. We'll call you."

"No checked bags. Just this carry-on."

The World's Nastiest Booby Traps

More dangerous than women, the insidious snares on these pages serve as outstanding examples of human ingenuity and depravity. From now on watch your step.

One moment you're walking along the sidewalk, thinking good thoughts, humming that new Clannad song and wondering what new sandwich wrap you're going to have for lunch. The next you're trying to stuff your intestines back into your abdominal cavity. You, my friend, have been booby-trapped.

Don't be so disappointed: This happens all the time. Since the first caveman learned to dig a pit and cover it with leaves, booby traps have lent a sense of danger and unwelcome surprise to our lives. With them we've maimed, killed, and mangled each other with spectacularly bloody and satisfying results. And just think what they do for the environment! In the spirit of that fine tradition, we bring you the Booby Trap Hall of Fame, a selection of the most sinister snares ever devised. But be careful when turning the pages. This whole thing is rigged.

JIVARO CATAPULT
■ **Goal:** Turn you into a human pincushion.
"Fancy invading Ecuador?" asked a Spanish nobleman in the 16th century. "Yeah," replied another, "it'll be a slam dunk. Just a bunch of natives down there, the Jivaros." *Thwaaaaannnnnngggggggg!*

■ Here's what the Jivaros were really good at: They'd take a paddle-shaped piece of wood, embed spikes in it, and horizontally attach it to a springy vine that stretched between the ground and an overhead tree limb.
■ The paddle was then pushed 'round and 'round the vine. When the vine couldn't be wound any tighter, the paddle was held in place with a delicate trigger, connected to a trip line.
■ The first clumsy Spaniard to stumble into the trap found out why everyone else in South America gave the Jivaros a wide berth. There's nothing like a spike-studded paddle to ventilate your chest. It was this special trap that helped turn the Jivaros into such fine interior designers. They decorated the walls of their jungle homes with other people's shrunken heads—particularly invaders'.

THE MACE
■ **Goal:** Smash you into a bloody pulp. Grunts went flying like skittles when the Viet Cong used this medieval-looking killer. The trip wire released a rock covered with sharpened stakes that swung like a giant pendulum, mashing anything in it's path. Don't try it on a grizzly bear, though. Alec Baldwin and Anthony Hopkins gave it a go in *The Edge,* and it just annoyed the man-eating bruin pursuing them. Too bad it didn't take out Baldwin.
■ A trap based on the same pendulum principle neatly sliced a couple of inches off Tim McManus' cheek in 1995. McManus, the manager of a self-storage building in California, opened the door to a unit that a renter hadn't paid for, and tripped a hatchet that swung down from the ceiling and gave him a closer shave than he ever got from his barber.

SHEEPEATERS' ROCKFALL
■ **Goal:** Human pancakes, anyone? Afghan rebels may have been short on guns when the Commie Russians invaded, but they had plenty of great big rocks. Big rocks hurt.
■ The Afghans turned rockfall traps into an art form. First they'd make a platform balanced on sticks about 200 yards above a trail on a mountain slope. The platform would then be loaded with more than 10,000 pounds of boulders. Wires running from the sticks ran all the way down the slope to a trigger mechanism designed to yank the sticks from under the platform when Russian vehicles rolled over it.
■ Anyone in an area 70 yards wide below the trap became Commie custard—which tasted, oddly enough, like borscht.

Boobs Trapped!

These guys flunked the first lesson in Booby Traps 101: Don't forget where you put the trap.

■ Three eastern Kentucky marijuana growers, eager to protect their crop from rivals, booby-trapped their isolated field with explosives in 1994. Sadly, they stumbled into their own trap and unwittingly set off the explosives. All that remained was a trio of three-foot craters.

■ A 60-year-old Polish man was so scared of burglars that he planted 28 lethal booby traps throughout his house in Warsaw. His last words were likely to have been a Polish version of "Oh shit" as he absentmindedly opened the doors

to his garage—which was guarded by two booby-trapped guns.

■ After gunman Anthony Allen shot a store clerk in the head in December 1997, he holed up in a motel in Anaheim, California, with a stash of homemade grenades, an assault rifle, and body armor. But he gave himself away—and then some—when cops heard an explosion. They discovered that Allen had blown himself to bits with one of his hand grenades while trying to rig a booby trap.

buddies got to see what he had for breakfast—when he spilled his guts in the mud.

CARTRIDGE TRAP

Goal: High-velocity ventilation of the foot.

■ The Viet Cong would take a bullet and place it on top of a nail or firing pin inside a bamboo sleeve. Then they'd bury it all in the ground, leaving just the tip of the round exposed.

■ Any grunt who trod on the round forced the cartridge down onto the pin and literally shot himself in the foot. According to experts, this really hurts.

PUNJI TRAP

Goal: Punch a hole through your foot with a shit-smeared spike.

■ Despite appearing in just about every Vietnam War movie ever made, it was Napoleon of France who first put the punji trap to widespread use. At its simplest it's a piece of wood with nails punched through it that's placed on a trail, sharp end up. More sophisticated versions were built into little pits in the ground or on pivots so they closed in on the ankle and not the sole of the foot. Shit-smeared spikes through the foot aren't particularly welcome in the tropics, where infection generally means that your foot will rot and drop off unless you get medical help fast.

■ Vietnam vets report one good thing about the treatment: It hurt so much that it took your mind off the pain caused by the hole in your foot. Medics soaked a rag in strong antiseptic, poked it into the hole, and pulled it right through.

■ Trying to beat the punji sticks, grunts inserted steel plates in their boots. But if they stepped on a cartridge trap instead of a punji spike, the metal plate turned into shrapnel and blew their toes off.

Between January 1965 and June 1970, punji stakes caused 2 percent of all combat casualties to U.S. forces in Vietnam.

SWINGING MAN TRAP

■ **Goal:** Impale you in the face. Tread on a broom head and the handle swings up and slaps you in the face. The swinging man trap works the same way, but is much, much funnier.

■ One end of a wooden board is studded with steel spikes. The other end is placed over a pit. Tread on the part that's over the hole and the studded end flies up and smacks you in the kisser.

■ Filipino fighters used this one against the Japanese during WWII. Any Japanese soldier trapped on his own either starved or bled to death. Unless wild animals heard his cries. Then it was one big party all around.

THE EXPLODING PHONE

Goal: Decapitation by phone.
When the Israelis discovered that Arab terrorist Yehiya Ayyash was behind a series of bus bombings in 1995, it took just one telephone call to put a stop to his activities. The Israelis learned that Ayyash—known as The Engineer for his bomb-making prowess—had sent away his mobile phone

to be repaired. So they offered one of his buddies $1 million to "lend" the terrorist a cell phone they'd rigged.

■ The earpiece was fitted with high explosives, which could be detonated by an audio signal. When the phone was in place, the Israelis dialed the number.

■ As soon as Ayyash answered, they played the audio detonation signal and blew his head clean off his shoulders. He did not recover.

THE BAMBOO WHIP

Goal: Stick a sharpened bamboo stake in your guts.

■ Between 1963 and 1966, the British SAS fought Indonesian insurgents who were trying to destabilize northern Borneo. Clever jungle hunters, the Indonesians adapted a pig trap called the bamboo whip to hunt SAS prey. The Viet Cong used it in Vietnam too.

■ A sharpened bamboo stake was lashed to one end of a springy shaft laid horizontally across a trail. The springy shaft was then pulled back across the path, so that it was at a right angle to its original position. It was then held under tension by a toggle trigger attached to a trip wire.

■ When a soldier tripped the wire, his

Other booby traps and mines caused a further 15 percent of casualties and 4,000 deaths. Famous punji victims include General Colin Powell, who was awarded a Purple Heart after he slipped and fell into a pit, and Joint Chief of Staff General Henry Shelton.

SNAKE-ON-A-STRING

Goal: To insert fangs in your face. Few booby traps are as scary as the snake-on-a-string. Drug barons in Southeast Asia's Golden Triangle use it nowadays to keep sneaky cops out of their opium poppy fields.

■ A venomous snake is hung at face level over a trail by a piece of string tied to its tail. The first cop along the trail comes face-to-face with one very pissed off reptile. We try this in the office corridors all the time—except we use Kerr1 Strug instead of snakes.

GRENADE TRAPS

Goal: Make mincemeat out of humans. The Viet Cong used to place grenades inside tin cans that were small enough to keep the ignition lever depressed. When the can was kicked, the grenade rolled out and exploded.

■ Slightly more sophisticated was the idea of putting grenades in cans on either side of a trail and connecting them by a trip wire. Hit the wire and out popped the primed killers.

■ Fortunately for the grunts, VC grenades were notoriously unreliable and didn't always explode.

■ Soldiers going back for their dead or wounded buddies were also easy booby-trap targets. The weight of a guy's body depresses the grenade lever—until he's lifted.

CHINESE CHOPPER

Goal: Crush your skull with a spike-studded log.

■ The chopper nailed lots of Japanese in northern Burma in WWII. The locals had been taught how to use it by Chinese fighters—hence the name. A 900-pound log with nails or hardwood spikes in the bottom is suspended over a trail by a rope that's connected to a trip wire. Tripping the wire yanks a notched piece of wood off a peg, which is the only thing holding the log up. When it drops, so do you. Permanently.

THE JUNGLE SNARE

Goal: Break all of your bones. The origins of this trap are lost in time, but it's still quite popular, maiming people from the upper reaches of the Amazon to the jungles of Africa.

■ Trappers find a log about three times the weight of a man. They tie a strong wire around it and throw the free end over a sturdy tree limb. The log is hauled onto the limb, and the free end of the wire is tied to a notched piece of wood that is then pegged on a nail hammered into the bottom of the tree. A looped snare is run out from the notched wood. The victim snags the loop, yanks the notched trigger off the nail, and is hoisted up in the air by the weight of the log. Ideally, trappers use a tree with a slope on one side so when the log drops, it keeps on going, dragging the victim over the tree limb and breaking most of his bones in the process. Funny, chiropractors charge 70 bucks for a similar treatment.

Big-Screen Booby Traps

■ *Home Alone* ranks as the all-time classic booby-trap movie. OK, so the kid's knowledge of booby traps would put a Navy SEAL to shame, and he rustles them up in an evening, but who can forget the swinging paint cans on the stairs, the trip-wired flamethrower that burns Joe Pesci's head, or the Christmas baubles under the window that shred the barefoot bandit's feet?

■ Check out *The Specialist* for bomb booby traps. Oh, and for Sharon Stone's butt in a G-string. Look out for the cup-and-saucer bomb: When the cup is lifted off the saucer, it explodes and takes out bad guy Eric Roberts.

■ "You really think this Boy Scout bullshit is going to work?" asks a skeptic in *The Predator*, as Arnie sets up a jungle snare to catch a homicidal flesh-eating monster. The Boy Scout bullshit *doesn't* work. The monster slips the snare, but of course Arnie nails him later with the counterweight on another trap.

■ *Nightmare on Elm Street* has a great pendulum hammer trap. When Freddie Kruger opens a door, a sledgehammer swings down from the ceiling and delivers a Tyson-style blow to his gut. Next he trips a wire that ignites a lightbulb full of gunpowder.

LEISURE EDGE

PLANES, TRAINS, & AUTOMOBILES

Get where you're going in style.

What to do, where to do it, and how to milk it for all it's worth

What good is having a Trump-size bank account if you suck at the important things—kicking back and avoiding responsibility? Leisure is a skill, just like anything else. We'll teach you everything you need to know: How to have a kick-ass road trip, how to cheat at board games, and how to shave your odds in Vegas. There's a lot of crazy, wild, fun things to do out there— someone's got to be man enough to handle them. We'll help you be that man.

"Any higher, baby, and my ears will pop."

Scam the Friendly Skies

You deserve a better in-flight experience. Here's how to take matters into your own hands.

FLY FREE, PRACTICALLY: Save up to 85 percent off a regular airline ticket to anywhere in the world—and even scoop up an occasional free ticket—by offering your services as a courier. All you have to do is give up most, and sometimes all, of your allotted baggage space. (Many air courier companies find this method cheaper and quicker than the regular air cargo route.) You're not allowed to touch the freight or documents the company is shipping, and you are never personally liable for the contents. You're on board simply to provide the courier company with room in the baggage hold of a commercial airliner. One caveat: You need to find a legitimate courier service. Check with the International Association of Air Travel Couriers for more information (561-582-8320).

ANOTHER ROUTE TO A CHEAP TICKET: Let the airlines come to you. At least five airlines—American, Continental, TWA, USAirways, and Cathay Pacific—will e-mail you low fares that become available at the last minute when they realize a flight is not completely booked. Fares are sometimes discounted as much as 70 percent. Of course Priceline.com and some other travel

Web sites are now offering similar discounting services, but you'll have less control over the flight you get by going the online route.

UPGRADE YOURSELF: You've got a coach ticket to Vacationland but can't stand the thought of getting stuck sitting next to an overweight woman with a snoring problem. Since you can't trust the vapid airline crew at the gate to realize you're the most deserving person on the flight for an upgrade, try the following. Wear a suit and tie to the airport to look businesslike and, let's face it, wealthy. Don't board when the attendants call your row number. Hang around just beyond the waiting area until everyone else has boarded and it looks like the flight attendants are about to close the gate door. Then sprint up to the counter, hand over your ticket, and sprint down the runway. When you're on the plane, sit in the first first-class seat available, huff and puff, and say to no one in particular that you're happy and relieved to have made your flight. When a flight attendant walks by, ask her for a Bloody Mary and a pillow before she even suspects that you're pulling a fast one. Your huffy, puffy panic, combined with your new authoritative calm and your nice clothes, will be enough to convince anyone that you belong in the lap of luxury.

PLEAD ILLNESS: Or...if you're already on the plane and decide that you simply cannot sit in a confined space with the demon-child in the next seat, find a flight attendant (not a steward—men lack the sympathy-for-other-men gene). Mess up your hair, look as pale and drawn as possible, and wheeze, "Could you put me somewhere quiet? I'm not feeling very well." If it doesn't work immediately, casually toss off the fact that you're a frequent flier. Any flight attendant with half a heart will set you up with a recliner in business class. As with every other scam, this works particularly well if you're wearing a suit and look trustworthy.

AVOID BEING NICKEL-AND-DIMED: Some airlines charge you for the headphones, without which your in-flight movie is just a silent flash of distracting light. But all airlines also provide a second jack in the arm rest for your Walkman headphones, ostensibly for the free radio broadcasts. But no one's figured out a way to block out the movie soundtrack from the Walkman jack. So carry your own headphones, switch on the movie soundtrack and it's showtime.

Fully loaded, with AC, CD, AM/FM, and IOU

LINGO PARLOR

BEHIND THE WHEEL

...and man invented the wheel

When you *can* drive 55 but just don't want to.

Ferrari-Faking

Key words, slang, and phrases to throw around a Ferrari dealership so you sound like you know your shit.

Maranello
What it is: The place in Italy where all Ferraris are born.
What you say: "When I retire next year, I'm thinking of making the pilgrimage...to Maranello!"

Pininfarina
What it is: The Italian firm that designs Ferrari bodies.
What you say: "The Pininfarina design of the F355, now that's art."

Shift gate
What it is: The cover over the car's gears, where the shift knob protrudes.
What you say: "I like the Ferrari's exposed shift gate; it's cool to watch the channels as you shift."

Fiorano
What it is: The official Ferrari test track, near the factory in Maranello.
What you say: "Yes, but how did she run at Fiorano?"

Cam-belt service
What it is: Necessary repair of the belts that drive the cam, which opens and closes the fuel and exhaust valves.
What you say: "Does this '88 have all its service records in order? I don't want any cam-belt service any time soon."

Enzo Ferrari
What it is: The man behind the car and the legend, who died in 1988.
What you say: "Enzo was a demanding SOB, but boy could he build a racing machine."

Retail balloon refinancing
What it is: It's like leasing a car, but you retain ownership of the vehicle.
What you say: "Let's talk payment: My accountant mentioned retail balloon refinancing..."

The 1990 Formula 1
What it is: A sad year for Ferrari fans.
What you say: "I could kick myself, thinking about how close Alain Prost came to a Formula 1 championship for Ferrari back in '90."

Good mileage, but you have to supply the "vroom" sound yourself.

How to Score Yourself a Primo Car

It'll have guys' jaws and girls' panties dropping left and right.

BUY A USED ONE:

According to Werner Pfister (love the name) of Miller Motor Cars in posh Greenwich, Connecticut, there are plenty of good used Ferraris priced between $30,000 and $60,000 out there. Not too shabby. A year-old Ferrari was good enough for Aerosmith drummer Joey Kramer—a rocker who requested that the car not come with a stereo so he could just listen to the roar of the engine. Now that's sweet emotion.

RENT A NEW ONE:

Owning a Ferrari means committing yourself to its costly maintenance. Maybe what you really want is just one day or an afternoon behind the wheel. No problem. When in Maui, visit Island Riders (800-529-2925). For $199 you can cruise the beach for five hours. "Our cars are very popular," attests proprietor Kriss Lambert, "because of *Magnum, P.I.*" If mustachioed Tom Selleck isn't your

speed, how about renting the car Al Pacino commandeered in *Scent of a Woman*—an F355 Spider—for only $1,100 a day at Beverly Hills Rent-a-Car (800-479-5996)? Turn up the heat in Miami by renting a Spider from Excellence Luxury Car Rental (305-526-0000) for $1,500 a day, or prolong the excitement with a $9,765 weekly rental. A luxury rental is worth the dough. According to Nick Saridakis of Wide World of Cars in Spring Valley, New York (914-425-2600), to drive a Ferrari on the open road is, well, "simply the most fun you can have with your clothes on."

TEST-DRIVE A NEW ONE:

Ferraris are sold at authorized dealers, like any other car, so it would follow that a trip to your local luxury-car outlet would have you revving the engine of, say, a brand-new 550 Maranello (list $204,000) in no time. Well, you'll have to do some serious sweet-talking if you don't have a billfold thicker than the Earth's crust. "We're not running an

amusement park here," cautions Saridakis, who, like all the dealers *Maxim* spoke with, appraises customers carefully. Saridakis will only share the intense roar of a Ferrari's engine with buyers who've put the paperwork in motion. And don't expect to fool the dealer elite with a fancy Italian suit to match your Italian dream machine. "We get guys in cutoffs who are serious buyers," says fellow Wide World salesman Gary Konner. "We'll entertain anyone, but if the first thing they say is, they want to go for a ride, then I'm suspect." Still, it's worth a bit of bravado to get behind the wheel. As one Volkswagen-owning Illinois man put it: "My whole life has been fucking *Fahrvergnugen,* but get me in a Ferrari just once and I'll die a happy man."

"The hearse is in the shop. Will this do?"

Crazy Events

Boy, what in the hell is the matter with you?

Welcome to Condé Nast Publishing!

Running of the Sheep

September
Info: Reedpoint Community Club , Reedpoint, MT (406) 326-2193
A cuddlier version of the running of the bulls. Hundreds of hairy, dumb beasts charge down the main street of Reedpoint. Then the sheepherders have a poetry reading. These people need to be mocked, big time.

Once a year the good old boys down in Spivey's Corner try to revive the lost art of hollering. As an American—a member of the loudest country on earth—you owe it to yourself to check this out.

Before you decide to hit the road, it's nice to have a destination in mind, or else you run the risk of waking up drunk in the middle of nowhere (unless, of course, that is your destination). Here are some wacky events worth driving for:

Fancy Rat and Mouse Annual Show
January
Info: AFRMA
Riverside, CA
(909) 685-2350
The purpose of this exhibition, which was begun in the early '80s, is to encourage the breeding of these suckers as urban pets. Like dog or cat shows, this one features competitors in different categories vying for the title of Most Obsessive and Friendless. Trap a few of the critters that frequent your hovel through the hole in the wall you keep meaning to patch up, and bring them here to see how they stack up!

International Leisure Suit Convention
March
Info: WHO Radio
Des Moines, IA
(515) 242-3671
Only Dow Chemical has a more impressive array of man-made fabrics. A fashion show is the highlight of this event, but there's plenty of mingling. Just don't light a match near these people.

World Championship Cow Chip-Throwing Contest
April
Info: Beaver Chamber of Commerce
Beaver, OK
(405) 625-4726
This event is...well...it's a good chance to see a whole lot of flying shit. 'Nuff said.

National Hollerin' Contest
June
Info: Spivey's Corner Volunteer Fire Department
Spivey's Corner, NC
(919) 567-2156

Great Klondike Outhouse Race
September
Info: Klondike Visitors Association
Dawson City, Yukon, Canada
(867) 993-5575
Yep. Outhouses on wheels, dozens of them, racing along a 1.5-mile course through the streets of Dawson City. The best part is, if you don't have your own wheeled outhouse, you can rent one. Bring your friends back a photo...or some other memento.

Nudes-a-Poppin'
Two shows a year (check Web site for dates: www.nudes-a-poppin.com)
Ponderosa Sun Club, Roselawn, IN
(219) 345-2268
The biggest, raunchiest outdoor nude beauty pageant you can find. And it's frequented by actual porn stars!

Ugly Truck Contest

"That's one purty truck."

July
Info: Jeff Johnson , Pelican Rapids, MN (218) 863-6693
Entrants bring their farm and pickup trucks to this event, where they're judged on categories like most rust, most dents, worst paint jobs, shattered or missing glass, most exhaust smoke, worst interior, and overall appearance—the ugly truck equivalent of winning Miss Congeniality. Bring your bib overalls and your cousin-wife.

Crazy Museums

Please, no flash photography.

Some of our favorite monuments of meaninglessness:

The National Knife Museum
Chattanooga, TN
Thousands of knives and other dangerously pointy shit—from blades used by headhunters to Nazi trinkets—fill these halls. There's a Rambo shrine, exhibits of the world's largest (5' 4") and smallest (1/4") blades, and the knife Donny and Marie used to get a new show.

Exotic World Burlesque Hall of Fame
Helendale, CA
Feather boas, elbow gloves, nipple pasties—you'll think you've died and gone to Larry Flynt's secret back room. Thrill

high Titan and reminisce about the apocalypse that almost was. Fun prank: While a tourist is leaning over some critical piece of equipment, inflate a paper bag and pop it in his ear.

The Madison Museum of Bathroom Tissue
Madison, WI
Come in, sit down, and check out this collection of 3,000-plus rolls "liberated" from famous locales like Graceland, Churchill Downs, and a Milwaukee Sizzler. Guaranteed to wipe that frown off your face. (No taking exhibits to the men's room.)

Belhaven Memorial Museum
Belhaven, NC
Linger over the items

The Elvis Museum

"You gonna finish that mayo?"

Wright City, MO
Impersonator Bill Beeny's roadside shrine will give you sideburns in no time. Snap pics of the 16-foot plywood Elvis and hang out by the satin-lined coffin complete with Elvis mannequin. Then choke down greasy burgers like The King himself used to do. Just don't say he's gone.

---

to sexhibits including one of Jayne Mansfield's ratty old ottomans. (If that footrest could talk, eh?)

The Museum of Questionable Medical Devices
Minneapolis, MN
Head-bump measurers? Prostate gland warmers? These quacky medical gizmos and treatments represent more than 200 years of Gestapo-like health experimentation. You'll thank your lucky stars you waited so long to be born.

The Titan Missile Museum
Green Valley, AZ
At this decommissioned launch site, you can climb into a silo housing a 103-foot-

collected by Mrs. Eva Blount Way during her lifetime, like fetuses in jars, pickled tumors (one weighing 10 pounds), a two-headed kitten, a dress worn by a 700-pound local woman, 30,000 buttons, and hideous ingrown toenails and cataracts. Bring the kids!

The Cockroach Hall of Fame Museum
Plano, TX
If you like dead roaches dressed up and positioned in little scenes—and who doesn't?—this is a must-see. "Ross Peroach" and "Marilyn Monroach" are only two of the proof-there's-no-God bug puns tacked onto this creepy collection of crawlers.

"Aw, chute!"

What You Need to Know About Skydiving

■ **Dress warm.** The sky at the typical jumping altitude of 14,000 feet is cold enough to send your balls up into your body cavity—and make 'em stay there. And no, it doesn't matter that you're only up there for only a few seconds.

■ **Track.** During freefall you spread your arms and legs out, put your hips forward, and arch your back. This gives you more stability and prevents you from twirling round and round as you plummet helplessly to the ground.

■ **Keep symmetrical.** When changing your position—like when you pull the ripcord—you have to make sure both sides of your body mirror each other in order to stay level in the air. As you reach over and across to pull the lever with one arm, the other arm should come under and across in the same way.

KILLING TIME

This is my rifle. There are many like it, but this one is mine...

Channel the homicidal urges brought on by endless rest stops and AM radio into a paintball war. You've heard about it—now get online and get into the action at www.warpig.com, a truly disturbing Web clearinghouse of all the ranges, equipment, salespeople, and just plain weirdness surrounding the sport. Here's how to win once you're in:

■ **Shampoo your goggles.** A tiny bit of shampoo or liquid soap on the inside of the goggle plastic will keep it from misting up, which will blind you and get you hit by 15 people. A little bit of your own spit can also decrease the dreaded misting effect.

■ **Hang behind loud people.** It's like the old joke of the two hunters running from the bear. One says, "We'll never outrun him." The other says, "I don't need to outrun the bear. I just need to outrun you." You should spot someone from your team who is loud and inept enough to get shot, and hang back just enough so you won't be in the crossfire. He'll be your little lightning rod, drawing all the stray shots away from you.

■ **Shoot first.** Rental guns have been banged up a lot, and many of them didn't start out all that accurate in the first place. While you're running to get into place, shoot that sucker a hell of a lot of times to judge the ridiculous way it tracks off the target, and how far it really shoots. It will come in handy.

MR. HANDS

"Good God! I just crapped my pants!"

POKER 101: WHAT BEATS WHAT

1. **Five of a kind** (if playing with wild cards, but only complete pansy-ass wusses play with wild cards)
2. **Straight flush**
3. **Four of a kind**
4. **Full house**
5. **Flush**
6. **Straight**
7. **Three of a kind**
8. **Two pair**
9. **Pair**
10. **High card**

The trouble is the middle range—**full house, flush, and straight.** To keep track, imagine a house surrounding a toilet with a straight piece of something floating in it.

Liquor in the Front, Poker in the Rear

When you think you know when to hold 'em, and know when to fold 'em.

If your road trip brings you into Sin City, you'd better know your shit or you'll be begging for change outside The Mirage.

"Have some free Kenny Rogers' Roasters coupons."

LINGO Throw some of these phrases, compiled by poker expert Jan Fisher, into your conversation and show 'em you're a round-er. (Sorry, but saying "three of black thingy" or "Queenie" will get you a quick ass-stomping.)

ABC: A-2-3	**Dr. Pepper:** 10-4-2	**Nits and lice:** two pair, treys and 2s
Aces and spaces: one pair only, A-A	**Drinking age:** 2-A	**Oldsmobile:** 9-8
Ajax: A-J	**Fishhooks:** J-J	**Pinochle:** QS JD
All blue or All pink: flush	**Flat tire:** J-4	**Pocket rockets:** A-A
American Airlines: A-A	**Girl's best friend:** diamond flush	**Presto:** 5-5
Assault rifle: A-K-4-7	**Gravedigger special:** spade flush	**Puppy feet:** club flush
Baskin-Robbins: 3-A	**Hard eight:** 4-4	**Quinine:** Q-9
Bicycle or Bike: A-2-3-4-5	**Heinz:** 5-7	**Raquel Welch:** 3-8
Big slick: A-K	**Huey, Dewey, and Louie:** 2-2-2	**Railroad:** J-6
Black Mariah: QS	**Hooks:** J-J	**Route:** 6-6
Blizzard: five facecards in razz	**Hookers:** Q-Q	**Snowballs:** 8-8
Broadway: A-K-Q-J-10	**Jack and Jill:** J-J	**Snowmen:** 8-8
Broderick Crawford: 10-4	**Benny:** 3-9	**Speed limit:** 6-5
Bug: joker	**Jesse James:** 4-5	**Tension:** 10-10
Bullets: A-A	**Joe Montana:** A-6	**Thirty miles:** 10-10-10
Canine: K-9	**King crab:** K-3	**Treys:** 3-3
Computer hand: Q-7	**King Kong:** K-K	**Trombone:** 7-6
Cowboys: K-K	**Kojak:** K-J	**Twiggy:** 2-9
Crabs: 3-3	**Ladies:** Q-Q	**Union Oil:** 7-6
Dame: Q	**Little slick:** A-2	**Valentines:** heart flush
Dead man's hand: aces and eights	**Lumberman's hand:** 2-4	**Waitress hand:** Q-3
Dolly Parton: 9-5	**Michael Jordan:** 2-3	**Washington Monument:** 5-5-5
Doyle Brunson: 10-2	**Mighty Wurlitzer:** 8-8	**Wheel:** A-2-3-4-5
Deuces: 2-2	**Montana banana:** 9-2	**Woolworth:** 5-10
Devil's hand: 6-6-6	**Mop squeezers:** Q-Q	**Yo eleven:** 6-5
Ducks: 2-2	**Motown:** J-5	

Poker Plays

Variations of the classic game you should know:

"Huh-huh. He said 'Jack.'"

SEVEN-CARD STUD

Deal two cards down and one up to each player. Betting starts with whomever has the high card showing. Deal three more cards up to each player, with additional betting rounds after each deal. Each player should now have four cards up and two down, and the pot should be swollen with the green (unless you and your chump friends are playing for the loose change in your pockets). The last card is dealt face down ("down and dirty") to each player, and a final betting round ensues. Players form their final hand using the best five cards they are holding.

"Gimme all your Queens!"

TEXAS HOLD 'EM

Deal two cards face down to each player; follow with a betting round. The first active player to the dealer's left bets first in each round. Next, three cards (called the "widow") are dealt face up in the middle of the table. These are "community cards" and are used simultaneously by each player to make their hand. There is another betting round, and then a fourth and fifth card are dealt face up to the widow, with a betting round after each deal. In the showdown each player selects his best five cards from the seven available. Beware that the strong cards showing are shared by everyone. It usually takes two pairs or better to win this game.

CINCINNATTI (ALSO CALLED UTAH OR LAMEBRAINS)

Deal five cards face down to each player and five more face down in the middle of the table. The cards in the widow are exposed one at a time, with a betting round after each one. In the showdown

each player may select any five cards from among his hand and the five cards in the widow. With 10 cards to choose from, it usually takes a flush or full house to win, since all strong cards are shared.

FIVE-CARD DRAW WITH THE BUG

This is a variation of the most popular form of draw poker. There is one joker in the deck, which is used as the "bug." It can be used only as an ace, or to represent the missing card in a straight or flush. The joker cannot be used, for example, to turn two kings into three. Deal each player five cards face down. There is a betting round and then each player in turn may discard and replace any of his cards with the goal of improving his hand. There is another betting round, and then the showdown, in which the highest poker hand wins. With the presence of the bug, most pots are won by two pairs or better.

LOWBALL

This is the most popular form of poker played for the lowest-ranking poker hand. Deal five cards face down to each player. There is a betting round, after which each player may discard and replace any of his five cards with the goal of making an even worse poker hand. A good low poker hand contains no pairs, and your highest card should be a 10 or lower. The best possible low hand is the "bicycle," or "little wheel" (5-4-3-2-Ace). Straights and flushes are ignored, and aces are low only.

Sorry kid. I got 3 kings and, uh, 2 popes

JACKPOTS

This is five-card draw with an opening requirement "jacks or better to open." Deal five cards face down to each player. There is a betting round, but a player must

have at least a pair of jacks to place the first bet. If no one opens the betting round, the dealer collects everyone's cards but leaves their antes in the pot. The deck is shuffled, each player antes again, and the game is redealt with the same opening requirement. This process repeats until someone bets with at least two jacks. After the first betting round, each player may replace any of his five cards with new ones dealt from the deck. There is a final betting round, followed by the showdown in which the best high hand wins the pot. The average winning hand is a high pair, but remember that the player who opened was dealt at least two jacks!

ANACONDA

This popular game combines the feature of betting on gradually exposed hands with the basic principle of the knock-poker family (the ability to obtain cards from other players). Each player is dealt seven cards face down and there is a betting round. Each active player then passes any three cards to the player on his left. There is another betting round, and then each player discards two cards from his hand and arranges his remaining face-down, cards in a strategic order. Each player flips his first card over simultaneously, followed by a betting round. This continues for each card until the showdown, with the highest hand winning the pot. Note that if you are dealt a strong hand (like a full house), you are forced to break it up when you pass three of your seven cards. When choosing the cards to pass, you should anticipate receiving low or midrange replacements. The key is the arrangement of your face-down cards. Since they are revealed one at a time, sort them in an order that will keep your opponents guessing to the end.

COUNTING CARDS

Yeah, definitely counting cards, yeah…10 minutes to Wapner…

Even if you become a master at casino blackjack strategy—and always know when to hit, stand, split, and so on—the house is still left with an advantage (albeit a very slim one—less than 1 percent) in the game. But learn to count cards and you can gain a small advantage over the house...the only game in Vegas in which this is possible. (Of course, the edge is small, particularly in multiple-deck games with lots of cards to count. And remember, card-counting doesn't help you *win* any more hands than you'd win otherwise. What it does do is tip you off as to when you're slightly more likely to win or slightly more likely to lose on the next round, so you can bet accordingly.)

■ Because the dealer has to hit everything short of a 17, the greater the ratio of high cards (10 through ace) to low cards (2 through 6) left in the deck, the more likely he is to go bust. Keep track of whether more high or more low cards have been played and you'll know what's left in the deck. This will allow you to bet more if a high card is more likely to come up and drop down to the table minimum when the advantage swings the house's way.

■ Count this way: Cards 2 through 6 are worth one point each; 10's, face cards, and aces are worth minus one. (Ignore 7's, 8's, and 9's.) Start from zero with a new deck, and as each card's flipped over, add or subtract. At the end of each round, if the number in your head is positive, bet big (more low cards have been played, so the deck's rich in high cards and bad for the dealer). If it's negative, bet the table minimum, or even sit out a round. Start with the number in your head for the next round, but begin at zero again when the deck's reshuffled.

■ That's all there is to it. Of course if you don't know basic blackjack strategy, card-counting won't help you. Also try to sit in the "first base" seat—the first hand the dealer distributes in each game. This'll give you a solid block of time after playing your hand to leisurely count cards before you have to place your next bet. One last tip: Don't bet more than three or four times the table minimum when the situation's advantageous; casinos that catch on to card-counting will boot your ass.

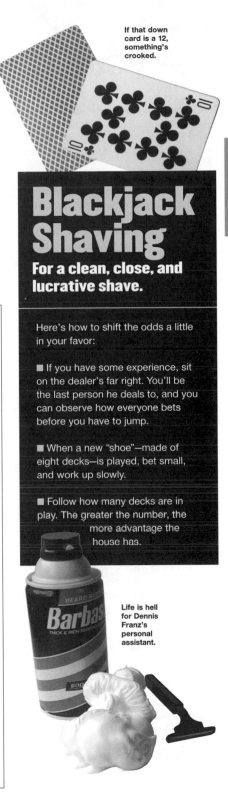

If that down card is a 12, something's crooked.

Blackjack Shaving

For a clean, close, and lucrative shave.

Here's how to shift the odds a little in your favor:

■ If you have some experience, sit on the dealer's far right. You'll be the last person he deals to, and you can observe how everyone bets before you have to jump.

■ When a new "shoe"—made of eight decks—is played, bet small, and work up slowly.

■ Follow how many decks are in play. The greater the number, the more advantage the house has.

Life is hell for Dennis Franz's personal assistant.

Bar Pool
Nice rack.

OK, so the poker and blackjack tables left you barely enough money for beer. Play some bar pool, and try to win back some self-respect. Here's how to look like a pro:

■ **Cut in line...gracefully.** Sign at the bottom of that "Who's got next?" chalkboard and you could be waiting all night. Instead check out the board and pick a common name three or four down from the top, like "Jim." When it's Jim's turn, saunter over and start racking up for the next game. If anyone challenges you, keep the charade going for another minute—"Well, maybe somebody's name got erased, but I know I'm up next!"—before giving in with, "It's bullshit, but whatever, I'll take the winner."

■ **Manage your image.** Project the perfect image—confident, cool, slightly menacing—and you've won half the battle. Don't try a trick shot unless you've got it mastered; no one will be impressed when you rip the felt and send a ball flying into a biker's crotch. (Same goes for that behind-the-back stuff.) Don't roll the stick across the table to check the warpage—sighting down the cue with your eyes is a more accurate, and cooler, method. And don't even think about using that wooden cuestick bridge, a.k.a. the sissy stick. That's only for escalating bar fights.

■ **Choose the right cue.** Never tote a custom cue to a bar—if you're not good enough to own the table all night, you're gonna look like a true jackass. When choosing one of the crappy ol' bar cues, the trick is to focus on the stick's tip rather than its weight. As Bob Jewett, an instructor certified with the Billiards Congress of America, explains, "To cushion the shot, the cue's leather tip should be about the thickness of a nickel, and evenly curved, like a thumbnail." Whichever way your stick is warped, just turn it so the bend is facing up for each shot and you'll be fine.

■ **Chalk it up.** You're always on display when you play bar pool, and there's no bet-ter way to look like you know what you're doing than to chalk up before every shot. And if done right it will also help your game. The key: "Boring the tip into the center of the chalk doesn't do the job," Jewett warns. Better: Use the edge of the chalk to scrape it onto your tip in one thin coat, then strategically place the chalk on the rail in your opponent's line of vision when he's shooting to break his concentration.

■ **Build a bridge.** Your bridge guides the front of the cue, so make it stable by planting all five fingers firmly on the table. A "closed" bridge, where the cue hangs in your looped index finger, is more accurate. But if those tequila shots are kicking in, consider the easi-er "open" bridge, where the cue sits in the groove between two knuckles. On the break bridge from the rail for the most stability. And while you're waiting to shoot, don't hold your beer in your bridge hand—the sticky scum will hinder a smooth slide.

■ **Count your beers.** Yeah, yeah, pool wisdom has it that a few beers loosens your game and makes you play better. That, however, is a crock. The more beer you drink, the worse your coordination becomes. Period. And yet, if you're not tak-ing the occasional chug, you look like a big, fat wuss. The best advice? Nurse 'till you lose. Then drown your sorrows.

■ **Make the break.** When you rack for your opponent, always put the six ball up front. Because it's dark green, the color of most bar tables, he'll have a tougher time making a solid break, and he'll look like a ninny. When it's your break, take the advice of Steve Mizerak, a three-time World Open Champion: "Aim for the front man and hit it straight on with as much power as you can muster. Hitting the second ball pays off with greater ball dispersion, but you have a higher chance of scratching."

■ **Take your best shot.** Now it's time to run the table. Plan to set up and shoot quickly, before the babes gathering behind you bump your stick and muff your shot. Mizerak advises: "Keep your head down, about 16 to 18 inches off the cue, and follow through with your stroke." When your oppo-nent sets up to shoot, murmur to your friend and shake your head ominously for effect.

■ **Play for drinks.** There's nothing worse than getting taken by a shark. Instead of playing a stranger for money, suggest an ante of a free beer: If he's a hustler, it's like offering garlic to a vampire—he knows he plays his best when he's sober. Either way you know what you're up against.

■ **Know when to lose.** It's always better to lose the table than have your knuckles crushed by an ex-con you've thoroughly humiliated. Go ahead and throw the game. Shake his hand, buy him a beer, ask him about his buddies at Rikers. Remember, it's not whether you win or lose, it's whether you need reconstructive surgery.

Throw Deadly Accurate Darts

■ Hold your arm up, straight in front of you, bent at a 90-degree angle. Your shoulder should be at a 90-degree angle from the board. And keep your forward foot at a 90-degree angle to your behind foot for greater balance.
■ Pinch the dart with at least three fingers. The longer the barrel, the more fingers you use. Any fingers not hold-ing the dart should be away from the dart or in the same rough position as your other fingers. Don't curl them up in your palm or your knuckles might nudge the sucker out of its flight path.
■ Align your eyes, the dart, and the bulls-eye in one line. Focus on the tar-get, not the dart.
■ Sweep straight back, and use your elbow, not your shoulder. Don't rush—many beginners rush or do not pull back far enough.
■ Guide the dart on a parabolic curve. For those of you who failed math, the idea is, when you release the dart, its path should form a perfect curve from when it leaves your hand to when it reaches the target.

RULE AT ARM WRESTLING

'Cause all yer fancy word-talkin' won't help ya here, boy.

To help you bust the knuckles of guys twice your size, we wrestled some tips out of one of the world's top-ranked professional arm wrestlers, Jason Vale.

FEEL THE BURN:

■ Build the right muscles.
■ Strengthen your upper body with some basic weightlifting.
■ Perform resistance exercises to fortify your joints: For your hands repeatedly squeeze a tennis ball. For your arms take an old bicycle tire and attach it to the ceiling or another stable object and pull, simulating the arm-wrestling motion.
■ Vale recommends: "Eat the gristle from the ends of chicken bones: It makes the joints and ligaments strong."

Yech...umm, we mean, right on!

TIME TO RUMBLE:

■ Go mental.
■ Clear your mind through deep breathing, prayer, or a quick shot of tequila.
■ Make sure you have some enthusiastic friends cheering you on.
■ Intimidate your opponent with a steady, steely stare.
■ Put a swatch of leather (your belt will work just fine) between your teeth and bite on it like a mad dog right before the match to scare your opponent.

RIGHT TO WIN:

■ Brace your feet on the table legs.

■ Push your thighs and hips right up to the tabletop to improve your leverage.
■ Wear big-soled boots so that your feet don't slip.
■ Keep your elbow near your chest, and don't hunch your shoulders—this way you can use a swinging motion to win.
■ End the match in the first second by pinning your rival's arm down the moment the ref's whistle blows (or the bartender yells, "Go").
■ Or go "over the top" by positioning your fingers over your opponent's knuckles and snapping his wrist back for the easy pin.
■ If you start to lose, distract your opponent with rude remarks about his mother, or quote Stallone in *Over the Top.*

Win at Monopoly
Be a cardboard tycoon.

You think you're any cooler than the Dungeons and Dragons kids?

Four or five times in every man's life, a game of Monopoly will be played all the way to its conclusion. We asked Roger Craig, current U.S. Monopoly champion, and Irvin Hentzel, mathematics professor at Iowa State and author of a scientific study called *How to Win at Monopoly,* for tips.

Tip #1: Never buy hotels. Build your properties to three houses and stop. The return on three houses, factoring in the cheaper purchase price, is as good as that on a hotel; and if you buy hotels and need to pay off an opponent late in the game, when all the houses are taken, you'll be unable to downsize to cash and houses.

Tip #2: Pay attention. Monopoly's won and lost at the bargaining table: From the first round keep track of the property color groups each opponent is trying to amass, so you'll know both who you can make deals with and when to make your move.

Tip #3: Color-coordinate. In a fast-paced game, where your opponents are

building up like Donald Trump on diet pills, go for the red properties to make a quick KO. They have heavy bankruptcy-inducing rents. Plus, they're affordable and people hit them often, unlike that overpriced green and dark-blue crap. In slower games go with orange and light blue properties. They're the best value.

Tip #4: First pay the rent. Don't upgrade or buy new property until you get past the board's high-rent corridors. Otherwise you could be hit bad.

Tip #5: Don't fear the cooler. Going to jail is bad in the game's early, property-acquisition phase, but it's a good thing later. "Send me to jail, please," says Craig. "Because then I'm not rolling the dice, and everyone is jumping around, landing on my stuff."

Tip #6: Be the iron. "It's the smallest game piece and sits closest to the table," notes Craig. "If people aren't paying attention, you can slide it onto their property and

they won't notice." If the next two players roll, you've just legally avoided paying rent.

Tip #7: If you're losing, "accidentally" sweep the board off the table. Secretly, your opponents will be grateful you ended it.

CHEAT AT SCRABBLE
Know your limits.

Maybe Vegas just isn't your speed. Take it slow by playing some common household board games—but still play to *win,* dammit! Here's how:

TIP #1: Try Braille in the letter bag, feeling for blanks and—when you need them—those elusive, 10-point *z*'s and *q*'s.

TIP #2: Turn over any tile in your tray that doesn't get along with the others, and use it as a blank to make a "bingo" (a seven-letter word that earns 50 bonus points).

TIP #3: Pick up a *Franklin Wordmaster,* which spits out dozens of combinations for even the most miserable, ragtag collection of letters. Brazenly use it during the game, pretending it's a pocket calculator you're keeping track of the score with.

TIP #4: Unload any letters you can't use or don't like by dragging a few of them back into the tile bag when you're fishing for replacement letters. They'll never call you Four *I*'s again.

TIP #5: Make up your own words and play 'em with impunity by first burning your opponent on obscure but legit words from the *Official Scrabble Dictionary*—like *ae, xi,* and *xu.* After he loses a couple of turns after unsuccessfully challenging these words, you'll be able to play whatever ridiculous outlaw combos you want as you smile your way to another victory.

JIFFY LUBE
Don't drink and drive. *Do* drink and pass out in your hotel room.

Since no road trip is complete without copious amounts of alcohol, we let you in on some coveted booze info. Guard it with your liver.

HOW TO SCAM FREE BEER
Sitting in a bar and you're out of cash? To squeeze 'em for one more golden brewski, try:

■ **The Bamboozle (also known as the "beerboozle").** Take your empty beer bottle into the men's room and fill 'er up. Then belly up to a hectic stretch of the bar and tell the 'keep he's mistakenly given you a warm one. He'll clutch the bottle, look puzzled, toss it, and fetch you another coldie. Maybe he'll even apologize!

■ **The Switcheroo.** Gravitate with your almost-empty toward a big, tipsy group ordering a monster round. Get in close and wait for their dozen cold ones to land on the counter, then "accidentally" pick up one of the new beverages instead of your backwashy bottle.

■ **The Butterfingers.** Pick a well-heeled patron, shadow him until he jogs your arm, and drop your near-empty beer. Nine times out of 10, the guy will buy you a new one—and if he doesn't, the bartender will.

■ **The Mourner.** Appear down in the dumps at a friendly tavern and any self-respecting bartender will ask what's wrong and pour a freebie. Go ahead, embellish: Losing a job or girlfriend merits a free draft by law in most states.

Open a Beer Anywhere
You got it. Now get it open.

Any putz can open a brew with a key or flip the lid off with a table edge. But what if there's no key? Or the only table is a family heirloom? What if you just feel like showing off? Try these alcohol-access techniques.

■ **Window lock.** Unlock a window and place the lip of the bottle cap under the lip of the latch. The beer is now upside down. Pull the base of the bottle toward you and down (and quickly, for minimum spillage).

■ **Bathtub faucet.** Settled into the tub but forgot the opener? Insert the top of the bottle into the spout (make sure the water's turned off, Bozo). Push the base of the bottle away from you, and ease the top off.

■ **Belt buckle.** Unbuckle your belt. Put the end of the buckle under the lip of the bottle cap, then pry the cap off. You can also use the "female" part of any door lock just like a belt buckle.

■ **Fire sprinkler.** If no one's around at the office, climb up on a chair and use the metal band, or collar, around the emergency sprinkler.

(Remember to take the cigarette out of your mouth first.)

■ **Seat belt.** Designate somebody as the sober driver (pray you don't draw the short straw), then use the hole in the "male" end of the seat belt to pop the lid off your beer.

■ **Hubcap or trunk.** Use a slot in a hubcap, or pop the trunk and employ the hole in the "male" part of the latch.

■ **Fridge handle.** Put the bottle cap between the handle and the door, and slide it down (most refrigerator handles angle toward the door at the bottom) until it sticks. With a quick karate chop, knock it down a bit more, then twist the bottle and the top comes off. (But sometimes the handle breaks too.)

■ **Beauty tools.** Flag down any woman sporting a decent manicure. Ask her if she has nail clippers or a cuticle shaper (a device with a pointy metal end) that you can use to loosen the bottle cap all the way around until it slips off. Then offer to split your beer with her.

Cure a Hangover

You gotta pay the price sometime. Here's how to keep the price down.

The Cure: Painkillers and water
The Theory: "Pain...killing...me. Doctors are smart...pills will fix anything."
The Lowdown: Princeton U's Pamela Bowen, M.D., says acetaminophen (e.g., Tylenol) is easier on your stomach than ibuprofen (e.g., Advil). Water helps with dehydration, the cause of most hangover pain (alcohol makes you piss too much), and reduces burning acids in your stomach.
The *Maxim* Test: This is the cure doctors advise most, but our guys didn't feel better until 2 P.M.—and by then it was time to start drinking again!

The Cure: Evening Primrose Oil
The Theory: "Ow...brain needs lubricating."
The Lowdown: Nutritionists advise a spoonful to boost liver activity, specifically to increase production of the enzymes that break alcohol down, speeding your recovery.
The *Maxim* Test: No noticeable effect—and trying Pennzoil as an alternative was an unmitigated disaster.

The Cure: Orange Juice
The Theory: "Stale beer taste. Want sweetness."
The Lowdown: Fruit and veggie juices flush your system of toxins while restocking your supply of vitamins and minerals. Dr. Linus Pauling, winner of the Nobel Prize for chemistry, suggested massive doses of vitamin C (try chuggin' 250 glasses of O.J.) as the best hangover cure.
The *Maxim* Test: The megadose had our boys *running* to the bathroom, if you know what we mean, and the O.J. added acid to their bellies, leading to problems at both ends.

The Cure: Hair of the Dog
The Theory: "Beer made head feel good last night—why not this morning?"
The Lowdown: Although drinking a smaller amount of the stuff that got you plastered in the first place might make you feel a bit better, Delaine Lisk, R.N., assures us

that it's all purely psychological. Plus, even if you drink away your current hangover, you're still going to pay for your new drunk tomorrow. You can only put off the inevitable for so long.
The *Maxim* Test: Works great as long as you don't have to go to work.

The Cure: Vigorous Sex
The Theory: "Must balance extraordinary pain with extraordinary pleasure."
The Lowdown: Kingsley Amis, author of *How's Your Glass: A Quizzical Look at Drinks and Drinking,* claims that "the exercise will do you good, and you'll feel toned up emotionally."
The *Maxim* Test: Needless to say, this is the official *Maxim*-endorsed remedy.

The Cure: Shit Tea (dried rabbit dung brewed with tea in hot water)
The Theory: "Well, I already feel like shit..."
The Lowdown: No medical foundation, but badass American frontiersmen drank this crap (sorry) every 30 minutes until their hangovers were gone. Bonus: Will prove you're a badass.
The *Maxim* Test: We wouldn't wish this on our worst enemy.

The Cure: Hot 'n' Cold (an ice pack for your head and a tub of hot water for your feet)
The Theory: "Must...confuse...pain receptors."
The Lowdown: Doctors in the 1800s believed this setup would make the blood rush to your feet, relieving that cranium-pounding pressure up top. In reality the ice slows blood flow.
The *Maxim* Test: It was strangely soothing—but as soon as Ted got up, he felt awful and fell down. Fortunately, we had the ice pack...

The Cure: Prairie Oyster
(two raw eggs, vinegar, and a dash of Tabasco sauce)
The Theory: "Raw eggs...will make me

feel strong like Rocky."
The Lowdown: Raw eggs have been a popular cure ever since ancient Roman Pliny the Elder started downing six raw owl's eggs after a night in and out of the vomitorium.
The *Maxim* Test: Like drinking spicy mucus.

The Cure: Herring Delight (herring, vinegar, juniper berries, cloves, and water)
The Theory: "Well, I drank like a fish..."
The Lowdown: The blend of spices and seafood helped Vikings pillage their way through another day—but the salt may make you more dehydrated.
The *Maxim* Test: The assumption, "Drinking this will impress Vendela," was wrong. Very wrong.

The Cure: Hangover Breakfast
(tomato juice, black coffee, two greasy fried eggs)
The Theory: "Just like mom used to make...I want my mommy."
The Lowdown: This one covers all the bases: juice to replenish you, caffeine to revive you, greasy food to settle your gut.
The *Maxim* Test: Enough of a remedy to get you to the couch in time for football, but overeat and you may be sorry by halftime.

The Cure: Bloody Mary
The Theory: "Veggies are healthy—I shoulda had a V8 last night."
The Lowdown: Nurse Lisk tells us the tomato juice is a good source of vitamin C, especially if you don't feel like guzzling orange juice.
The *Maxim* Test: This combination of Hair of the Dog and The Hangover Breakfast actually worked—just crunch that celery as quietly as you can.

"I feel like a pig shat in my head."

Sometimes a cigar ain't a cigar.

You've exerted all this energy scamming flights, beers, board games—but what about *your* needs?

It's time to start looking out for number one, and friend, it doesn't get any better than this.

Just like Mom used to make.

Mix a Perfect Martini

If you say the words "shaken" or "stirred," we will kill you.

Since the ultimate casino-hound was unquestionably the suave and debonair 007 (Timothy Dalton notwithstanding), here's how to mix yourself a Bond-worthy drink that would make M proud.

STEP 1: **Get a haircut.** Hey, if you're looking for a quick fix, go slosh yourself a rum and coke. The martini is a poised, delicate, finely balanced instrument of inebriation that requires a total commitment to excellence. So clean up your act: Get a haircut and a shave; carefully trim your nose and

ear hair. Pick out a nice suit-and-tie combo, something conservative but with a little flash: Armani and Nicole Miller make a great couple. For best results, don't loosen the tie until your first sip.

STEP 2: **Have a bad day at work.** Unless you lay down a solid base level of stress, a martini has no *raison d'être*. Of course the bitterness of a *really* lousy day can adversely affect the taste: If you were fired over lunch and came home to find your wife in bed with the mailman, the drink you're looking for is called straight whiskey. For a martini, you should arrive on a red-eye in the morning, sit through tedious meetings all afternoon, and suffer a few pre-ulcerous stomach rumbles from an ongoing crisis somewhere in between.

STEP 3: **Gather your hardware and software.** Tally-ho, on to the drink. You will need: a real martini glass or two (they can both be for you), and either a capped glass shaker with a strainer lid or a metal cup with a separate strainer. You will also

need gin, sweet vermouth, dry vermouth, cubed (not crushed) ice, and a jar of olives.

The choice of gin is obviously important but is largely a matter of personal preference: Choose from any of the crystal-clear, butter-smooth, lovingly textured high-end gins on the market. (You can use Fred's Bargain Gin too, but in that case why not just mix the drink in a radiator cap and stir it with your dick?) A word or two about olives: The olive is the aesthetic anchor in the martini's cone of clarity and contributes an ever-so-slight Levantine twang to the taste. Most

important of all, though, the olive is critical because *that's the fucking drink*.

STEP 4: **Mix it up.** Take off your jacket and roll up your sleeves. Pack your shaker solid with ice, unscrew the tops of both vermouth bottles, and pour a healthy slug of each over the ice. It doesn't matter how much you pour in altogether—you'll see why in a minute—but the 1:1 sweet-to-dry ratio is important: It's what makes this a "perfect" martini.

Next cap your shaker and shake it up. Don't bruise the vermouth by "jerking off" the canister: The correct shaking procedure is a little manual twist-and-roll that's a combination of playing maracas and trying to crack your wrist joint. When you're doing it right, the ice makes a crunchy, low-decibel *chukka-chukka-chuk*. After shaking for 15 seconds, strain the vermouth—all of it, mind you—down the sink.

This seems an appropriate place to point out that in its heart of hearts, a martini isn't really a mixed drink: It's a showcase for gin. Accordingly the vermouth's not there to cut the gin, the way cranberry juice cuts vodka, but to *accent* it, like a spice. And now that your ice cubes have been lovingly frosted with the perfect vermouth mix, you've established an ideal environment for your best gin.

Stop to admire your handiwork. Your cubes will start melting, introducing an element of (cringe) water to your drink. After you've drained the vermouth, pour approximately one drink's worth of gin into the ice. Cap the shaker over the gin and vermouth-ice, and shake for another 15 seconds; then uncap and strain the martini slowly into your glass, leaving a half-inch or so of breathing room at the top. Roll in an olive with a splashless bloop; raise the glass to the light to better appreciate its perfect clarity; swirl the gin to admire its texture. Then...well, you can take it from there, James.

The Perfect Steak
Mmmm...steak.

Chop suey!

LEISURE EDGE

Nothing says "good livin'" like a hunk of prime meat grilling in the open air. Here's how to—*Bam!*—kick your steak up a notch.

1. THE MEAT
Start with a prime cut: a big, ugly slab surrounded by a layer of dry, gray fat and stamped "U.S.D.A. Prime." Get one fresh from a butcher—shrink-wrapped supermarket steaks are hockey pucks in comparison. A prime cut is marbleized with tenderizing fat and will have hung in a meat locker for about 21 days until its tissues are torn and soft. Most of the fat will burn away as it cooks; trim off whatever remains.

2. THE FUEL
Charcoal and gas grills are damn convenient, but serious carnivores prefer dangerously large wood fires. Hardwood chips produce great-tasting smoke that really soaks into the meat. Hickory and mesquite are best, though oak and pecan are close enough. (Never use lighter woods like pine, spruce, and sassafras, which contain harmful tars and resins.) Let the chips burn down to a bed of coals before you start cooking. You can try to salvage a gas or charcoal fire by throwing in some wood chips, but the real thing still rules.

3. THE MARINADE
Bottled Italian salad dressings (the oily kind, not the creamy) make fast and easy marinades—particularly red-wine or vinaigrette dressing, which helps break down tough tendons in the meat. Soak and refrigerate for a few hours before cooking: Four hours on each side is optimal to turn even the leatheriest chunk of cow's flesh into a buttery-smooth crowd pleaser (but you can settle for less than four hours if you're running late). After marinating the meat, place it on a dish or clean cutting board until it reaches room temperature. While you're waiting, light your fire and beat the meat—that's the steak, of course—with a meat pounder (or maul it with a fork) for 10 minutes per side.

4. THE EVENT
A typical eight-ounce steak should grill about eight minutes per side. Cook it until the internal temperature reaches 160 degrees (do the knife-split test for pinkness, or stick in a wimpy meat thermometer when nobody's looking). Ideally, you should flip a steak only once: Overzealous flipping cools the surface of the beef, steaming the meat on the outside instead of grilling it. Take the steak off the grill just before you think it's done (it continues to cook), and set it aside for five minutes so its juices settle. Then kick back with some cactus juice and dig in.

Jerkying-Off
Make your own beef jerky.

This is the only recipe you really need to know.

Ingredients
(makes two dozen pieces):
1 cut of choice tenderloin
1/2 cup Worcestershire sauce
1/2 cup dark soy sauce
2 cloves fresh garlic
1 Tbsp brown sugar
1 tsp salt
1 Tbsp liquid smoke (optional)

Cut the tenderloin into strips about 1 inch wide and 1/4 inch thick. (You can substitute chicken, turkey, emu, or any animal your conscience allows you to eat.) Mix the ingredients well in a medium-size bowl, then toss in the meat. Cover with plastic wrap and refrigerate overnight. On the next day preheat the oven to its lowest setting (usually 150°), put the meat on an aluminum-foil-covered cookie sheet, and cook until it's cooked through—about three hours, depending on the meat's thickness. Broil it to where it's fairly dry but still tender.

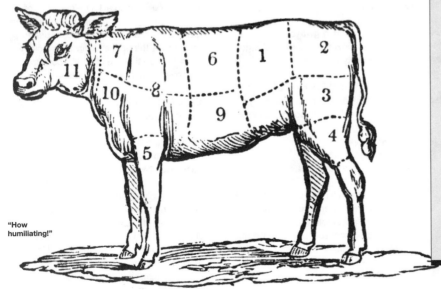

"How humiliating!"

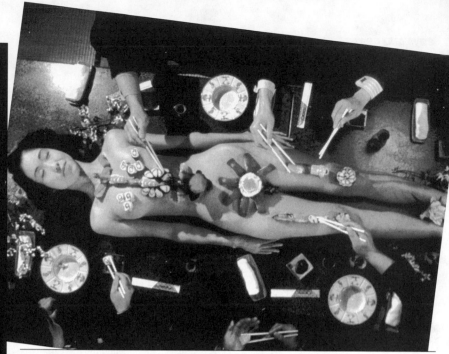

STAYIN' AFLOAT

Eat—check. Drink—check. Be merry? Um…this is gonna take some work, Twinkle-toes.

Sure, you cheated on your college and even bartender exams, but how the heck are you going to fake dancing? Don't worry: If you have even an ounce of rhythm, you're halfway there.

■ "First of all, don't look down," notes Melina Burdusi, dance instructor at the Towson Dance Studio in Towson, Maryland. "Women like a man with confidence, so always look up."

■ As with sex, concentrate more on the experience and not on the mechanics or you'll embarrass everyone involved. "Try to move your hips in time with the bass, and don't stop or pause," adds Burdusi, who also notes that "side-to-side dance moves are good, but never bounce, and never do the chickenhead; that's a big no-no."

■ Keep your elbows in an L-shape and uniform. "If everyone breaks out into uncontrollable laughter, get your ass and feet to the nearest dance studio."

"Eek! A giant bug!"

Roll Your Own Sushi

Could the power to turn raw, dead meat into a gourmet treat actually lie in your clumsy hands? Quite possibly. Phillip Yi, vice president of the celebrated California Sushi Academy in Venice, California, demonstrates how you, too, can make the tasty delight that's been a staple of Japanese cuisine for untold centuries: The California Roll.

Step 1: Hunt and gather

Pick up the following essentials at a gourmet or specialty food store:

■ a makisu (a rollable woven bamboo mat)
■ short-grain rice
■ grated wasabi (a fiery-hot green horse-radish)
■ pickled ginger
■ soy sauce
■ nori (a.k.a. sheets of seaweed)

For the filling you'll need some julienned veggies and either crabmeat or kanikama, a vegetarian substitute that's engineered to taste like crab and seal cracks in weather-stripping. Dressing yourself in a colorful silk robe may not help, but it certainly won't hurt, either.

Step 2: Line the roll

Cook half a cup of rice with salt and vinegar, and put out a bowl of water. "Wet your hands before you touch rice," says Yi. "Otherwise your hands will turn white." Heavens! It'll also keep the rice from sticking to you. Place a sheet of seaweed on the mat, then blanket it with about a half-inch of rice, leaving a 1 1/2-inch strip of uncovered seaweed running parallel to the grain of the mat. Place a sheet of cellophane over the rice, and flip the whole thing over so the rice is on the bottom. Remove the mat and set it aside.

Step 3: Fill 'er up

Cover the seaweed with another layer of rice, leaving a half-inch uncovered. Make a furrow in the rice along the opposite edge, in which to put the crabmeat, avocado, and cucumber. Moisten the exposed flap of the seaweed. Now use the mat to roll the seaweed into a cylinder until you've overlapped the moistened edge. Then light up the fat end of the roll and...no, wait...Wet a sharp knife and cut the roll into inch-wide wheels (practice on Ho Ho's). Chill in the fridge for an hour; serve with wasabi, soy sauce, ginger, and geisha girls.

CABLE GUY!

If your idea of leisure is entertaining the unemployed or invalid masses, then it's time to produce your own cable access TV show.

If you have cable (and what kind of hellish life are you leading if you don't?), you've seen public access television: cheap, bad, boring programs produced by people who you can only hope don't live near you. One approach to public access is to watch it in mute horror for a few seconds, then flip the channel and get to safety. The other is to realize that this can be your road to fame and TV Land fortune. We turned to the public access directors at Century Cable in Santa Monica, California, for their advice:

■ **Figure out what kind of show you want.** People have different motivations for producing programs. Some wish to be informative *(Ask Mr. Traffic),* while others take a lower, though arguably more entertaining, road *(Colin's Sleazy Friends).* Unlike success in most of TV Land, which depends on ratings, success in public access ultimately depends on how much you, the producer, like the final result. Colin, whose show consists of him interviewing porn starlets who then dance naked during the closing credits, considers his show a success. We agree.

■ **Take the producers' course.** Stations require that would-be producers attend a course to attain a minimum competency level (with the emphasis on *minimum*). Over two long and pointless weekends, you will be briefed about the rules and regulations of the station (i.e., no advertising), and the nuts and bolts of production (get your show done in two hours, because the crew won't stay late for you). To find out how to enroll in your local producers' course, call your cable TV supplier.

■ **Book interesting guests.** Your cousin is not interesting. Your drinking buddy is not interesting. The sad truth: You're not all that interesting. People with freakish talents are interesting. Nude people are interesting. Nude freaks are fascinating.

■ **Plan what will happen every minute.** This is where most shows fall apart. Too often hack producers book guests and figure that their work is done. Prepare a "breakdown" sheet, which divides the program into smaller segments. Every part of the show should be scheduled: introductions, skits, video roll-ins, time spent on

given topics, public service announcements, etc. Script the segments that can be scripted. If you know what's meant to happen during each and every minute of your show, you stand a better chance of not looking like a complete dickhead.

■ **Have a gimmick.** Public access producers talk constantly about *Squirt TV* and *Mister Pete*—two shows that made it onto legitimate TV networks. *Squirt TV* featured a prepubescent boy frolicking in his bedroom, while *Mister Pete* sported a magnificent mustache worthy of an Eastern bloc dictator. The take-home lesson? Weird is good.

■ **Bring your own set decorations.** The fake dogwood tree provided by the station has been on thousands of shows. Don't rely on it to liven up yours.

■ **Ignore the naysayers.** One director told us bluntly, "Don't do it. Back out now while you still have some dignity. Almost all public access shows suck. Yours will too." Of course you'll be on television. And when babes ask you what you do, you can tell them you're a producer.

Man's Laziest Friend

No other animal can share your leisure time better than a pooch.

"To some, I am only an ingredient."

You're going to want a little company during your new life of leisure, but if you're not careful, your pup'll grow up and kill your family. How can you be sure that the dog you pick is right for you?

DECIDE BEFORE YOU GO. "Consider what you're looking for in a dog, even before you get to the shelter," notes Jacque Schultz, director of special projects for the ASPCA. Are you looking for a serious commitment involving exercising, socializing, training, and grooming? In all

likelihood the answer is no (after all, that's why you're single). In which case you're better off with what Schultz calls the basic wash-and-wear pet.

MEET AND GREET. "Look for a dog who comes to the front of the cage and greets you in a social manner," explains Schultz. That shy pup shivering in the corner reminds you of your little brother, but it's probably even more neurotic than he is. Does Fido pay attention to you and seem to make a connection? Ask if you can take

him to a "get acquainted" room or area. Then just stand there and see if the dog's interested in you or in whatever may have urinated recently in the corner. After two or three minutes, put your hand down to stroke him. Does he kind of run up and meet your hand, or is he freaked? "Always go for the happy dog who's interested," says Schultz. "It'll be the one that'll fetch the paper for you."

If the dog's mean make sure nobody's watching you, and then kick him in the ribs.

THE ANSWER MAN

Screw with Telemarketers

If you can't avoid evil phone salespeople, you might as well have some fun with 'em.

"Hello, Mr. Jones! How're you today?" wonders the telephone voice that just spoiled your dinner, interrupted your coitus, or pulled you off the can. Don't get mad...get freaky. That telemarketer on the other end of the line is so starved for attention, he'd love to play any of the following games with you. Honest!

Game: Secret Agent Man
How to play: Ask repeatedly if the conversation is being recorded. Claim that the CIA's been listening in ever since you got back from "the operation in Grenada." Neither confirm nor deny any of the information he may have obtained.

You win when: He acknowledges that he hears the clicking, too.

Game: Say What?
How to play: Explain that you've just returned from a Limp Bizkit concert and your hearing is shot. Ask him to speak louder... louder...louder! Make him keep starting his pitch from the top.

You win when: He slams the phone down and you finish your meal or bathroom trip or stewardess in peace.

"That's right, sir. You've been very naughty and are in need of a good tongue-lashing."

Game: Holy Roller
How to play: Ask him if he has accepted the Lord Jesus into his heart. Deliver the "righteous man" speech from *Pulp Fiction*. Ask him to get on his knees and pray with you.

You win when: You get him to repeat after you, "Hallelujah."

Game: Tourette's Sufferer
How to play: Act interested in whatever he has to offer—but stutter. Explain that you have a neurological disease and that you can't bitch! control what goddamn man-titties! comes out of your assface! assface!

You win when: He apologizes to you.

Game: Finger Mutilation
How to play: Tell him you're chopping some onions for your spaghetti sauce and that you're interested in hearing what he has to say. After he starts his pitch, interrupt him with a piercing, obscenity-laced howl. Tell him that you just sliced your finger off while screaming hysterically. Act as if you're trying to handle the situation, but makeit apparent it's getting progressively worse.

You win when: He offers to call for help.

Q : Is it legal to download and/or post pornography on the Internet?

ANSWER: Yes and no. While states and communities can legally ban "obscene materials," the U.S. Supreme Court grants you a "zone of privacy" that generally permits you to possess obscene materials in your own home, including computer files. So it's perfectly legal to download a picture of adults playing consensual naked Twister; even such, uh, exotic tastes as S&M and bestiality could fall under that protection. Posting images is another story: Now you're officially "promoting," and it could be worth up to five years in the federal pokey. As in real life it gets worse if she's under 18: You face a heavy fine and up to 10 years in prison, under Title 18, Chapter 110 of the United States Code, for downloading (much less posting) kiddie porn. And that's no idle threat: A recent New York State sting, *Operation Rip Cord,* identified more than 2,000 suspects who downloaded kiddie porn through E-mail and chat rooms, and this led to more than 120 arrests and 31 convictions.

Q : In the song "Yankee Doodle Dandy," why would somebody stick a feather in his hat and call it "macaroni"?

ANSWER: In England in the late 1700s, the term *macaroni* referred to the members of the Macaroni Club, a group of dandies who favored the styles of continental Europe over those of their native land. (First rule of Macaroni Club: Don't talk about Macaroni Club.) Swishing around London in short coats, big wigs, and polka-dot stockings, they were universally loathed on both sides of the Atlantic—even the Germans hated 'em, and you know how hard it is to piss off the Germans. During the Revolutionary War, when soldiers waged battle by trading insults as well as bullets, the Brits would call their opponents "Yankee" (from a Dutch phrase meaning "cheese breath"), "doodle" (which meant they were morons), and "dandy" or "macaroni" (this last barb was by far the worst of them all). According to Richard Lederer, author of *The Word Circus and Crazy English,* "these words began as terms of derision for the colonists, but after the war they became terms of pride." Gosh, maybe all those guys who called you "douche bag" in high school really did like you.

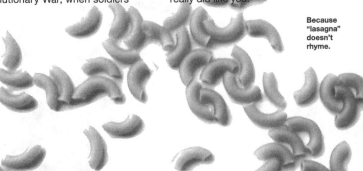

Because "lasagna" doesn't rhyme.

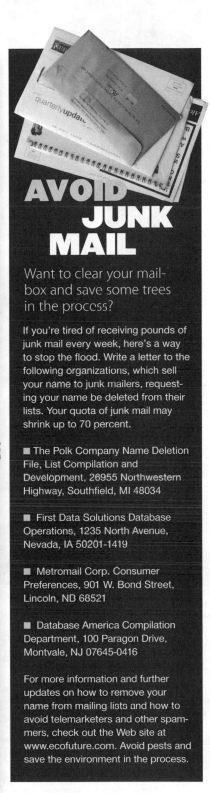

AVOID JUNK MAIL

Want to clear your mailbox and save some trees in the process?

If you're tired of receiving pounds of junk mail every week, here's a way to stop the flood. Write a letter to the following organizations, which sell your name to junk mailers, requesting your name be deleted from their lists. Your quota of junk mail may shrink up to 70 percent.

■ The Polk Company Name Deletion File, List Compilation and Development, 26955 Northwestern Highway, Southfield, MI 48034

■ First Data Solutions Database Operations, 1235 North Avenue, Nevada, IA 50201-1419

■ Metromail Corp. Consumer Preferences, 901 W. Bond Street, Lincoln, ND 68521

■ Database America Compilation Department, 100 Paragon Drive, Montvale, NJ 07645-0416

For more information and further updates on how to remove your name from mailing lists and how to avoid telemarketers and other spammers, check out the Web site at www.ecofuture.com. Avoid pests and save the environment in the process.

LAST 10 STANLEY CUP CHAMPIONS

1999–00	New Jersey 4, Dallas 2
1998–99	Dallas 4, Buffalo 2
1997–98	Detroit 4, Washington 0
1996–97	Detroit 4, Philadelphia 0
1995–96	Colorado 4, Florida 0
1994–95	New Jersey 4, Detroit 0
1993–94	NY (Rangers) 4, Vancouver 3
1992–93	Montreal 4, Los Angeles 1
1991–92	Pittsburgh 4, Chicago 0
1990–91	Pittsburgh 4, Minnesota 2

SPORTS EDGE

Because it's not whether you win or lose, but how badly asses are kicked.

Why do we love sport so much? As with most activities, it likely has a lot to do with the preponderance of alcohol that accompanies any athletic event. There's also our need to kick the crap out of others and make fun of their mothers while they wallow in abject defeat.

Watch your ass, Canada.

America's Pastime

Everything you need to lay down the lumber, throw a wicked curve, or simply be a spectator from your La-Z-Boy—this is our guide to the greatest American sport since the 100-meter get-the-hell-away-from-the-pissed-off-natives dash.

Get Slammy like Sammy

Learn how to knock the stitches loose…on the ball, not your pants, Ruthie.

All right, so maybe your shot at the majors is still sitting in your sixth-grade gym bag. That doesn't mean you can't go yard at the company picnic.

Use the wind. If it's blowing in to one side, knock the ball with it. If it's coming straight at you, a low line drive will go further. And if it's blowing from behind you, hit the ball up for a better chance of clearing the fence.

Have some balls. Boog Powell, 1970 American League MVP and power hitter extraordinaire, says he trained by carrying a tennis ball wherever he went, constantly squeezing it to develop hand strength.

Set it right. Billy "Sweet Swing" Williams, 1987 Hall of Famer, said you should set your hands in a position four to six inches back, before swinging...and practice using the whole field.

Attack the Pitcher. Bite, kick, and knee him in the... no, wait. One bit of advice coaches give is that you should walk out of the dugout, mentally preparing to lay waste to the ball. The pitcher should feel like you're the hunter, and he's the prey.

Handle the bat well. In the base of the fingers, not the back of your hand, for greater control. Also, hold the bat loose, free of tension.

Don't get out front. According to Tommy Davis, a career .294 hitter, "'Get the bat out front' is a misnomer." Instead, he says, you should hit the ball on an angle. On an inside pitch, for example, the head of the bat should be in front of the plate. When it's down the middle, the bat will be even with your navel. And when the pitch is outside, you should angle the bat down and back toward the catcher. Finally, if the pitch is square at your head, you should grip the bat tightly and hold it high as you go after the pitcher.

Stride. Move forward, toward the pitcher, as you swing, with your front foot coming down as softly as possible. When your "stride foot" comes down, your hands should still be behind, or even with, your back leg.

"Squash the bug." This is the way you should pivot your back foot as you swing—as a turning movement, not a push. You release your backside and turn, your hands swinging inside the flight path of the ball. Practice with the roaches at home.

Steal like Robin Hood

It's your only chance to burgle without going to jail, and here's how to do it right.

Be sure to get your greens.

GPG. No, it's not something Alan Greenspan manipulates. It's the rule for stealing used by Bert "The Roadrunner" Campaneris, who's one of the top base stealers in the game with a career total of 649. GPG stands for Get a good lead, Pick the right pitch to run on, and Get a good jump.

CLOCK THE PITCHER. Check his timing. If he has a slow delivery, or a big leg kick when winding up, he's like a baby with candy. Or a fool with money. Or...oh, hell, you get the idea.

RATTLE HIM. One way to do this is to act like you're going to steal any minute. Lead a lot, as long as your jump is good. That way, when you do steal he'll have a crucial half-second when he'll think you're faking.

WHEN TO BAIL. If all game you've been stealing third base, the traditional boon to runners, be cautious. You're apt to get stung.

Dangerous Curves

"Position your fingers just right..."

Learn to hurl the three basic curve balls—standard, screwball, and slider.

General Rules: Shorten your stride from a normal pitch, and throw with a little less speed. Also, lead with your chest, and pull forward and across your body to the opposite knee when you hurl. When you're done you want your elbow and the back of your wrist facing the batter. And not just because you've dislocated them.

STANDARD CURVEBALL: Hold the ball wedged down between your thumb and forefinger. Cock your wrist to the left when you throw—the ball will snap down and to the right when you release, then curve to the left.

SCREWBALL: Throw like you would a curveball, only reverse your wrist, cocking it first to the right, and then turning it over to the left as you release. The ball will whip down and to the right.

SLIDER: Throw the ball like a football, with the wrist cocked at a 90-degree angle. Note: If you use this pitch too often, it can damage the connective tissue of your forearm. Use sparingly, for God's sake.

Diamond Decrees
Baseball's trickiest rules made so simple, even a blind umpire will understand.

The long off-season can make you a little hazy when it comes to remembering players' nicknames, their slugging percentages with runners on third, and even, *gasp,* the rules. To get you up to speed, here's a quick refresher course:

INFIELD FLY RULE.
Why it's necessary: To rein in wily infielders.
When it's used: You're a third baseman saddled with runners on first and second, and maybe even third, and you've got fewer than two outs. Next batter pops it up for an easy out. But if there were no infield fly rule, you could let the ball bounce and then pick it up, tag a bag, and toss it to second for a freebie double play. To nip that shit in the bud, the infield fly rule declares any infield pop-up an automatic out—regardless of whether it's caught—and the runners must hold their positions.

GROUND RULE DOUBLE.
Why it's necessary: Because every ballpark has its quirks, from hyperactive AstroTurf that sends choppy grounders sailing over fences to ivy that can trap a ball against the centerfield wall.
When it's used: Before every game, the managers and umpires meet at home plate and review the specific idiosyncracies of the field they'll be playing on. When an in-play ball strikes an out-of-play obstacle, bounces over the fence, or rolls under a rain tarp, the batter is automatically awarded a double.

THE BALK.
Why it's necessary: Because pitchers would have a vast arsenal of sneaky pick-off moves, and a huge advantage over base runners, without it.
When it's used: When a pitcher is standing on the rubber, he's announcing to the batter and the base runners that he's going to make a pitch. If he changes his mind and wants to attempt a pick-off, he must step directly toward the intended base, clearly indicating that he's no longer pitching. If he does anything else—steps toward home and throws to first, or fakes a throw to first, even if he simply drops the ball—he's committing a balk. If the balk is called, the runner(s) advances one base.

RUNNER INTERFERENCE/ DEFENSIVE OBSTRUCTION.
Why it's necessary: To make sure runners and fielders don't turn the base paths into warpaths.
When it's used: You usually see "offensive interference" calls when base runners are trying to break up double plays. Here's the scenario: Player on first with fewer than two outs. Ground ball to the shortstop, who flips it to the second baseman for the force-out. But the second baseman is upended by the base runner and can't complete a double play. If the umpire thinks the runner has gone out of his way to make the second baseman's job difficult—it's called willful interference—the runner is automatically out, and so is the hitter running to first. On the defensive side, the second baseman can only obstruct a runner's progress to the base if he's (1) making a play on the runner, or (2) trying to catch the shortstop's flip. Like the "intentionally interferes" call, obstruction comes down to the umpire's judgment. But few umps like to make judgment calls, since they result in irate managers and dirt-kicking. So willful inteference and runner obstruction calls are rare, and turning a double play is still a dangerous proposition.

Break in a Mitt

How are you gonna snare one at the wall if your mitt doesn't fit like a glove?

When your father told you that the best way to break in your mitt was to slather it with fish guts, stick it in the freezer, then park the Caddy on it, he was—how to put this delicately?—completely fucking wrong. Ken Higdon, longtime equipment manager for the Anaheim Angels, has broken in hundreds of mitts for the pros. Here's how the big boys do it.

STEP ONE: The very first thing you should do after buying a new mitt is to play catch with it. "I usually get the mitts ready by tossing a ball around," says Higdon. "It sounds obvious, but this helps to form the pocket and ease the stiffness of a new mitt." Two hours of catch over two days, he says, is about right.

STEP TWO: "There's this stuff called Dr. Glove made by Franklin Sports," Higdon explains. "Grease the mitt thoroughly with Dr. Glove softener every other night for a week. This softens the leather, which is the key to a good mitt."

STEP THREE: Now you're ready to form the perfect pocket. "At the end of the week, dunk the mitt in a bucket of water for 10 minutes," says Higdon. "Then put a ball in the mitt, let the mitt form around it, and tape it shut with duct tape. Put the mitt in your closet, and leave it there overnight. This gives the mitt the right form."

ET VOILÀ: No more excuses for muffing those pop-ups.

THROW LIKE A PRO QB
Flinging the perfect pass.

Just because Ryan Leaf hasn't learned doesn't mean you can't.

1. Your fingers should grip the ball over the laces, with your index finger near the back of the ball for proper guidance. Leave a little space between your palm and the ball.

2. Keep the ball in a ready position at the armpit before raising it straight up to throw. Your elbow extends out and leads the ball toward the target. Your front foot should also be pointed toward the target to ensure accuracy.

3. When releasing the ball, keep your thumb and wrist facing down. The index finger should be last to leave the ball, and it should be pointing directly at the target.

SUPER BOWL CHAMPS SINCE 1989

2000	St. Louis 23, Tennessee 16	1994	Dallas 30, Buffalo 13
1999	Denver 34, Atlanta 19	1993	Dallas 52, Buffalo 17
1998	Denver 31, Green Bay 24	1992	Washington 37, Buffalo 24
1997	Green Bay 35, New England 21	1991	NY Giants 20, Buffalo 19
1996	Dallas 27, Pittsburgh 17	1990	San Francisco 55, Denver 10
1995	San Francisco 49, San Diego 26	1989	San Francisco 20, Cincinnati 16

FOOTBALL'S GREATEST RECORDS

Most Wins in a Season:
The 1972 Miami Dolphins. 19–0, including the playoffs and Super Bowl

Most Super Bowl Wins:
The San Francisco 49ers and the Dallas Cowboys are tied with five apiece.

Most rushing yards (Season):
Eric Dickerson 2,105 yards (L.A. Rams, 1984)

Most Rushing Yards (Game):
Corey Dillon 278 yards (Cincinnati Bengals, 10/22/2000)

Highest Rushing Average (Career):
Jim Brown 5.2 yards per carry

Most Touchdowns (Career):
Jerry Rice 187 (and counting)

Most Touchdown Passes (Career):
Dan Marino 420

Most Touchdown Passes (Season):
Dan Marino 48 (1984)

Most Passing Yards (Career):
Dan Marino 61,361 yards

Most Passing Yards (Game):
Norm Van Brocklin 554 yards (L.A. Rams, 9/28/51)

WORKHORSE DRILLS FOR A QUARTERBACK

THE DROP-BACK
Take the snap from the center, and practice backpedaling, taking three-, five-, and seven-step drops. Vary this by doing crossover backpedaling and rollout drops, where you move sideways to the line of scrimmage. This trains you to get into firing position quickly and cleanly, no matter who's barreling down at you.

SET, PICK, AND FIRE
Take the snap, do a quick drop, and set to deliver the ball. Station three or four receivers downfield, spaced out evenly, facing the QB. If you have a coach, he calls out a number and the quarterback resets his feet and fires. A harder variation involves the coach calling out a series of numbers. The quarterback has to set and aim for each player, in sequence, and deliver the ball to the last.

Signs and Signals

Here's the last, best guide you'll need to understand all the ref's signals. Tape it to the snack caddy for a handy reference.

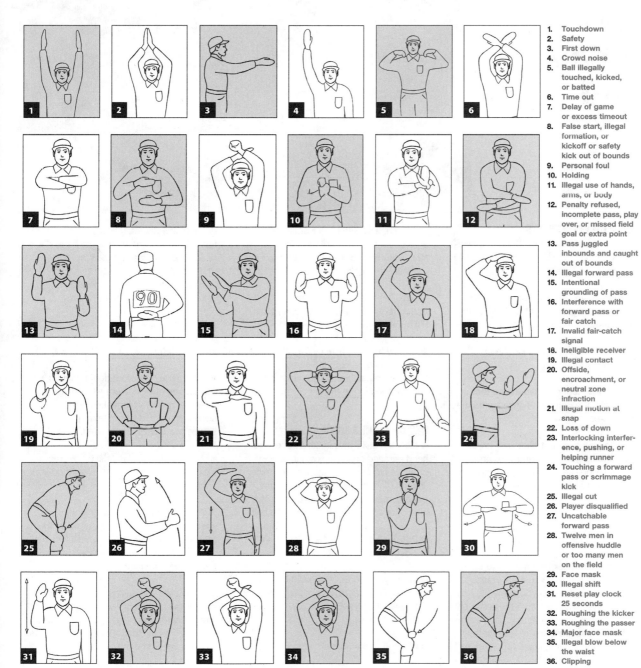

1. Touchdown
2. Safety
3. First down
4. Crowd noise
5. Ball illegally touched, kicked, or batted
6. Time out
7. Delay of game or excess timeout
8. False start, illegal formation, or kickoff or safety kick out of bounds
9. Personal foul
10. Holding
11. Illegal use of hands, arms, or body
12. Penalty refused, incomplete pass, play over, or missed field goal or extra point
13. Pass juggled inbounds and caught out of bounds
14. Illegal forward pass
15. Intentional grounding of pass
16. Interference with forward pass or fair catch
17. Invalid fair-catch signal
18. Ineligible receiver
19. Illegal contact
20. Offside, encroachment, or neutral zone infraction
21. Illegal motion at snap
22. Loss of down
23. Interlocking interference, pushing, or helping runner
24. Touching a forward pass or scrimmage kick
25. Illegal cut
26. Player disqualified
27. Uncatchable forward pass
28. Twelve men in offensive huddle or too many men on the field
29. Face mask
30. Illegal shift
31. Reset play clock 25 seconds
32. Roughing the kicker
33. Roughing the passer
34. Major face mask
35. Illegal blow below the waist
36. Clipping

Small Ball

Sure, golf's a game for arthritic old men. Learn these tips now so you can play it when you become one.

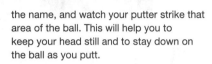

"Listen up, gopher. You and the Judge are goin' down."

PUMP UP YOUR PUTTS

No, this doesn't belong in the dating section. Keeping these tips in mind will make you mean on a green.

■ Stand so you're well-balanced, with 70 percent of your weight resting on the leg nearest the hole.

■ Bend a little at the knees to keep your base strong.

■ Keep your feet no more than a foot apart, with the golf ball slightly inside the foot nearest the hole.

■ While taking your stroke, your lower body should not move, and your arms should swing like a pendulum. Keep them relaxed and swing 'em freely.

■ A common cause of shooting past the hole is letting your wrists "break." Keep them locked in position.

■ Keep your putter face square to the line you want to shoot. If you mark your ball and clean it, when you place the ball back in position, make sure the name printed on the ball is visible and is on the side of the ball you are going to hit with the putter. When putting, keep your eyes on the name, and watch your putter strike that area of the ball. This will help you to keep your head still and to stay down on the ball as you putt.

■ Use the reverse overlap grip, with thumbs to the front, palms on the side, and the left index finger outside the right fingers.

■ Keep your eyes directly over the ball and directly parallel to the line of putt. If they are outside or inside, you'll compensate by shooting to the left or right.

REV UP YOUR DRIVES

■ Hold the ball tightly in the palm of your hand perched on the tee, which should protrude out between your first and second fingers. Plant that sucker firmly into the ground, making sure the top of your club will not come up below the center of the ball.

■ Position yourself so the ball is roughly opposite your left heel.

■ When you address the ball, keep your feet slightly wider than your shoulders and your weight centered, with your right side down and relaxed.

■ Make sure the right shoulder is dropped down below the left, never pulled up or forward. Your right arm should hang down relaxed, slightly behind the ball.

■ Your backswing should be wide and full, with your weight behind the ball.

■ At the top of your backswing, you're going to change direction. You have to give yourself plenty of time to do this.

■ During the drive your right shoulder, hands, and clubhead are all moving forward. You need to make sure the clubhead always leads and stays firmly behind the ball when it makes contact.

■ When driving make a full 90-degree turn, ending up with all the weight on your right foot.

■ When aiming don't simply look for the line of trees and try to stay between them. Most likely you will subconsciously drive toward one or the other. Instead find a fixed target and hit it.

■ Make sure you avoid trouble. Don't just aim for the middle of each fairway. Instead find the safest way to approach the green and you'll steer clear of hazards and get a lower score overall.

GOLF'S MAJOR TOURNAMENT WINNERS SINCE 1990

THE MASTERS

2000	Vijay Singh
1999	José María Olazábal
1998	Mark O'Meara
1997	Tiger Woods
1996	Nick Faldo
1995	Ben Crenshaw
1994	José María Olazábal
1993	Bernhard Langer
1992	Fred Couples
1991	Ian Woosnam
1990	Nick Faldo

U.S. OPEN

2000	Tiger Woods
1999	Payne Stewart
1998	Lee Janzen
1997	Ernie Els
1996	Steve Jones
1995	Corey Pavin
1994	Ernie Els
1993	Lee Janzen
1992	Tom Kite
1991	Payne Stewart
1990	Hale Irwin

BRITISH OPEN

2000	Tiger Woods
1999	Paul Lawrie
1998	Mark O'Meara
1997	Justin Leonard
1996	Tom Lehman
1995	John Daly
1994	Nick Price
1993	Greg Norman
1992	Nick Faldo
1991	Ian Baker-Finch
1990	Nick Faldo

PGA CHAMPIONSHIP

2000	Tiger Woods
1999	Tiger Woods
1998	Vijay Singh
1997	Davis Love III
1996	Mark Brooks
1995	Steve Elkington
1994	Nick Price
1993	Paul Azinger
1992	Nick Price
1991	John Daly
1990	Wayne Grady

GOLFERS WITH THE MOST MAJOR TOURNAMENT VICTORIES

Jack Nicklaus 20
- 6 Masters
- 4 U.S. Open
- 3 British Open
- 5 PGA Championship
- 2 U.S. Amateur

Gary Player 9
- 3 Masters
- 1 U.S. Open
- 3 British Open
- 2 PGA Championship

Harold Hilton 7
- 2 British Open
- 1 U.S. Amateur
- 4 British Amateur

Bobby Jones 13
- 4 U.S. Open
- 3 British Open
- 5 U.S. Amateur
- 1 British Amateur

Arnold Palmer 8
- 4 Masters
- 1 U.S. Open
- 2 British Open
- 1 U.S. Amateur

Gene Sarazen 7
- 1 Masters
- 2 U.S. Open
- 1 British Open
- 3 PGA Championship

Walter Hagen 11
- 2 U.S. Open
- 4 British Open
- 5 PGA Championship

Tom Watson 8
- 2 Masters
- 1 U.S. Open
- 5 British Open

Sam Snead 7
- 3 Masters
- 1 British Open
- 3 PGA Championship

Ben Hogan 9
- 2 Masters
- 4 U.S. Open
- 1 British Open
- 2 PGA Championship

Tiger Woods 8
- 1 Masters
- 1 U.S. Open
- 1 British Open
- 2 PGA Championships
- 3 U.S. Amateur

Harry Vardon 7
- 1 U.S. Open
- 6 British Open

Q: Why do golf balls have dimples?

ANSWER: The same reason Cheech and Chong had a multichambered hookah: to help them get high. As a golf ball soars over the green and makes a beeline for the water hazard, a pocket of turbulent air forms behind it, creating an area of low pressure. The greater the difference between the air pressure in front of the ball and that behind it, the more resistance to forward movement there is. Dimples minimize this difference, enabling a pock-marked ball to travel twice as far as a smooth one would. Most modern-day golf balls have 360 to 460 dimples, each one .12 to .16 inch in diameter. "There's no advantage to going outside that range because the air flow around the ball isn't as efficient if you use any fewer or any more dimples," says Matthew Stanczak, the dimple development engineer for Maxfli, one of America's largest golf ball manufacturers. Hmm...wonder how much range Gary Coleman's head has?

Betting Tips to Make You Quick Dough

Ah, who needs a 401(k) anyway?

While there are many ways to get your legs broken, none are quite as satisfying as when you take your bookie to the cleaners.

"Hey, hey! What's the rush?"

How can you cash in on a hot tip that the Cubs will sweep the Series? (Actually, we'll take that bet.) If you live in Vegas, it's easy: Get thee to any big-casino sports book. If you live outside Nevada but value your kneecaps too much to get involved with heinous, evil-smelling bookies, there's always the Internet. The no-sports-gamblin' law makes it verboten to accept wagers over state lines but OK to place wagers over state lines. Savvy cyberpreneurs have taken advantage of this loophole by setting up gambling sites outside the U.S. Experts estimate that more than $800 million in sports bets will be wagered online in the year 2000, and as much as $1.6 billion by the end of 2001.

How do you know these places will still be operating tomorrow? That's your problem.

(In fact at press time, a few of these off-shore gamblers' havens were under criminal investigation.)

However you do it, here's the basic strategy for making a living at sports gambling:

RULE #1: Do your homework.

Read preseason guides and the dailies, watch *SportsCenter* (and all sports shows) religiously, and listen to the experts for anything that might affect a game: Slumps and streaks, injuries, trade rumors. Watch the news too: When a star player gets arrested for assault, drug possession, or DWI, it's bound to have an effect on your team's morale. Place a bet without first arming yourself with good info and you're just pissing into a fan, but without that cool staccato sound.

RULE #2: Only bet games you feel you've got an edge on.

If you don't have an angle on a particular game, save your money: Picking a side "to keep things interesting" is amateur shit. You must be able to recognize the real plays from the dogs, regardless of what they are. If the smart bet at the time is the duration of two mules fornicating, you gotta make it, no questions asked.

RULE #3: Prepare to lose...a lot.

Even with inside dope, you're going to lose nearly half of your games—there are just too many factors be able to take them all into account. At any given time, any team can defeat any other team. Human desire and emotion account for a lot and can overcome mammoth point spreads.

RULE #4: Understand the spread.

Most people wrongly assume that the spread reflects two teams' relative abilities. Actually, it's simply the oddsmakers' attempt to choose a score that will divide the game's total betting pool in half (so sports books don't take a bath because of too many winners). This is why the spread "moves" as bettors vote with their dollars. Say the Denver Broncos start the week as a 10-point favorite at home over the Miami Dolphins, a.k.a. "Denver −10 over Miami." If Fins fans crawl out of the woodwork and pick Miami to beat the spread, the spread can decrease (say, to Denver −7 over Miami), reestablishing that voting equilibrium. How does this help you? Games are played on the field, not in the sports bar. If you think the general public's wrong and the spread's an inaccurate reflection of the scoring potential of the two teams, then it's time to take your chances.

RULE #5: Avoid sucker bets.

Multiple-winner bets, such as parlays and teasers, offer high payoffs but are extremely difficult to pull off. When was the last time you picked five winners in a row while playing the spreads? You won't know enough about all the contests involved to bet sensibly...and if you have to rely on luck, you may as well play craps. And don't waste time on 900-number picks-of-the-week lines. If you could reliably pick the winners of ball games and, hence, could make millions watching sports for a living, would you bother with the hassles of running a 900-number business, or would you live in Caesar's Palace, sharing a Jacuzzi with identical-triplet hookers? We rest our case.

"Shit! My contact lens! Nobody move!"

HOUSES OF THE HOLY

The definitive list of the best stadiums in the world.

■ Fenway Park

Fenway franks, the Green Monster, and the spot on the bleachers Ted Williams nailed. It's baseball nirvana. The only problem? It's surrounded by Boston. For reservations and information, call (617) 236-6666, or visit www.redsox.com.

■ Lambeau Field

Named after Earl L. "Curly" Lambeau, founder of the Packers, this stadium is everything you want in a football arena. The seats are all close to the action: There are no upper decks, and the backs of the end zones are mere yards away from the first row. More to the point, it's every bit as cold as you expect a football game to be. Jaw-clenching, ball-shriveling cold. And you either scream rabidly with the rest of the fans, surreptitiously drinking bourbon to keep away the chill...or you die, pal. This too is what the sport is about. (Note: A major renovation is set to take place from 2001 through 2003, so move quickly to visit Lambeau in its current "old school" shape. Call (920) 494-3328, or visit www.packers.com.

■ Madison Square Garden

The 18,000-plus seats of this colossus are made more impressive by the fact that during Rangers and Knicks games, each one of them is packed with a screaming, sociopathic New Yorker who probably already has your wallet. Whether hockey or basketball is your game, you must see what hell would look like if you had to buy a scalped ticket to get there. Call (212) 465-6040, or visit www.madisonsquaregarden.com.

■ Charlotte Coliseum

The home of the NBA's Hornets and the WNBA's Sting, the Charlotte Coliseum is undoubtedly the chummiest, most down-home 23,000-seat stadium you'll ever visit. High numbers of season ticket-holders make for plenty of familiarity among fans. Plus, being Bible Belters, the crowd often actually joins in for a pregame prayer. A perfect place to find God and watch some serious ass-kicking in the process. Call (704) 357-4701.

■ Wimbledon

Yeah, Wimbledon may conjure up images of stuffy folks with prissy accents, monocles, and crooked teeth who would have been taken over by the Germans long ago if it weren't for us. Nonetheless it's the world's tennis Mecca. With 20 grass courts, seating for more than 13,000 people in Centre Court, and atmosphere to spare, this is the place you must be to see the world's best tennis. The tournament has been running since 1877—from its present location since 1922. For more info visit www.wimbledon.org.

"Which one of you is the guy they call Shorty?"

Roundball

Everything you need to know to turn B-rate game into A-game.

STRAIGHT SHOOTING

If you can't hit the side of a barn with a dart from 10 paces, these quick hints will help improve all your shots across the boards.

ONE-HANDED JUMP SHOT:

■ Don't let your helper hand keep in contact too long. And make it a light, light touch.

■ Your shooting hand should rotate out until your middle finger is sticking straight up—that's when you're ready to shoot the ball (insert your own flipping-the-bird joke here). This way when you throw it, it will assume a straight, backward rotation, which will keep it stable and prevent it from winging off the backboard.

■ As you rotate your hand and prepare to shoot, the foot on the same side as your shooting hand should be coming up and slightly ahead of the other foot as you jump. Both feet should be shoulder-width apart.

■ Any shot within eight feet of the hole needs some backboard. Don't try to net it or you'll look like a chump when it wings someone off the court.

■ Don't shoot short. The main cause of this is shooting while your body's coming down, which forces your arm to work against the momentum of your body. Make sure you launch that ball when you are at the top of your arc. And don't try to jump so high, either, or you'll run out of steam.

HOOK SHOT:

You should be within 10 feet of the basket and start with your back to it for this to work.

■ Keep your legs flexed, with your feet shoulder-width apart or more.

■ After you get the ball, chest it with two hands, then pivot on your right foot to take a long step into the lane with your left leg. Keep your left foot turned toward the basket.

■ Land with the heel of your left foot, roll forward to the ball of your foot, rotate like a bastard, lifting your right knee straight up, and with both hands lift the ball past your head.

■ Keep the wrist of your shooting hand cocked as you move it toward the net, and rest the ball on the pads of your fingers so you can release it easy and light.

■ Release your helper hand before your shooter hand lets go, or you will tip the shot off to one side.

FREE THROW:

■ Keep your elbows tucked in. By keeping them tucked, you eliminate the risk of shooting off to one side of the net.

■ Don't take your position too soon—wait until the ref has the ball to hand you. Otherwise you'll be standing there sweating, getting so nervous and twitchy that you'll fake yourself out.

■ Find the hole that marks the center of the free-throw circle. Pace your toe on the same side as your shooting hand one inch behind that point.

■ Always bounce the ball the same number of times whenever you shoot. This relaxes you and gets you into a rhythm. Also breathe deep, and then exhale.

■ Don't heave the ball in a straight line toward the backboard. Shoot a gentle one-handed jump with plenty of arc.

BASKETBALL'S GREATEST RECORDS

Most NBA Titles:
The Boston Celtics have won 16 NBA titles (1957, 1959–1966, 1968, 1969, 1974, 1976, 1981, 1984, and 1986). Too bad they've sucked ever since that last one.

Most NBA Season Wins:
Chicago Bulls 72 (1995-96)

Most Points (Career):
Kareem Abdul-Jabbar 38,387

Most Points (Season):
Wilt Chamberlain 4,029 (Philadelphia, 1961–62)

Most Points in a Game:
Wilt Chamberlain 100 (Philadelphia, 3/2/1962)

Highest Scoring Average (Career):
Michael Jordan 31.5 ppg over 930 games

Highest Scoring Average (Season):
Wilt Chamberlain 50.4 ppg (Philadelphia, 1961–62)

Most 3-pt. Field Goals (Career):
Reggie Miller 1,867 (and counting)

Most 3-pt. Field Goals (Game):
Dennis Scott 11 (Orlando, 4/18/96)

Most Rebounds (Career):
Wilt Chamberlain 23,924 (that's a 22.9 rebound per game average, folks!)

Most Rebounds (Game):
Wilt Chamberlain 55 (Philadelphia, 11/24/60)

Most Assists (Career):
John Stockton 13,087

Most Assists (Game):
Scott Skiles 30 (Orlando, 1990)

Sneak Booze Into a Stadium
Because you're tired of paying $6 for a 12-oz. brew.

MAXIM

Shots from the hip.

CANS AND BOTTLES

■ Purchase one of those big foam "We're #1!" hands and hollow the fingers out. Who's going to suspect that you, the team's biggest fan, have five brewskies stuffed up there?

■ Confound the security dudes by wearing a big coat over your sweatshirt. They'll search your outer pockets but miss bottles hidden in the sweatshirt tucked into your jeans.

■ Buy a sandwich at any of the big chain sandwich shops (Subway, Blimpie, Togo's, Quizno's, etc.) along with an empty sandwich roll. Eat the sandwich and save the paper it was wrapped in. Then, cut the roll in half lengthwise and stick a pint of Jack Daniels in there. Wrap your "sandwich" in the wrapping paper and stick it in your bag. When the clueless security guard looks inside he'll just be seeing your dinner. Even if he squeezes your sandwich, he'll just feel the bread, not the bottle stashed safely inside. The beauty of this one is you can make several different kinds of "sandwiches" and enjoy a full range of cocktails during the game.

■ Buy some "Barnoculars," realistic looking binoculars that are really cleverly disguised dual flasks. Available in most joke and gag stores, or online at www.fakecrap.com ($15).

■ Buy a container of contact lens solution, empty it, then refill it with your booze du jour. Once inside, squirt some of that extra-strength saline into your stadium cola.

■ Before heading to the stadium, inject oranges with vodka. Tell security that you're diabetic and must have fruit with you at all times. (Keep the syringe for added effect.)

■ Dump a shot or two of hard stuff into spill-proof plastic sandwich bags. Slip the half-filled bags into the pockets of your baggiest pant, under your hat, down your crotch, and in your socks. (The last two places are also ideal for flasks.)

KEGS

Rent or borrow a wheelchair. Strap a keg underneath the seat, sit a buddy down, cover his legs (and the seat) with a blanket, and wheel him on in. Section 37 will thank you. Add a flask shoved in a fake leg cast and you rule this game!

TIPS ON TECHNIQUE

■ Enter the stadium during peak periods, when security is busiest.

■ If you and your friends arrive late, split up and stagger your entrances. Security will view a guy arriving alone as a pitiable loser and let him pass with a gentle pat down.

■ Ask Dad to sneak it in. No one will expect your gray-haired pa to have six pints of Jameson wrapped in his stadium blanket.

■ Bring women along. The guards will think you're more benign if some straight-laced-looking gals accompany you.

"We never talk anymore, you know? Just talk."

HEAVYWEIGHT CHAMPIONS SINCE 1980			
1980–82	Mike Weaver (WBA)	1992–93	Riddick Bowe (WBA, IBF)
1980–85	Larry Holmes	1992–94	Lennox Lewis (WBC)
1982–83	Michael Dokes (WBA)	1993–94	Evander Holyfield (WBA, IBF)
1983–84	Gerrie Coetzee (WBA)	1994	Michael Moorer (WBA, IBF)
1984	Tim Witherspoon (WBC)	1994–95	George Foreman (WBA, IBF)
1984–85	Greg Page (WBA)	1994–95	Oliver McCall (WBC)
1984–86	Pinklon Thomas (WBC)	1995–96	Frank Bruno (WBC)
1985–87	Michael Spinks	1995–96	Bruce Seldon (WBA)
1986	Tim Witherspoon (WBA)	1995–96	Francois Botha (IBF)
1986	Trevor Berbick (WBC)	1996	Mike Tyson (WBA, WBC)
1986–87	Mike Tyson (WBC)	1996	Evander Holyfield (WBA)
1986–87	James "Bonecrusher" Smith (WBA)	1997	Michael Moorer (IBF)
1987	Tony Tucker (IBF)	1997	Lennox Lewis (WBC)
1987–90	Mike Tyson	1997–99	Evander Holyfield (WBA, IBF)
1990	Buster Douglas	1999–00	Lennox Lewis (WBC, WBA, IBF)
1990–92	Evander Holyfield	2000	Evander Holyfield (WBA)

SEX EDGE

Doin' and doin' it and doin' it well...

We all want the kind of sex life that would make Hugh Hefner seem like a Carmelite nun. You know...the kind of acrobatic sex that can peel the paint off walls. Guess what? Anyone, and we mean *anyone*, can have great sex. Better, longer, weirder, and illegal in most states. After you read this chapter, women will worship you...and they'll bring friends. Welcome to your new life.

Talk Her into Bed

The Osmond nobody talks about.

Baby steps, young Jedi.

Before you worry about holding it longer and doing it better, you have to get yourself a partner (there's always a catch, isn't there?). Before you commence with the mattress mambo, use these surefire lines to rope her in, cowboy.

You know who gets a woman into bed on the first date? A man can subtly trigger the female mating instinct by revealing himself to be the kind of guy she'd like to mate with. And bragging about your job or your ride isn't the way to do it. No, what will really melt her heart (and her panties) are words and phrases that strike her on an almost Darwinian level.

Don't take it from us. Geoffrey Miller, a cognitive psychologist and the author of The *Mating Mind,* says there is evolutionary evidence for why girls fall for the sappy crap we dole out. Like how she melts when you say you love cats. Heck, you don't even have to love them; just saying you don't mind them can promote you from putz to prospect in a matter of seconds. Try putting some of these phrases on display during your next date and she'll be purring all the way back to your place.

"I CRIED LIKE A BABY."

These five words say worlds about you symbolically—not only that you've used your tear ducts on at least one occasion, but that you're comfortable enough with your masculinity to gush forth with such a fountain of feelings. Miller believes that you earn extra points if your tears are emotional (from watching *The Champ*) rather than pain-related (from getting the crap beat out of you in middle school). "Women want to see that you have the emotional capability to sympathize, which is crucial in relationships," says Miller. "Especially if it's for someone you're not even related to, like a fictional character in a movie."

"YOU'VE GOT THE MOST GORGEOUS EYES/BEAUTIFUL COLLARBONE/AMAZING LAUGH."

Rather than telling the woman you're with that she "looks great," compliment something unique about her. This, by the way, works best when expressed in a revelatory tone, as in, "Wow, I hadn't really noticed until the light hit your face in that certain way" or "...until I saw you smile from across the room." Steer clear of features that get Hooters girls hired, like her breasts, butt, legs, and lips (or at least save those compliments for later, when she's hopefully stripping down and wants you to notice these features). "Complimenting a woman on her primarily sexual features is a powerful way of saying you're not in it for the long term," explains Miller. And while you may not be in it for the long term, we suggest you keep that to yourself for the short term.

"SOME JACKASS WAS TRYING TO START A FIGHT WITH ME."

While every woman has had a fantasy about two men fighting to the death over her, in the real world of supermarkets and sports bars, women don't like men who fight. "A hundred thousand years ago, our ancestors wanted men who could maintain peace to keep their children out of danger," says Miller. "This is the same way dominant male chimpanzees act: like policemen who break up fights rather than start them." So don't think you're impressing them with

your tough-guy speeches. They'd much rather hug the big hairy ape who can calm those ready-to-rumble types down.

"IT WAS FOR CHARITY."

You don't feed the homeless in soup kitchens or run the bingo game at the nursing home or anything like that. But, yeah, you did run a 5K for cancer last month. And that new painting in your apartment? Well, sure, you bought it at an Art for AIDS auction. Women don't want to date telethon hosts, but she'd love to hear that every so often you do something that benefits a greater good, however inadvertently. "Our species evolved to be incredibly altruistic because our ancestors were into mates who displayed traits of sympathy and kindness toward others," says Miller.

"I'M GOING HOME TOMORROW TO HELP MY MOM INSTALL HER NEW COMPUTER."

Can't go for lunch on Saturday? Oh. Can't go because you promised your mom you'd drive her to IKEA and then assemble her new three-tier portable bookshelf? Oh! It warms a woman's heart to hear that a guy is happy to spend time with his family. "Think about it," says Miller. "You can't choose your family. And because our family members are often not people we would have chosen as our friends if we weren't related, being close with his family indicates that a man can adapt socially to other people he can't choose—like his in-laws." Not to mention that she's thinking if all goes well, she might be spending time with your family, too.

"I LIKE TO COOK."

It's every woman's domestic fantasy: A handsome man, shirtsleeves rolled up to his elbows, is in their kitchen, cooking her a gourmet meal. And here's the great part: You don't even have to be good at it. If you're whistling while you pour pancake batter into the shape of silver dollars, women

don't care that you can't make crepes. Dating you would bring them that much closer to living out one of those scenes in a J.Crew catalog, where barefoot men in log cabins crack eggs into cast-iron frying pans. "Culturally, this implies that a man doesn't allocate traditional gender roles—he's not going to come home from work and ask, 'Where's my dinner?'" Miller explains. "Women find it attractive that a man will share home responsibilities."

"I'M TAKING VACATION NEXT WEEK."

You'll do whatever it takes to get ahead in your job, you love jetting around the world for business meetings, and you plan on being a CEO by 35. Sounds great—to a Palm VII. Women want men who love their jobs, but trust us when we tell you that no woman wants a workaholic. So if you tell her you work to live—rather than live to work—she'll sigh with more relief than a metope on the Parthenon. "When a woman selects a mate, she ideally looks for a man she can raise a family with, and she wants to know that he'll be there for it, too," says Miller, who suggests talking to her about the vacations you want to take. "Talking about time off," he says, "is a good sign that you take time off." Plus, talk about the warm sand and the tropical breezes you're looking forward to and she'll wonder if you might not want a travel companion.

"I WAS TAKING CARE OF MY NIECE THE OTHER DAY..."

Drip...drip...drip...That's the sound of a woman's heart melting at the thought of a man tying a two-year-old's sneakers. "When our ancestors chose sexual companions, they were also choosing fathers for their children," says Miller. "It's still crucial for women to anticipate how interested a man is in child care, should she ever make a baby with him." While most guys would rather do a shot of Similac than bring up the subject of children, you should know that mentioning your soft spot for kids will just about bust a woman's biological clock. Throw in the fact that you think little girls are sweeter than boys and she'll be grinning like the cat that ate the canary.

"I'll be Mike Tyson and you'll be Evander Holyfield."

SWEET NOTHINGS

Dirty Talking

Turn that sweet girl into a foul-mouthed tigress.

A great way to spice up your sex life is to employ, um, "colorful language." But beware: There is a difference between sounding provocative and sounding like a porn star with Tourette's syndrome. We asked some ladies for tips on how to keep from scaring them off.

■ Speak first

If you want to get your babe talking dirty, initiate it yourself—before making a beeline to the bedroom. "When my date asked if he could sit next to me during dinner so he could look into my beautiful eyes, I was hugely turned on," says Jill, 33. Another woman had an Italian lover who made her knees go weak when he whispered, *Ti voglio coccolare,* which means "I want to cuddle you." She didn't know it meant that at the time; with her minimal Italian, she knew only that he wanted to do something to her. But heck, she said: "He could have said he wanted to clip my toenails and I would have melted."

■ Be specific

Focus on the unique attributes that make your lady luscious so she knows you're not using lines your best friend swears by. Does she have long eyelashes? A shapely waist? A collarbone that could balance a bottle of wine? Compliment it all. And for God's sake don't mumble. Nick Nolte may get away with it, but nothing can make a woman more uncomfortable than hearing "Mumble, sexy, mumble, harder, mumble" from you. In the same way a joke's not funny when you have to explain the punch line, you shouldn't have to repeat what you meant by wanting to "come fall over" her.

■ Pose a question

Ease your way into spicy speak by asking her if you can do certain things rather than telling her. This not only shows a woman you respect her but also lessens any pressure she may feel to perform like a porn star. Try, for example, "May I slide my hands up your skirt and slip off your panties?" If she responds with, "You could, but I forgot to wear panties," you're well on your way to delectable disrobing dialogue.

■ Be a master of disguise

Don't shock your girlfriend with trash talk

Words That Work

If she takes to phrases like these, she may be ready to grant your big promotion.

■ "My boyfriend and I were at a coffee bar, and while I was pouring nonfat milk into my grande Sumatra, he whispered, 'I'd like to cool you off with an ice cube between my lips and then heat you back up with my tongue.' I started to melt right there."—*Allison, 32*

■ "One guy said, 'I've had a huge crush on you all night—can I kiss you?' and it totally sent tingles through my body."—*Gillian, 31*

■ "I was at this party with a ton of gorgeous women who were all decked out, and my boyfriend said, 'You're the most beautiful woman in the room; every guy here is jealous of me.' We had amazing sex that night."—*Annie, 37*

■ "The most arousing phrase a man ever murmured to me was 'I want to look at your face while I touch you so I can see your pleasure.' And what a pleasure it was!"—*Monica, 25*

■ "I was playing pool, and my boyfriend leaned in as if he was going to help me with my shot, but what he actually said was, 'Your ass looks so hot in those jeans, I can't wait to take them off you later.'"—*Amy, 28*

■ "I was on the third date with this guy, and before we sat down to dinner, he whisked me away to the bathroom, kissed me, and said, 'You are so delicious, I could eat you with a spoon.' Needless to say, we went home for dessert."—*Lisa, 30*

that would make Deion Sanders proud. Instead, toy with your words and employ a little double entendre as a way of getting into your lioness' den. Maybe you want to pet her kitty or munch on a late lunch. This is a lot more fun than calling her body parts by the clinical names in Gray's Anatomy. (Not to mention that those won't get her wet unless you're talking to her in a swimming pool.)

■ Remember, it's just talk

In the land of naughty talk, you're not required to follow through on the promises you make, so let your imagination run wild: Tell her you'd like to lather her up and oil her down. Tell her you want to strip her naked and lick every inch of her body for the baseball stadium JumboTron. Usually just picturing such scenarios is enough to send currents of desire through her body (and in the case of the JumboTron, a little bit of fear).

per dirty words, and the hotter he got, the wetter I got; it worked like a charm. Now I talk like that in bed all the time." This is just as effective if the two of you happen to live in the same town—or are, perhaps, on opposite sides of those soundproof prison windows.

■ ID her private parts

Try getting your girl to open up about what she likes to call her anatomical jewel. This prevents those awkward moments when you're complimenting her big jugs or bazoombas when she'd much rather you were calling them breasts. Sometimes having her utter the words she likes can be libidinous. "As soon as I told my boyfriend I liked to use the P-word for my special spot, the floodgates opened. I got hot simply mouthing the word to him," says Laura, 29.

■ Use your own words

Reciting cheesy lines from Bryan Adams' songs or *Deepthroat IX* is only

Unclasp a Bra With One Hand

Send the signal right from the start that, hey, you know what the hell you're doing…

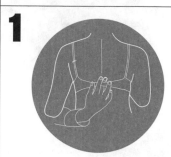

1

With the palm of your dominant hand facing her, slide your middle finger under the bra strap, right between the clasp and her unbelievable body.

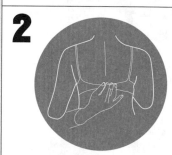

2

Pull the clasp out and away from her with your middle finger, and pinch the strap between your thumb and ring finger. Pull your middle finger out, and begin to hum "Moon River."

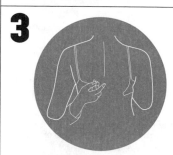

3

Slowly snap your fingers to accomplish mission. If she has a double-clasp bra, you may have to snap twice; don't get flustered. Practice on department store mannequins if necessary.

Tell her you want to strip her naked and lick every inch of her body for the baseball Jumbotron.

■ Eat, drink, and be merry

"The best bottle of Dom Pérignon I ever drank was off my boyfriend's body," says Rose, 36. "The bubbly added these really fun tingles, and I went down on him for days." The best thing about using food is that you get to talk about it. Go on a field trip to the supermarket with your girl and ask her what she'd like to taste on you. Or if you're in a restaurant, dip your finger in the crème fraîche and ask her if she'd like to nibble on it. Think about it: If she's willing to lap up that cream...

■ Turn your telephone calls into phone fantasies

One way to matriculate your girlfriend in the school of lewd lingo is to use the telephone; not looking each another in the face can be freeing. "When my boyfriend went overseas for a few weeks, we started fooling around over the phone as a joke," says Jill. "I'd whis-

going to arm your girlfriend and her friends with scathing criticism: "And then he said, 'Bow before my purple-helmeted soldier of love.'" Just keep it real. Most women like to think kinky, but if you offer to pierce them with your steely sword, they may be more nervous than receptive.

■ Star in your own role-play

In the same way that phone sex allows you to let go of inhibitions, creating alternate personas can facilitate some titillating talk face-to-face. "My boyfriend and I changed our names, met in a bar, and picked each other up as if meeting for the first time," says Amber, 27. "Because I was playing this wild woman, I used the most explicit words I could think of." Pull it off in public and you'll have every woman in the joint wanting to see the magic potion in your pocket.

Tantric Sex
Put your leg there...OK, now hold it for six to seven hours...

Don't try this at home.

It's an Eastern tradition that allows you and your woman to get in touch with each other's inner spiritual energies. But you don't care about that. What you want is eight hours of screaming multiple orgasms for the both of you, right? Here's all you need to know to get there without burning any fucking incense:

GET IN SYNC.

You and your girlfriend or wife should spoon up, both lying on your left side (ancient Tantric principles say this is the best way to achieve closeness; we'd like to add it makes it easy to grab her ass.). Both of you should inhale, holding it a few seconds, exhale, holding a few seconds, and so on, until you're breathing comfortably in unison. You practice this a few times—say, every morning—until you do it easily.

FACE-OFF.

The next step is to sit cross-legged, opposite each other. You should hold hands, look into each other's eyes, and start breathing in unison. There's a bunch of other mystical shit you can say to each other—but that isn't the point now, is it? No, the point is get into the moment, enjoy it, and whatever you do, don't rush. After a little while, you and she should reach over and start fondling each other, slowly and rhythmically. Don't worry how much time it takes or where you're going. Focus on your breathing and the sensations you're feeling together. No moaning, wiggling, or writhing. Try to keep calm and aware.

LET'S GET IT ON.

Eventually, you can have sex. Get into the missionary position—it's better for control at the beginning—and put an inch or two of your penis into her. No thrusting. Just rest it there for a few minutes. Take your penis out, and rub the head all around her clitoris and vagina. Repeat the process and take your time, Flash.

RINSE, LATHER, AND REPEAT.

You should practice, slowly building up to the point where you're going to come, and then relaxing. Obviously you will eventually let go. But practice going further and further to the edge without falling off (called "riding the wave" by Tantra masters) and you will get better at it. Eventually, you and your girlie will have "full-body" orgasms, a sensation that will wrap around you instead of being just a small, local explosion down at the "point."

Get Her in the Mood for Nookie
Before you do it, of course, you gotta set the stage.

Milwaukee's very best.

Here's how to do it right. A great way to put her in the mood without saying, "Hey, you wanna do it?" is to wait until she's just out of the shower and help her towel off. It's suggestive without coming on too fast too soon. Or lay the groundwork that morning by leaving her a suggestive note where she'll find it on her commute, when she can't see you right away, according to Sari Locker, sex educator and author of *The Complete Idiot's Guide to Amazing Sex.* This way, she says, you get her to think about it all day—kind of like 12-hour foreplay, only without the wear and tear.

GO SLOW AND START SMALL.

Don't break out the Orgasminator 2000 and that Best of Jenna Jameson tape just yet. A good place to start is the Web site of Good Vibrations (www.goodvibes.com), a San Francisco-based sex emporium that's very good for women, couples, newcomers...you get the point. Their sight is frank and easy to use, and doesn't make the whole thing sound seedy. A good place to buy porn that nice girls will like is at www.royalle.com. This is the Web site of Candida Royalle, a porn star from the '80s who made it her mission to create erotic films that women would get into. And God bless her for it.

DO HER MIND FIRST.

The female imagination is your greatest tool to getting some quality tail. That isn't some bullshit Mars-Venus claptrap, either. A Hite study and a Kinsey study found that women's sexual fantasies were strong and pronounced—a small percentage of women can actually come just by fantasizing about sex, with no other help! Write her an erotic story, or call her on the phone and tell her what you'd like to do. Either way, your mission is to get her thinking about it.

MAKE GUILT WORK FOR YOU.

Nobody really wants to cheat. It makes you feel bad, it makes her feel bad, and it's more trouble than it's worth. But, according to sex guru Nancy Friday, an expert on female fantasies, nothing compares with the thrill of having forbidden sex—because our earliest sexual feelings and adventures are linked to sneaking behind our parents' backs. Your mission, if you want to really drive her wild, is to bring back the feeling that you two are doing something naughty or prohibitive. Checking into hotels under assumed names, wearing costumes, or even an old fashioned fuck in the back seat can do the trick. Be creative.

"Whoops! Time for my 8:19 orgasm."

MAKE HER COME LIKE CLOCKWORK

These approaches to her runway will have you flying the very friendly skies.

It's not an ego thing, it's not for bragging rights, and you sure can't get a degree in it. But if you can bring her to the moon every time, she'll want to take the trip more often. Here's how to get her there:

■ **Memorize this stat: 30/40/30.** Thirty percent of women can come from intercourse alone, 40 percent can come from their man's hand, and 30 percent are down with the mouth, according to a Hite report. The easiest moves to make are also the most effective. For a good hand job, several women we talked to say the key part is to start outside and move in. "Don't go for my clit like it's the buzzer on *Jeopardy,*" says Marcy, a legal secretary who's been given rough treatment before. Instead, start by massaging her legs, stomach, inner thighs, pubic hair, then her lips before hitting the spot.

■ **Keep it light and lubed.** Use her lubrication to keep things slick, and massage her clit in tiny circles. Since the clit is so sensitive, it sometimes hurts when you rub it too soon. If she's not there yet, continue to rub her clit from outside of her lips or on top of her clitoral hood—it will dull the sensations just enough to keep them warm and pleasant.

■ **Go all over.** Some women love it when a guy gently slips one or two fingers inside her while stimulating her clitoris.

■ **Cheat.** Get her to help. She gets all the excitement of having a partner, but it's just as efficient as if she did herself in the shower. In fact, according to Kinsey's research, women can reach orgasm from masturbation in about four minutes! That's practically the time it takes a guy (if there are distractions). So, ask her. Or better yet, just guide her hand down there so she's helping you out at first, and then pull back subtly and watch her go. You get to help her reach orgasm without any carpal tunnel problems, and—here's the kicker—you can start studying her moves.

■ **Bonus round.** Here's how to get her there again. While her clit may be too sensitive for direct stimulation right after she comes, keep lightly touching around the area. She should start breathing slowly and deeply, and gently rocking her pelvis in time—you can help her with this part. In some cases this is all it takes to get her warmed up again and ready for action. In fact, it might even get you up again, so it's certainly worth a try. But then again, sometimes it's so tempting to just turn over and go to—zzzzzzz...

Mouthing Off

According to a *Redbook* study, 90 percent of women like getting head. (Who says we're nothing alike?) Keep these tips in mind and you can't go wrong:

LICK AROUND THE ENTIRE AREA.
As with giving her a hand job, you should start outside and work your way in. Don't go right for the clitoris until you know she's ready. Instead, get her aroused by licking her inner thighs, belly, vulva. Wait until she starts subtly moving herself up to meet your mouth before you go for it.

FINGERS.
A lot of women like it if you use your fingers to gently pull their lips apart. Gently, dammit. You're not shooting rubber bands here.

ROAM AROUND HER BODY.
Use your hands to rub other parts of her body, like her breasts or the small of her back. Go gentle, but firm.

VARY YOUR STROKES.
Use the flat of your tongue and lick the whole length of her slit like warm, fleshy ice cream (OK, not a great image). But use your tongue to make flat, light strokes until she's good and warmed up, then start flicking her clitoris with the tip of your tongue in a gentle rhythm as she gets more and more into it.

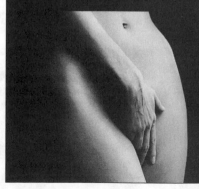

DUMB FUCKS

Bedroom Blunders

OK, since you're on your way to Casanova-hood, it's time to identify some possible flaws in your technique. To have her moaning, not groaning, avoid these moves.

HEADING STRAIGHT FOR THE BUSH: There is such a thing as going Down Under too soon, mate. "As charming as a guy is and as much as I may be attracted to him, I don't get instantly aroused," says Amy, 26. "I need some foreplay—you know, kissing, caressing." More specifically, points out Jennifer, 28: "There's more to a woman's body than her vagina. Just because guys like women to reach right for their penises doesn't mean women go for that, too."

KNEADING THE BREASTS: Grabbing or kneading boobies like bread dough doesn't give women maximum tingle or make them feel sexy. In fact, many women find this downright painful. The bosom bottom line? Larger breasts are usually less sensitive. "Tweaking the nipple or gentle biting is the only way I can really get off on it," says Susannah, 31, a 34DD. Women with smaller breasts will prefer you to run your fingers or tongue across their nipples.

PRETENDING YOU'RE A PORN STAR: "Just because you like us to talk dirty doesn't mean we want you to," says Cassie, 24. Even if your girlfriend works as a phone-sex operator, she may not be into dirty dialogue at home. Feel free to test her tolerance of pornographic prose, but don't be surprised if she cringes—or cracks up.

STRIPPING HER HALFWAY: "I like a guy to undress me *slowly,*" says Vicki, 27. Only on those occasions when both parties instinctively know that it's quickie-sex time should you tear off her pants and proceed to have sex while she's still zipped into her coat. Otherwise, you'll make her feel silly and used.

SHOVING HER HEAD DOWN: Pushing your girlfriend's head down will get you a blow, but it won't be the kind you want. If she wants to go head-to-head, she'll work her way down the happy trail in her own sweet time. Patience is a virtue.

PUTTING HER IN A PAINFUL POSITION: New and exciting positions may spice things up, but keep in mind that most women are not contortionists. You must be considerate, especially when trying something new. Lisa suggests: "If we're sitting on your face, we're essentially doing squats, so we'd be happy to have your strong arms helping to hold up our asses." Well put.

FARTING: If we have to explain why this is a no-no, perhaps you should consider donating your reproductive organs to science.

REFUSING TO QUIT: True, control is great, but extended intercourse gets painful, especially when the big "O" is just not gonna happen. "Guys have to learn to give up," says Jamie, 27. "It's like they think they know something we don't. They keep going, but you're so sure it's not going to happen that you're mentally rearranging your sock drawer."

SKIPPING THE LUBE JOB: If she's not wet it won't work. It's that simple. Even a lubricated condom won't do the trick if she's not a little bit moist. If you're antsy try licking your finger before touching her, "Or better yet," says Jill, 22, "get your tongue down there." You heard the lady.

PLAYING GYNECOLOGIST: One sure way to get a girl out of the mood fast is to make her feel like she's about to have a pelvic exam. "When a guy shoves my legs apart, it's anything but sexy," says Tara, 31. A gently prodding knee or kissing her thighs will usually do the trick.

BOLTING FOR THE BATHROOM: "I knew a guy who used to run to brush his teeth every time we had oral sex," says Sue, 26. "It was so humiliating." C'mon guys, if you expect her to swallow any bodily fluids, you've gotta give a little here. Pour some wine beforehand and take a swig from the glass on the bedside table. Cheers!

Pole Positions

Add these to your repertoire and you're on your way to legend-hood.

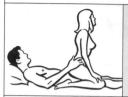

SQUAT THRUST. She's on top of you, squatting, facing your feet. She can pace your lovemaking and do some work if you're tired. Plus, according to Masters and Johnson, positions with the woman on top allow for greater stimulation of her clitoris than the regular old missionary. When tired she can lie back and draw her legs together, still keeping you inside her. As she closes her legs, there will be mega friction down in her place.

KINKY SPOON. You lower yourself down on her while she's lying on her back. But she draws one leg up and across her body, bending at the knee, so you are going into her partly from the side and rear. While you two crazy kids are going at it, you can rub her clit. This acts as a double-whammy and gets her off quick. But note: Let her stretch her legs first gently. And be careful—there's nothing sexy about a charley horse.

PELVIS HAS LEFT THE BUILDING. She gets on her back and you are on your knees, entering her. The trick is, you put your hands on her hips and pull her pelvis up level with your thang. Plusses: Great stimulation of her G-spot. Try this with a girl who's light and petite or you'll drop her ass flat on the floor, ending things right there.

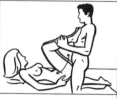

ROLLING TICKLE. Tantric sexpert Margo Anand recommends this as a great way of rubbing her all the right ways. You are on your knees, and she is on her back with her legs up in the air, feet resting on your chest. You gently thrust, while she swivels her hips in little circles. You two end up giving each other sensations from another friggin' world, without hookas and brownies. The force vectors at work here could tear the roof off a tank!

X POSITION. This was popularized by Dr. Comfort back in the swinging '70s. You sit facing each other, pelvises together, with legs extended and arms back for support, seesawing gently back and forth. The great part about this is that you can do it forever because tension builds slowly.

TAKIN' YOUR TANTRIC TIME. This is a Tantric position that allows for long, slow bouts of doing it. Basically, it's just the missionary position, except the woman wraps her legs around the guy's back, and, instead of thrusting madly, he lets her pull him in gently.

SILENT BUT SEXY. This is a position where you lie side by side, facing each other, while you're inside her. You both move your thighs up and down, and rub, instead of having normal-thrusting monkey sex. This allows for a slow buildup of pleasure because you and she rub more surface area of each other. (This position also cuts down on movement noise, so it's great when visiting your parents.)

SEX EDGE

SET IT UP.
"Set up the room for lovemaking," advises Kuriansky. So stow the Scrabble board, lower the lights, clean-up the scraps of that leftover burrito you ate in bed last night, and lay the music, candles, and mood lighting on thick. Keep the room temperature warm—you want to be able to remove clothes here, not have to stay bundled up. Remember the pillows, too, Kuriansky adds. No one likes rug burn.

PRESS IN.
Slide your hands up and outward toward the shoulders and then toward the neck, wrapping your fingers around her shoulders and pressing your thumbs right into the muscle.

GO BACK.
Start at the lower back again and make circles outward to the sides of the body, as though you're spreading the muscles like dough, and then work your way up. Another trick: Start from the spine and trace your thumbs outward, as if you were tracing her rib cage. Work your way back toward the butt.

Give An Erotic Massage
She *will* be putty in your hands!

While this'll make her feel all warm and turned-on, what it really does is show her you think of her as more than a sex toy. And don't worry if your technique is off—with women, you definitely get A's for effort. And just like when you were in school, you can trade these points in for playtime. Dr. Judy Kuriansky, sex therapist extraordinaire, helps us get there. No talking. School's in session.

START WITH THE BACK.
Kneel by her side or sit down on her booty and place one hand on either side of the spine at the lower back. Slide up to the neck and back, warming the spine. "Be careful not to put direct pressure on the spine," Kuriansky says. A little dab of massage oil, to warm her and keep you from pulling at her skin, is just what you need right now.

ESTABLISH A RHYTHM.
"At this point you can get creative," Kuriansky says. You should be confident that you know her well enough to explore all sorts of body parts. We'll leave that to your twisted imagination. Have fun—and bring back pictures.

That'll keep her from grabbing the damb remote.

NIGHT OF 1,000 SEX STUNTS
Don't stop now. You're getting closer to godhood.

OK, so you think you've done it all. You've mastered the tongue exercises, memorized the entire Kama Sutra, and can say with confidence that by flicking this switch and adjusting that knob, you can send your woman to planet Yes. But if you've decided to stick with any routine, there's a good possibility your girlfriend is getting sick of your syndicated reruns.

So, the next time she's expecting the same old song and dance, here are some sex moves you can surprise her with that'll make her jaw drop.

■ **Grab a chair.**
Because a pool table, the kitchen counter, and the bathroom sink are about as comfortable as a convention of your ex-girl-friends, pull up a chair. Settle into an armless upholstered dining-room-type throne and have her straddle you with her legs dangling. Boner bonus: Sitting allows more blood to pool in the pelvic region, which means you'll bring a better-than-average hard-on to the table.

■ **Make her bed.**
While guys can hump happily on week-old pizza boxes and dirty clothes, girls want the hay they roll in to be more refined. So make her bed with quality sheets. "Setting the scene for lovemaking shows you care enough to make an effort," says Kevin Leman, Ph.D., author of *Sex Begins in the Kitchen*. The absolute best are Egyptian-cotton Frette sheets (800-353-7388; www.frette.it/ index.html), which have found their way onto the beds of Madonna and the pope (separately, we hope). While the price goes as high as $3,000, you can get a $500 set that will still be light-years from the linens she owns.

■ Hum your way home.

The next time you're yodeling down her valley, hum a little ditty. While she'll probably think, *Why do I always get the weird guys?*, she'll change her tune once she feels the bass. "Humming creates a buzz on your lips that, when applied to her anatomy, works exactly like a vibrator," says Sandor Gardos, Ph.D., a San Francisco sex therapist. Warm her up with some prolonged low moans to insure that your rendition of "Smoke on the Water" won't be booed off the stage.

■ Hit her A spot.

She's heard truckloads about her G spot, but zip about her other hot button, the anterior fornix erogenous zone, or A spot for short. The scientists conducting an experiment in 1996 to find a cure for vaginal dryness got more than they asked for: Stimulating that spot lubed the ladies in less than 10 minutes, and 95 percent of them reported blowing a fuse—some more than once. To replicate these findings in your own lab of love, slide two fingers inside her vagina a third of the way up on the front wall, until you hit a small mass of spongy material (that's the G spot). Continue upward to find her cervix, which will feel round, like the end of your nose. Move back until you're about halfway between her G spot and her cervix, and move your fingertips clockwise over that spot.

■ Make fun of your willie.

No, we haven't gone crazy. Women know better than to laugh, smirk, or even smile at a guy's johnson (it shrinks things faster than a cold dip). But if you've been dating a woman for a while, give her permission to chuckle by drawing a smiley face on it. Or let her play ringtoss with it. "Women like a man who can treat his penis lightly because it shows he's comfortable with his sexuality," says Carol Queen, a San Francisco sexologist.

■ Say you don't want sex.

Telling her you just want to talk or "make out" will stump her. "Women think men always want sex," says Lou Paget, author of *How to Give Her Absolute Pleasure,* "so

they often wait for men to make the first move." But if you stop acting like a slobbery sex fiend, she'll be forced to become one herself. If she calls your bluff and forgoes sex for conversation, talk about your carburetor and she'll do you out of sheer boredom.

■ Toe her boat.

Give your toes a crack at making her come. Lube up your little piggies and lie foot to crotch with her, so your biggest one's in contact with her clitoris. (We suggest you clip your toenails if you're going to try this one.) You'll be surprised how much you enjoy it: The nerve centers for your genitals and your feet share a border in one parietal lobe of your brain.

■ Go for the glow.

Light up your night life with some recently FDA-approved Knight Light glowing condoms ($11.95 for a dozen; www.condomania.com; 800-926-6366). Or give your own light-saber a break by using a Light Up DickStick ($39.95 at www.xandria.com), a clear jelly dong with a removable Glow Stick inside. Afterward, rip off your face mask and tell her you're an alien and that her next baby will glow like a 50-watt bulb.

■ Reposition your pecker.

While thrusting gratifies your primal urges, it misses all her prime pleasure centers. Take the high road by aiming your penis toward her belly button, which will cause your rod to rub against her G spot and A spot. Or take the low road: Shift your hips higher than hers and aim your penis at her back; this will make your shaft kiss up to her clitoris with each fell stroke.

■ Give her a hand.

Because nothing dials God like a woman's own digits, try matching her masturbation technique mano a mano: Lie down facing your partner and slowly reach between her legs. Lubricate your finger with her juices, then lightly rub her clitoris with a slow circular motion. About every 10 seconds, give the little button a rest and tend to the folds below. By the 10th time you head back up into the hills, she'll be begging you to bring it on home.

■ Spice it up.

Warn her about this in advance or she'll think you've gone nuts; do it right and she'll declare you a genius. Keep a pepper shaker by the bed, and as she approaches the brink of bliss, sprinkle a dash of pepper under her nose. If she's gifted enough to time her sneeze to coincide with her orgasm, she'll be blown away in more ways than one. That's because, according to experts, sneezing both releases the same endorphins as an orgasm and causes a rapid alteration of her oxygen level that intensifies her climax.

Leave her undies on.
Since you're perpetually devising ways to get her dang panties off, she'll be surprised if you just let them be and instead apply warm, sloppy licks on top of and around that frustrating swath of material. Think of those undies as a buffer against

intercourse but not oral sex," says Tracey Cox, author of *Hot Sex: How to Do It*. Try this: Lift her thighs onto your shoulders, and raise her lower torso off the bed so she's, essentially, upside down: That way she's very open to everything.

Give her a wake-up call.
Unless she has an 8 A.M. meeting, your woman would probably be flattered to wake up and find you between her legs, working the early shift. Waking up to sex makes her think she turns you on so much, you can't control yourself until she's awake. That impulsiveness is exciting. But if you want to test the waters

a rookie rendition of *9 1/2 Weeks* and a pimply C-list porno.

Heat her up, chill her out.
Challenge her nipples to a taste test: Take a sip of a hot drink and touch her breasts with your warm lips; then take a sip of ice water and touch her again, firing up a set of nerve endings she didn't know existed. "Certain nerve endings respond to touch; others respond to temperature," says Jay Wiseman, author of *Tricks: More Than 125 Ways to Make Good Sex Better*. "So if you activate both, she'll get twice the buzz." For the best effect, go back

She'll be melting into the mattress by the time you reach the eight deep thrusts. Pausing after each one will set the stage for a cliffhanger of a climax.

your inborn tendency to pounce on her clit like a linebacker on a loose ball. Women's genitals can't handle too much direct stimulation during the early stages of arousal, so before you dive-bomb, put her shield up.

Pause between pumps.
"Monotonous thrusting can have a numbing effect on a woman, especially if she's not aroused enough to respond to intense sensation," says Felice Dunas, author of *Passion Play*. So vary the speed and rhythm of your old in-and-out, or try a Tantric technique: Start with one deep thrust followed by seven shallow ones, then follow two deep thrusts with six shallow ones, and so on. She'll be melting into the mattress by the time you reach the eight deep thrusts. Pausing after each one will set the stage for a cliffhanger of a climax.

Get her off upside down.
Although you've tried every intercourse position, from the Wheelbarrow to the Five-Legged Flying Serpent (you have tried those, haven't you?), don't forget there's more than one way to go down on her. "Most couples try new positions for

before you ruffle her R.E.M., mention that her skimpy nightgowns keep you up all night; if she throws on long johns, stick to waking hours.

Get a tattoo.
Imagine your girlfriend's face when she finds her name tattooed on your ass! To bypass that annoying permanence problem, order a temporary brand from Tatt 2 World (800-747-8016). For $89 you'll get 1,000 one-and-a-half-inch custom-made tattoos (yes, 1,000: Tatt 2 World doesn't usually sell them to individual wackos like you). They wash off with soap and water, but the memory of JIM AND JULIA 2-GETHA 4-EVER branded on your rump will last a lifetime.

Lend her a mirror.
The next time you dive south, give her a handheld mirror so she can see your mouth working its magic on her in a whole new light; when you're doing it doggy-style, put the mirror under her stomach for a front-row view of the genital junction. To increase the odds that she'll like what she sees, keep the lights dimmed: It'll make the difference between

and forth between touching her gently and playing a game of hot-and-cold. "Skin becomes insensitive to the same stimulus after a while, so the more you vary it, the more she'll feel it," Wiseman says.

Give her the mint treatment.
Ever since Monica Lewinsky talked about popping those "curiously strong" mints to give the former president a curiously kick-ass hummer, breath mints have become an oral-sex staple. But you've got news for her: Mints work even better on her because the menthol in the candy penetrates the mucous membranes of the vulva more easily than it does those of the penis. So dissolve one in your mouth, then head south. Surgeon General's Warning: Women have different levels of sensitivity to menthol, and some may experience a burning sensation if you use too much (that's also why you should avoid the cinnamon flavor). To be safe, start with one candy and wait five minutes; if she doesn't feel it, pop another and repeat. Hope you're hungry. She may want a tin's worth.

Timetables for Getting Her Pregnant

Because God has a sense of humor and a cruel streak, when a woman's flowing is also when she's at her randiest…

■ Do the ovulation:
A slew of studies in the '70s and '80s found that women masturbated more, had more sexual fantasies, and did the do with their partners more during ovulation. And a highly unscientific poll of the women we know confirmed this. "I get like Catwoman," one young actress told us. So mark your calendars and break out the extra-strength condoms. You're about to get lucky and unlucky at the same time.

■ For rocking her world:
According to Dr. Ruth, many pregnant women who cannot bear the thought of having sex during their first trimester find that sex during their second trimester is the best of their lives. Hang out by the ob-gyn and score!

■ For performing:
According to a Japanese study, male testosterone levels peak at 10 A.M. There's a second, slightly lower peak at 7 P.M. These are prime times for getting it up, hard, and off. So if you want to have a righteous quickie, that's the time. Your testosterone levels are lowest between 10 P.M. and 3 in the morning… so make your move earlier in the evening, before last call.

Halt the March

We break down the last line of pregnancy defenses.

NORPLANT: A group of six thin implants under the skin of a woman's arm. Cost: $500, and it's covered by Medicaid.
Effectiveness: 99+%

DEPO-PROVERA: A hormonal contraceptive injected into the woman that lasts three months. Cost: $35–$45.
Effectiveness: No numbers, but it uses the same drug as Norplant

PILL: Like Tylenol, only not. Cost: About $30 a month
Effectiveness: 97–99%

CONDOMS: If you don't know, drop this book now. Cost: About $12 for 20
Effectiveness: 97% (in most cases, because of mistakes, 88%)

DIAPHRAGM: Like a shower cap, but not. Cost: $13–$25.
Effectiveness: 94% (which is theoretical…in the real world, 82%)

IUD: A metal or plastic loop inserted into a women's uterus (by a doctor). Cost: $200–$300
Effectiveness: 98–99%

SMASHING BALLS WITH HAMMER:
Cost: About $7 (not counting missed work and hospital time).
Effectiveness: 100%

Condom Control
How to effectively wrap your rascal.

■ Store condoms in a cool, dark place. Exposure to sunlight, heat, or humidity can break down latex, causing them to rupture or tear more easily (don't leave 'em on the radiator).

■ Some dates are marked MFG, which indicates the manufacturing date. These condoms are good up to four years *from* the MFG date. Others are marked EXP, which indicates the expiration date, *after* which the condom should not be used.

■ Lambskin or natural condoms are not effective in the prevention of disease. Also, the jury is still out on how effective the new plastic, or polyurethane, condoms are at disease prevention. For the best protection, use latex.

■ Do not unroll the condom before putting it on. It can weaken the latex and make it difficult to use.

■ If your penis is uncircumcised, pull back the foreskin before slapping that jobber on.

■ Hold the tip flat just north of your wanger, while you unroll the condom with the other hand.

■ Put a drop of lubricant inside the tip of the condom for better sensation, and also less chance of ripping. Never use an oil-based product such as hand lotion, Vaseline, baby oil, or Crisco (unless you have a hot date with Betty Crocker), as it will weaken the latex and cause the jimmy to break.

■ After ejaculation, pull out while the penis is still hard, holding onto the base of the condom to prevent it from falling off.

■ If it breaks, it is important that women not douche; that can push sperm further into the body—oh, the humanity! Cover the entire genital area with a contraceptive foam, which has a high concentration of spermicide and will help neutralize any infectious agent. Try to figure out why the condom broke so that you can prevent it from happening again.

Sperm Busters?

Hazards that can leave your pearls in peril.

"Its, um, an aquarium filter, mom."

Man's first evolutionary directive is, of course: Protect the balls. But are we doing enough? To help you protect and nourish your own supply of wriggly microdependents, we've assessed a range of rumored sperm killers and separated the hype from the, uh, hard truth.

Apparent threat: Spilling a cup of coffee into crotch
Hard truth: Heat is the mortal enemy of sperm. Number-one rule: Avoid hot tubs and bumpy McDonald's drive-thrus.

Apparent threat: Wearing briefs or banana hammocks
Hard truth: Tighty-whitey wearers take heart: There is no evidence that normal cotton briefs reduce sperm count. Then again, Clinton wore boxers...

Apparent threat: Smokin' Dr. J
Hard truth: Regular wacky-weed smoking lowers the sperm count, decreases sperm motility, and increases the number of abnormally shaped sperm. Bummer, dude.

Apparent threat: Bicycling
Hard truth: Bad news, Greg LeMond: Tight pants plus hot exercise plus a crotch hump grinding into your nut cluster makes a man fit as a fiddle but infertile as, um, a turtle. Oh, hell—it rhymes, anyway.

Apparent threat: Getting a boot in the jewelry box
Hard truth: Rule of thumb: Never let people kick you in the balls really hard. It's hazardous to your reproductive chances. Oh, and it hurts like the bejeezus.

Apparent threat: Catching a bug
Hard truth: Hard science. Fever, adult mumps, and STD's are among a host of diseases that can hurt your sperm count, some of them permanently. Almost makes you want to live in a bubble.

Apparent threat: Sharing a locker with Ben Johnson
Hard truth: Beefcake warriors beware: Steroids may pump you up, but they make you a little girly man when it comes to sperm count. Also watch out for testosterone supplements, DHEA, and ginseng.

Apparent threat: Eating three-headed fish from Lake Chernobyl
Hard truth: As bad as it gets. If you're about to blast your gonads with major doses of radiation, make a deposit at your local sperm bank first.

Apparent threat: Getting an x-ray
Hard truth: Forget the lead shield and the doctors and dentists scurrying out of the way: Unless you're a bad NASCAR driver or a parachute tester, odds are you're not getting enough x-rays to worry about this.

Apparent threat: Listening to Kenny G
Hard truth: Scientists have not been able to prove that low levels of exposure to the lite-jazz musician causes permanent sperm-count damage. But is it really worth taking chances?

Love Potions, Numbers 1–4

Do aphrodisiacs really work? Here are the facts behind all the hype. Use this to plan your next romantic dinner.

BANANAS are rich in potassium, which is necessary for nerve and muscle functioning.

RAW OYSTERS are rich in zinc, complex sugars, and proteins, which help build testosterone—good for you, not so much for her.

CHOCOLATE has sugar and caffeine for an energy boost, but it also contains amino acids that help the brain build its own natural aphrodisiacs. In addition, the stuff also includes phenylethylamin (PEA), a natural stimulant and neurotransmitter. High levels of PEA have been linked to love and lust.

GINKGO increases blood flow to the brain and the penis, according to studies.

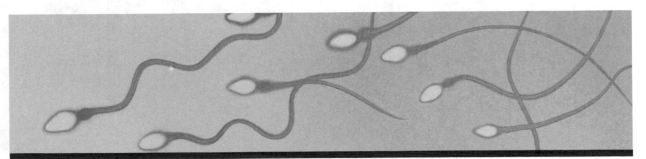

THE SEX OLYMPICS

Turn in your amateur status and go pro.

Now that you're confident in your technique, penis size, and overall macking skills, we issue you (and some of your equally pimped friends) a challenge.

We've compiled a list of risky public places to have sex. They're places everyone has access to (the beach, the office, the Gap), so readers all across the country can play. Simply grab the most adventurous girl you know, have your buddies do the same (we're assuming they'll be different girls, but hey, if that's your thing...), and see which couple can amass the most points. We've included strategies to help you score in each location. Feel free to substitute a particularly enticing landmark in your own community. Remember: It's not whether you win or lose. It's if you can avoid arrest.

IN A CLOTHING-STORE CHANGING ROOM—75 POINTS

You will need: *An empty shopping bag; enough money to replace any clothes you may soil in the process.*
Find a large store with banks of adjoining fitting booths. The female carries the shopping bag. To avoid suspicion, you must be perceived as strangers to each other. Shop separately until the agreed-upon signal is given. Proceed to the changing room, secure adjoining booths, and lock

the doors. Quickly slide under the barrier and into your woman's booth, stand in the shopping bag (just you), and enter her from behind.

Take your time—this little scam is pretty foolproof. Even if your partner moans too loudly and the changing-room attendant decides to peek under the door, all she'll see is one pair of legs and a shopping bag.

AT THE BEACH—100 POINTS
You will need: *bathing suits; suntan lotion; Floatties.*
Give a fake swimming lesson. Walk your woman to the water, whereupon she will display fear. (This shouldn't be too hard to fake, as you're exposing her to the risk of both arrest and shark attack.) Utter consoling phrases in a loud voice so everyone hears. Find an unpopulated section of ocean about waist-deep, and begin the "lesson."

Part one: Floating. She dons the Floatties, which allow her to float on her back while you stand at her side and cradle her in your arms. She lets her inside arm slip beneath the waves and into your suit. Practice this "stroke" together for a while until you're sure you've overcome any "shrinkage" problems caused by the cold water.

Part two: The crawl. She floats facedown, as if doing the crawl, with her legs scissored around your waist. In this position, your groin is close to that of your pupil. Under cover of the waves, slide her suit aside and enter her. This "interior" support will keep her afloat, and her thrashing motions will simply be interpreted as poor swimming technique. Encourage your partner with positive remarks such as "That's good. You're doing really well" and "Swim, woman, swim!" People will think you're an enthusiastic instructor.

150 PTS

IN A TAXI—150 POINTS
You will need: *a taxi; a short skirt; money.*
Be brazen. Hail a cab, jump in, and fall back into the seat in a passionate embrace. There are dirtier dogs than you out there, and taxi drivers have seen it all. If the guy behind the wheel doesn't say anything about your behavior right away, he's probably cool with it. Shout the address, shove a handful of money at him, and slide the little window shut. Psychologically, this

you are thus hidden from sight while your lower bodies are left unobstructed.

As a security measure, place some documents on the floor beside the desk. If someone walks in, stand up and say, "I dropped my TPS report." Use the report to cover your genitalia. We know, we know—it'd better be a big report, right? Cautionary note: Choose the right partner for the office competition. Do not opt for a "screamer" who will put you at risk for a common sexthletic injury— getting fired.

Your woman straddles you and undoes your fly. Her skirt conceals what you're really doing. You should look like a couple of crazy kids necking after the prom.

125 PTS

IN AN AIRPLANE— 125 POINTS
You will need: *airline tickets.*
Minutes after takeoff, you'll hear a ping that indicates the aircraft has reached cruising altitude, says our expert, former stewardess Jill Hammelman. The pilot will leave the seat-belt sign lit to keep passengers in their seats while the attendants bring the service carts. Before they start down the aisles with lunch, your girl dashes to the rest room and locks herself in. Wait a minute, then make your way to the rest room (make sure you move before the service carts come out). When you get there, don't knock. Instead look at the little sign on the door that now reads OCCUPIED. Below that is a little metal plate. Lift the plate and you'll find an emergency latch that opens the door from the outside. Let yourself in and relock the door. (Make sure you both agree on which bathroom she'll be in ahead of time so you don't walk in on some poor unsuspecting stranger.)

The attendants will then pass by with the carts, trapping the other passengers in their seats.

allows him to pretend that nothing's happening back there.

Your woman straddles you and undoes your fly. Her skirt conceals what you're really doing. You should look like a couple of crazy kids necking after the prom. Make it easy for the driver to ignore what you're doing and he probably will.

Ways to give yourself away include shouting "Tweak my nipple!" and ejaculating through the little coin slot.

IN YOUR OFFICE (DURING WORK HOURS)—175 POINTS
You will need: *an office; a desk; an official work-related document of some kind Your approach here depends on the size of your apparatus (your office, sicko). If your office is too small, use your boss' office.*
Time is of the essence. Synchronize watches and commence maneuvers in a state of readiness. Slide your woman face-up under the desk until her legs stick out (on the side facing away from the door). Get on top of her under the desk. You should be positioned like a pair of very well-acquainted car mechanics;

IN A SAUNA—200 POINTS
You will need: *A strong heart; Gatorade; a working phone nearby on which to dial 911.*
Why so many points for this semiprivate locale? Because sex in a sauna is not only physically strenuous, it's also really dangerous. Before you attempt this feat of sexual daring, understand the hazards.

The intense heat dilates your capillaries, causing hypotension (decreased blood pressure). The loss of sodium through sweating can lead to muscle cramps and heat sickness, and you risk dehydration. It's also really, really hot. These effects are beneficial over short periods, but prolonged exposure should be avoided. And that's just *sitting* in there. If you want the points, you have to engage in some truly hot *sex*.

Here's how to survive: First, both of you need to agree to listen to your bodies: If they're telling you to quit, quit. You don't

want to pass out on a bed of hot rocks. Especially not naked. Hydrate before, during, and after your attempt. Drink beverages that are high in glucose (a carbohydrate) and sodium

175 PTS

to replenish what you lose in the sauna; sports drinks are probably your best bet.

Don't lie down, because when you stand up again, the blood rushing into the already swollen veins in your head may cause you to faint. The best position is sitting, with her astride you. Hold her upright at arm's length to minimize the rather gross sensation of two sweaty bellies rubbing together.

Hot, dry air is bad for the respiratory system. Splash water on the walls of the sauna to make the atmosphere more pleasant.

Given its dangers, this might be the perfect way to eliminate unwanted competition. "Oh, yeah, that event's totally safe," you encourage your opponent. "It's just a little warm."

IN A RESTAURANT LADIES' ROOM—
300 POINTS
You will need: *A fake baby; swaddling clothes.*

Then you smile lovingly at each other.

Head to the ladies' room together. While you hold "Junior," have your partner check all the stalls. Once you're sure the room's unoccupied, pull down that little changing table and try for a real baby.

If you hear anyone coming in, have Mom stop her at the door and say, "I'm very sorry; my husband's in here. We're changing the baby together. I didn't think anyone would mind. Could we have a moment?"

"Of course," the woman will answer.
"What a supportive father, helping to change the baby. That's a good man you have there."
"Yes, he's quite special."
Quite.

ON A WASHING MACHINE—
400 POINTS
You will need: *Extra quarters.* Women love washing machines. Perhaps it's the April freshness, perhaps it's the sense of order and cleanliness, or perhaps it's the pressing of their tender regions against an enormous vibrating plate—we'll never really

Washing machines weren't built with this purpose in mind, so you may need a step stool. Slip some quarters into the machine and commence the wash cycle. Hold her shoulders firmly but affectionately to keep her upright. This maximizes contact between her and the machine's surface. When things heat up, press down on her hips so she receives the full effect of the washer's vibrations. That should spin her cycle. Kinky-sounding laundry tip: Only protein gets out protein.

IN A MATTRESS STORE—
500 POINTS
You will need: *Balls like freakin' melons.* Do you think the mattress guy doesn't know what you're thinking? If you were the mattress guy, what would you be thinking? Exactly. The mattress guy is on the lookout for two things: people ripping those little tags off and people "testing" the merchandise. He's watching the mattresses like a hawk. The

Everyone's always having sex in the back booth in restaurants. It's a cliché. The true sexthlete prides himself on finding innovative solutions to old problems.

Everyone's always having sex in the back booth in restaurants. It's a cliché. The true sexthlete prides himself on finding innovative solutions to old problems. The fake-baby ploy takes creativity, guts, and energy. You can't coach hustle.

Bring a baby doll to a not-too-crowded restaurant. Feed it, cuddle it, whisper snookie-snookums to it, and stare into your partner's eyes with love and obvious devotion. You're such loving parents.

In the middle of the meal, "Mom" exclaims loudly, "Oops, someone has a poo-poo!"

know. Whatever the reason, a washing machine—when used correctly—can be a great addition to your collection of marital aids.

Find a secluded, empty laundromat without an attendant in which to do the deed, or use the public washers in your apartment building. (Sure, you can do this at home if you own a washing machine, but you get zero points for being such a wuss.) Sit her on top of the machine and get between her legs.

mattresses. He's not, however, watching the floor between the mattresses. Enter the store during off-hours. Browse your way to the back, and when no one's looking, dive between two beds and go at it like a pair of maddened missionaries. When the mattress man eyes the room, he'll see a passive sea of Posturepedic peace. Little does he know that beneath the surface, the waves are crashing.

"For God's sake, Regis, yes, that's his final answer!"

FLICK CHICKS

Don't Try This at Home

What do you get when you cross six women with a dozen erotic videos? Seven trademark porn tricks that don't belong in the bedroom.

Why is it that when you watch porn videos, you see guys doing things that appear to come not only from a different playbook, but from an entirely different sport? Positions that couldn't possibly be enjoyable—or are they? Words and phrases that couldn't possibly turn women on—or do they? Things that fit in places they really shouldn't fit—or should they?

Yes, erotic videos can turn women on—and often make us feel more comfortable experimenting with new positions. But just because watching them may make our world a, ahem, wetter place doesn't mean we want you to try the twisted maneuvers the VCR offers up—or do we?

To separate the must-nots from the maybes, we sat down with a few women, loaded them up with booze, popped in some porn tapes, and...talked to them.

(C'mon, what kind of guys do you think we are?) They came clean about porn myths and realities.

Porn Fiction #1: Use your penis like a Whack-a-Mole mallet. This is a staple of porn videos: guys thwacking their limp johnsons on women like fly swatters. As a guy smacked his limp love muscle against a woman's nipples in *Tattoo: Your Fate Has Been Written in Ink,* Jill, a 26-year-old corporate events planner, explained, "I don't want to think of a guy's penis as a bouncy bath toy. I want it to look hard and sexy." When it comes to one-night scoring, take your penis seriously and she'll be more inclined to revere it, among other things.

Porn Fiction #2: When making love to a woman's body, ignore her head. Porn guys don't pay too much attention to whatever a woman's got going for her above the

shoulders. In *The Awakening,* a man actually has sex with a woman while her head is stuffed in a toilet bowl! "I kept waiting for him to get excited and start flushing!" said Rachel, a 25-year-old civil engineer. "Feel free to look her in the eyes," Rachel complained. "I mean, a guy who can kiss me passionately while we're having sex? That's hot."

Porn Fiction #3: Her nipples can double as PlayStation controllers. When a man poured red-hot wax on a woman's erect nipples during *Rope of the Rising Sun,* three women on the panel winced and yelled, "Youch!" Don't get me wrong. Women want you to engage in rough play. Just not there. "One guy I slept with used to grab my ass with both hands and yank me toward him," said Tina, a 22-year-old student. "We were like animals!"

Porn Fiction #4: Pretend her face is a dartboard, and aim between her eyes. One scene in *The Voyeur #12: Suck on This* looks like a "Got Milk?" commercial gone crazy. "She's drowning!" Jill cringed. Many women enjoy feeling your love juice on their bodies, but they'd rather you chose more acceptable receptacles. "Once a guy shot it in my eye," said Tina, "so I cringe when guys try that now." Instead aim for the smooth skin on her chest or stomach.

Porn Fiction #5: Grab her hair like a leash during sex. Sure, it seems logical for the ship's crew in *Conquest: High Seas, Low Morals* to use Louisa's long blonde curls as a joystick. Logical to you, that is. "Hey, if I wanted to be ridden by a cowboy, I'd move to Texas!" joked Wendy, a 29-year-old accountant. In reality, a woman wants the power to give you pleasure—where, when, and how fast she wants. But touching her hair does turn her on if you're doing it right. "I hate to have to stop while going down on my boyfriend because my own hair gets caught in my mouth," Rachel said, "so it's sweet when he holds my hair back."

Porn Fiction #6: Fill up all her orifices. Women in pornos sometimes resemble cars at Indy 500 pit stops, with a few men furiously pumping away from every angle. "Multiple stimulation is great," said Chris, 35, a literary agent, "as long as you're not

NON-PORN ALTERNATIVES

Tempt her with five titillating titles you can rent from the family store.

THE LOVER (1992)
Never mind that this film is set in French colonial Vietnam in 1929. The scene where the rich Chinese businessman undresses his pouty-lipped lover—while dressed in a three-piece suit—is sizzling.

BOUND (1996)
Tank-topped Gina Gershon seduces cleavage queen Jennifer Tilly in the busiest on-screen lesbian relationship this side of the Adults Only curtain—and all of it wrapped in a double-crossing Mafia-land plot.

BETTY BLUE (1986)
You could make a hot night from watching just the first 10 min-utes of this steamy French film a few times, as a very un-shy Beatrice Dalle shakes the bedsprings with her boyfriend. It's in French, but trust us—panting like this doesn't require subtitles.

MISSISSIPPI MASALA (1992)
Denzel Washington fulfills every woman's fantasy when he sings a sexy version of "Happy Birthday" to his young Indian lover; the succeeding close-ups of their smooth, sweaty skin are hotter than a vindaloo.

SEA OF LOVE (1989)
When Al Pacino is thrown up against the wall by Ellen Barkin, he doesn't know if she's a harmless sexpot or a murderer. But by the time she opens her bathrobe and rubs her naked body against his back...he doesn't care.

---

going so crazy that she feels like she's bedding Edward Penis-Hands!" Most women love a particular combo, like having their nipples touched while you go down on them. Or try Tina's favorite: "I like when a guy uses a vibrator on my super-spot and pushes his tongue inside me." The key is to start with one point of entry and add slowly so she has a chance to adjust to each layer of pleasure before you up the ecstasy ante.

Porn Fiction #7: Suddenly exposing your penis will make a woman melt.
In Porn World, sex happens at the drop of a hat. In *The Voyeur #13: Live in Europe,* for example, two blue-collar guys pull out their Mini-Me's for a blonde with a clipboard; she's so impressed, she gets down on her knees and does them double duty. "Yuck. There's nothing more disturbing than an unexpected penis," Chris said. So don't think stripping and jumping out of the bathroom will get her engine revving. Take a clue from the stars of *Fire & Ice* (in which a woman later rides an anatomically correct ice sculpture): "It's so sexy when the motorcycle guy kisses her breasts beneath her camisole and leather jacket," said Pam, a 29-year-old software developer.

The MacGyver Guide to Sex Tools

Sex expert Sari Locker, author of *Mindblowing Sex in the Real World,* cleans out the cupboards and finds some naughty toys hiding within.

■ Drag a fork down her stomach or along her back, but don't poke her like a porterhouse.

■ Get naked and rub flour all over each other. Throw some on a clean floor and roll in it. (Try not to think of the old joke: "Yo mamma's so fat, I had to roll her in flour to find the wet spot").

■ Cloak a zucchini wonder wand in a condom and use it as a dildo. (Try not to think of the airport scene in *This is Spinal Tap*).

■ Dip a sponge in warm oil and run it over her naked body, slow enough for her to savor it.

■ Bend your naughty girl over your knee and paddle her bare bottom with a wooden spoon.

■ Turn an electric toothbrush on low speed and circle her nipples. Do not insert it anywhere.

■ Brush her hair with long, slow strokes, and keep brushing down her bare back and behind.

■ Spread a new shower curtain on the bathroom floor, coat it with baby oil, and slither naked all over it.

■ Tie her wrists to the bedposts (or each other) with a clean pair of stretchy tube socks.

■ Drive a Matchbox car over her curves with "vroom-vroom" sound effects.

Bedtime Stories

We take one last peek behind the curtain to find out what's really on women's minds: Hot erotic daydreams that would make Larry Flynt blush.

DRAMA-SUSPENSE

When desire is in the director's chair, ordinary people and places can produce some pretty titillating takes. Yeah, you've probably come across these plots before, but knowing that the details were drummed up by the same hot young things you're trying to bed day in and day out makes them a lot more interesting, no?

"For the first nine years of my life, most of the men I came in contact with were the priests at my Catholic elementary school. Now I frequently fantasize about seducing one. First I'll picture myself opening my legs so he can see my white cotton underwear when I'm sitting in the front pew at mass. Then he calls me into his private chamber to chastise me. But when I lift his heavy black velvet robes, I discover a huge hard-on." —Maura, 23

"I have a really tough time grinding against a guy hard enough to have an orgasm. I start feeling self-conscious and usually stop before I finish. So while I play with myself, I'll fantasize that I'm a nurse who comes across a catatonic male patient with a stiffie the size of a Coke can. Basically, I get on top of him and ride to my heart's content." —Rayanne, 20

"During meetings with my boss, I picture him going down on me and getting really into it. It boosts my confidence and usually gets my nipples hard, which I'm sure he notices." —Naomi, 28

"I saw this sex swing on the Internet. When you're strapped into it, your move-

"No, I don't want to come look. Just flush, for Christ's sake."

ment is restricted and you can hang upside down, sideways, whatever. I can just imagine the creak of the leather, the clank of the chain, while I'm sort of floating in midair and being controlled by my man. De-e-e-lish." —Kay, 26

"In my favorite fantasy, I'm the only female teacher at an all-boys high school. I stand at the front of the room and slowly unbutton my blouse and lift up my skirt to reveal my lacy undergarments. The whole class starts touching themselves, and I choose one lucky 17-year-old to come up and have sex with me on the desk while the rest watch." —Teresa, 28

"This isn't exactly a fantasy, but when I meet an attractive guy, I'll look him straight in the eye while I visualize straddling him and rubbing my crotch against his. I like to think telepathy is possible." —Gretchen, 24

"During a meeting, the two male coworkers sitting on either side of me reach under the table and start stroking my thighs and taking turns bringing me to orgasm. Then they

get so excited, they come all over the inside of their designer pants." —Cara, 26

ACTION-ADVENTURE

Forget romantic, forget sensitive, and definitely forget gentle. When it comes to our ultimate fantasy man, most women want the kind of guy (or guys, as the case may be) who has rough hands, rides a Harley, and is more likely to rip our panties off with his teeth than quote Shakespeare. But don't take our word for it...

"A tough-guy cop handcuffs me to a bar in the back of his squad car and proceeds to strip-search me because he thinks I might be hiding a weapon. But once he gets my clothes off, he's so turned on that he decides to screw me instead. The red and blue lights are flashing, and he uses his night stick in some creative ways. Once in a while, I imagine his partner joins in, too." —Rosalyn, 19

"When I'm having sex with my boyfriend, I'll usually fantasize that he's some sexy international spy." —Yvette, 30

"You know in *Fight Club* when Brad Pitt tells Ed Norton to hit him as hard as he can? In my latest fantasy, it's me and Brad, and after I punch him, we wrestle and roll around until we're all sweaty. Then we have frantic sex—there's lots of hair-pulling, nipple-pinching, and shoulder-biting—in the middle of the parking lot with the cold, hard asphalt against my back." —*Hillary, 25*

"A bunch of medieval knights come across me in the woods and have their way with me, one, two, and three at a time."
—*Jessica, 29*

"I love to imagine that I'm trekking through the jungle when I come across a wild, muscular young man who's been raised by wolves and has never seen a woman before. He has 18 years' worth of raw, animalistic sexual energy pent up inside him and not an iota of shame. So he attacks me, drags me up to his tree dwelling, and ravishes me until he's too exhausted to move—which would be something like 15 hours later." —*Annie, 32*

"Sean Penn and I end up stranded on a tropical island. He carves my initials into his arm with a Swiss Army knife and screws my brains out morning, noon, and night, only stopping to hand-feed me papayas and rub coconut milk all over my body."
—*Noelle, 25*

"Horny young GIs have a birthday party in the bunks, and I pop out of the cake, wearing nothing but a smile. They cover me in frosting and take turns licking it off."
—*Andrea, 32*

SCI-FI/FANTASY
You may think we don't want you to pull any freaky, Spielberg–esque surprises on us in the sack, but there's something about the whole explore-the-possibilities outlook that can really rev a girl's engine. Here's what's going through your girlfriend's head when reality (no offense) starts to lose its luster.

"I've always wanted to do it with a hunky astronaut in the antigravity chamber at NASA. We could float around naked and assume any and every position. The one that usually comes to my mind consists of us sixty-nining while engaged in a slow, steady spin. In real life that'd probably make me puke. I can't even ride a roller coaster without getting queasy." —*Ruth, 27*

"My friends and I live on a planet of Amazons like in the old *Wonder Woman* TV series, and we go out into the galaxy to capture men and bring them back as our sex slaves. We chain their hands to the wall and torture them by going down on them for five minutes at a time and then stopping. At the end of the fantasy, I'm there alone when the chains fall off, and they pounce on me." —*Felicia, 31*

"Jimmy—the guy I lost my virginity to—worked as a clown at kids' birthday parties. A lot of the time we'd have sex while he was still wearing his red nose and big rub-

"A lot of the time we'd have sex while he was still wearing his red nose and big rubber shoes."

ber shoes. If I'm having trouble getting turned on, I'll picture the guy I'm with in Jimmy's clown outfit. It does the trick every time." —*Lauren, 24*

"When I'm sitting at my computer, I'll often think about how nice it would be if there were a guy who lived under my desk and just performed oral sex on me all day while I worked." —*Shelly, 26*

"Mine is a variation on Madonna's 'Cherish' video and the movie *Splash*. In the video, there are these two really hot male mermaids. Well, these mermen see me sunning myself on the deck of a cruise ship, so they pull themselves on board, their tales turn into legs the way

Daryl Hannah's did in the movie, and without saying a word, one makes me give him oral sex, while the other gets between my legs, pushes aside my bikini bottoms, and starts pumping away. After we all orgasm simultaneously, they jump overboard and turn back into mermen." —*Pat, 25*

"When a guy isn't doing what I need him to do to make me come, I'll imagine that he's a lifelike robot that's been programmed to make love to me any way I want. All I have to do is give verbal commands. So I'll start telling the guy what to do, as if the fantasy were a reality. The guy never seems to mind."
—*Vanessa, 22*

"I imagine making it with Jeri Ryan from *Star Trek: Voyager.* She and I get busy on one of the consoles, our bodies hitting all the buttons and setting off alarms all over the ship. After we work ourselves into a frenzy, we order a few of the guys to lose their jumpsuits and take us into hyper-speed." —*Madeline, 23*

PHOTO CREDITS

COVER
Photographer: Gene Bresler
Assistant: Chek Wu
Model: Vanessa
Hair/Make up: Maurine Walsh
Producer: A.S. Brodsky

FITNESS EDGE
Page 12
Man: Superstock

Page 14
Man with Barbell: Archive
Man Holding weights:
Superstock

Page 15
Medicine Cabinet:
Robert Glasgow
Steve Austin: Kobal
Weightbelt: Zoe Chan

Page 17
Atomic Explosion: Archive

Page 22
Sleeping Man: Superstock
Trainspotting: Everett Collection

Page 24
Gauze/Ambulance/Blood
Pressure: Comstock

Page 25
Boy with Clothespin: Corbis

STYLE EDGE
Page 26
Sean Connery: Kobal

Page 27
Tom Jones: Harry Longdon/
Shooting Star
Suit: Robert Glasgow

Page 28
Sexy Shirt: Gene Bresler

Page 29
Wild and Crazy Guys:
Photofest

Page 30
Arnold: Bruce McBroom/MPTV
Tattoo: Kobal
Lurch: Everett Collection
Dom Deluise: Kobal
Pee Wee: Neal Peters

Page 32
Carrie: Everett Collection
Airplane: Everett Collection

Page 34
Yul Brenner: Kobal
Burt Reynolds: Everett
Collection
Texas Chainsaw Massacre:
Photofest

Page 35
Night at The Roxbury:
Everett Collection

Page 38
Cake Lady: Photofest

CAREER EDGE
Page 40
Blinking dollar bill: Satoshi,
Jon Sosnovsky

Page 41
Wall Street: Photofest
CHiPs: Photofest

Page 42
Cardinal O'Conner: Liason

Page 43
Speedometer: Photodisc

Page 46
J.R.: MPTV

Page 48
Handshake: Superstock

Page 51
Man Giving a Speech: Stone

Page 52
Incredible Hulk: Kobal
Mailman: Corbis/Bettman

Page 54
Desks: Archive

Page 55
Anthony Perkins: Kobal

MONEY EDGE
Page 56
Monopoly board: Robert
Glasgow

Page 57
Trump: Retna

Page 58
Pamela Anderson:
Everett Collection

Page 59
Boss Hog: Everett Collection

Page 60
Bill Gates: Retna
Poodle: Stone
Famine Victims: Etienne
Werner/Archive

Page 62
Nightmare on Elm Street:
MPTV

Page 67
David: Superstock

Page 69
Mrs Howell: Photofest

Page 70
Willie Nelson: Globe

Page 71
Dracula: Photofest

Page 72
Cheers: Everett Collection

STREET EDGE
Page 74
Goodfellas: Neal Peters

Page 75
Rocky: Everett Collection

Page 77
Bullit: Kobal

Page 78
Dukes of Hazzard: Warner
Bros./Foto Fantasies

Page 79
Nascar: Jonathan
Ferrey/Allsport

Page 80
Falling Car: Everett Collection

Page 82
Used Car Salesman: Stone

Page 83
Interrogation: Archive

Page 84
Clinton: Robert Giroux/
Archive

Page 85
Gotti: Corbis

Page 86
O.J.: Sam Mircovich/Archive

HANDYMAN EDGE
Page 90
Bob Vila: Everett Collection

Page 91
Schneider: Globe Photos

Page 94
House: David J. Sams/Stone

Page 95
Three Stooges: Everett

Page 96
Lumberjack: Image Bank

Page 98
Edward Scissorhands:
Fox/Neal Peters

Page 99
Race Car: David
Madison/Stone